LEVEL III PRACTICE EXAMS – VOLUME 1

SCHWESER 2011 CFA LEVEL III PRACTICE EXAMS VOLUME 1

©2010 Kaplan, Inc. All rights reserved.

Published in 2010 by Kaplan Schweser.

Printed in the United States of America.

ISBN: 978-1-4277-2762-6 / 1-4277-2762-7

PPN: 3200-0084

2011 PRACTICE EXAM ANSWERS AND EXPLANATIONS ARE ONLINE AT WWW.SCHWESER.COM

Answers and explanations for self-grading all questions, essays as well as item sets, are available at the end of this book. For the essay questions, you will find both "For the Exam" and "Discussion" answers. "For the Exam" answers are short, to-the-point answers that would earn 100% of the available points for the question. They are presented to help you practice cutting down your actual exam answers to the bare minimum to conserve valuable time. "Discussion" answers explain the related concepts and help you to understand why the answer is what it is. In the process of taking the practice exams, the discussion answers will actually serve as a review.

Answers to item set questions are also available online at *www.schweser.com*. They contain embedded links to supporting curriculum material for the relevant Learning Outcome Statements. You also have online access to Performance Tracker, a tool that will provide you with exam diagnostics to target your study and review effort and allow you to compare your scores on Practice Exams to those of other candidates.

JUST USE YOUR SCHWESER *ONLINE ACCESS* ACCOUNT

All purchasers of SchweserNotes™ receive an e-mail with login information for Online Access. This is your login to view the video volumes in the Schweser Library, to use the Schweser Study Planner, to get Practice Exam item set answer explanations, to use Performance Tracker, and (if you purchased the Essential, Premium, or PremiumPlus Solutions) to get your questions answered during Office Hours. Simply log in at *www.schweser.com* and select Online Access to use any of these features. Access Practice Exam answers and explanations with the Practice Exams Vol. 1 left-hand menu item. If you need password help, go to *www.schweser.com/password* or use the Password Help link that appears if your login is unsuccessful.

PRACTICE EXAM ONLINE FEATURES AT A GLANCE

Item Set Answer Explanations
Our format contains expanded Practice Exam answer explanations to help candidates understand why one answer is the best of all the choices. When using Performance Tracker, you can choose to get detailed explanations for only those questions you missed or for all questions.

Links to Curriculum
Within the answer explanations, we have embedded links to the relevant content for review. This can include multiple Learning Outcome Statements, concepts, definitions, or formulas.

Exam Diagnostics
When you enter your answers in our Performance Tracker utility, you can request a breakdown of your overall score on the afternoon session of any exam. You can even get the Learning Outcome Statement references for questions you answered incorrectly to help you focus your review efforts.

HOW TO USE THE LEVEL III PRACTICE EXAMS

Save the Practice Exams for last. A good strategy is to take one exam in each of the three weeks prior to the exam. Plan ahead (e.g., actually schedule each practice exam and take it on the scheduled day) and do your best to mimic actual exam conditions: take the entire exam in one sitting, time yourself, have someone work on a computer in the same room; for distractions, have that person leave the room occasionally, turn the temperature in the room up and down, and talk to himself. Remember, no matter how challenging we make our Practice Exams, the actual exam experience will be different, because you and everyone else in the room will be nervous and fidgety with the pressures of the day. Also, your perception will probably be that the actual exam was much more difficult than our Practice Exams or even old CFA Exam questions you may have seen.

At times it can even appear that the material on the exam wasn't covered anywhere in our study products or the curriculum. This is because the Level III curriculum is far broader than it seems, and no one can anticipate everything that will be asked on the exam. It could also simply be that the material is asked in a form or language that is different from what you expect. Regardless, the important thing is to be able to think clearly and draw on your store of knowledge. As I have described my doctoral program experience, they teach you a lot of finance, but they can't teach you everything. They do, however, teach you to think on your feet and piece together your knowledge in several areas to arrive at a reasonable explanation.

Be ready for essay and multiple-choice questions. The morning session (3 hours and 50% of the exam) is entirely constructed response essay format. The afternoon session (3 hours and 50%) is 10 selected response item sets, each worth 18 points. For the 2011 exam, expect any topic (e.g., portfolio management, derivatives, GIPS®) in either format. The Level III topic area weights, as presented by CFA Institute®, are shown in Figure 1.

Figure 1: Topic Area Weights for the Level III CFA Exam

Topic Area	*Level III Weight**
Ethical and Professional Standards (total)	10%
Quantitative Methods, Economics, Financial Reporting and Analysis, and Corporate Finance	0%
Equity Investments	5–15%
Fixed Income	10–20%
Derivatives	5–15%
Alternative Investments	5–15%
Portfolio Management and Wealth Planning (total)	45–55%

* Note: These weights are intended to guide the curriculum and exam development processes. Actual exam weights may vary slightly from year to year. Please note that some topics are combined for testing purposes.

Figure 2 below shows the topic areas by study session. When you compare Figure 2 to Figure 1, the topic area weights in Figure 1 are a little confusing. For example, you will notice in Figure 2 that Study Session 7 is titled *Economic Concepts for Asset Valuation in Portfolio Management*. Then you will notice that the weight for Economics in Figure 1 is zero. As explained to me by a representative of CFA Institute, this is because Economics is tested as part of Portfolio Management. In fact, Study Sessions 3 through 18 fall under the umbrella of Portfolio Management. Just how the individual topics will be tested is somewhat of an unknown, so your focus is exactly the same as that for prior years' candidates; you must learn the entire Level III curriculum.

Figure 2: 2011 Level III Topic Areas by Study Session

Study Session	Topic Area	Title
1	Ethics and Standards	Code of Ethics and Professional Standards
2	Ethics and Standards	Ethical and Professional Standards in Practice
3	Portfolio Management	Behavioral Finance
4	Portfolio Management	Private Wealth Management
5	Portfolio Management	Portfolio Management for Institutional Investors
6	Portfolio Management	Capital Market Expectations
7	Portfolio Management	Economic Concepts
8	Portfolio Management	Asset Allocation
9	Portfolio Management	Management of Fixed Income Portfolios
10	Portfolio Management	Global Bonds and Fixed Income Derivatives
11	Portfolio Management	Equity Portfolio Management
12	Portfolio Management	Equity Portfolio Management
13	Portfolio Management	Alternative Investments
14	Portfolio Management	Risk Management
15	Portfolio Management	Risk Management Application of Derivatives
16	Portfolio Management	Execution; Monitoring and Rebalancing
17	Portfolio Management	Performance Evaluation and Attribution
18	Portfolio Management	Global Investment Performance Standards

Don't underestimate Level III. Many candidates believe that the Level II curriculum and exam are the hardest and Level III is the most enjoyable. However, do not take Level III lightly. Your best strategy is to come to the exam as prepared and confident as you can be. There is a lot of new material every year at Level III, and the Level III pass rate has been below 55% the last three years, so relying on the comments of those who took the exam last year, or even relying on last year's study materials, could be a prescription for disaster.

Write effective answers to the essay questions. CFA Institute's guideline answers for old exam questions are "perfect answers" (i.e., the one you would write if you had enough time). Also, CFA Institute typically gives you much more answer space than you need (often several pages for a one-paragraph answer), so don't think you are expected to fill all the answer space provided. Just like our "For the Exam" answers, your responses should be concise and, most importantly, address the command words. This way, there can be no doubt that you are addressing the question.

Give the CFA answer. Graders use an answer key and don't give points for creative thought, either yours or theirs! That is, they are not allowed to read anything into your answer, so you must be precise. Also, organize your work and think before you write. If the graders can't find or decipher your work, you will receive no credit. Although not strictly required, make sure to use the template for your answer, if one is provided.

Be prepared. It should go without saying that you should get plenty of sleep the night before the exam. Bring all necessary items (including snacks) with you, and arrive early enough at the test site to get a decent parking space. In fact, I recommend thoroughly checking out the site before exam day. *Important!* Be sure to read the CFA Institute guidelines for test day, which can be found on the CFA Institute website. Also, remember to answer *every* question, even if it means guessing. Graders can only award points; they cannot deduct points for wrong answers.

My thanks to the Schweser team. I would like to thank all of my colleagues at Schweser, especially Kurt Schuldes, CFA; Kristen Rindfleisch, Lead Editor; and Jeff Faas, Lead Editor, for their incredible work ethic and commitment to quality. Schweser would not be the company it is, nor could it provide the quality products you see, without all the Schweser content and editing professionals.

Best regards,

Bruce Kuhlman

Dr. Bruce Kuhlman, CFA, CAIA
Vice President and Level III Manager
Kaplan Schweser

Practice Exam 1 Morning Session Question Breakdown

MORNING SESSION		
Topic	Question	Points
Behavioral Finance	1A	4
Portfolio Management	1B	3
Portfolio Management	2A	6
Portfolio Management	2B	12
Portfolio Management	2C	2
Portfolio Management	3	16
Portfolio Management	4	9
Asset Allocation	5A	9
Asset Allocation	5B	6
Alternative Investments	6A	6
Alternative Investments	6B	4
Alternative Investments	6C	6
Alternative Investments	6D	9
Alternative Investments	7A	6
Alternative Investments	7B	2
Portfolio Management	8A	19
Portfolio Management	8B	4
Portfolio Management	8C	9
Alternative Investments	9A	6
Alternative Investments	9B	6
Alternative Investments	9C	2
Asset Allocation	10A	2
Asset Allocation	10B	3
Asset Allocation	10C	3
Asset Allocation	10D	4
Performance Evaluation	11	12
Asset Allocation	12A	6
Asset Allocation	12B	4
Total		180

PRACTICE EXAM 1 SCORE SHEET

MORNING SESSION		
Question	Maximum Points	Your Approximate Score
1A	4	
1B	3	
2A	6	
2B	12	
2C	2	
3	16	
4	9	
5A	9	
5B	6	
6A	6	
6B	4	
6C	6	
6D	9	
7A	6	
7B	2	
8A	19	
8B	4	
8C	9	
9A	6	
9B	6	
9C	2	
10A	2	
10B	3	
10C	3	
10D	4	
11	12	
12A	6	
12B	4	
Total	180	

AFTERNOON SESSION		
Question	Maximum Points	Your Approximate Score
13	18	
14	18	
15	18	
16	18	
17	18	
18	18	
19	18	
20	18	
21	18	
22	18	
Total	180	

Certain Passing Score: 252 of 360 (70%)
Probable Passing Score: 234

Please note that we write these exams to be as representative of Level III exam questions as possible. However, due to the relaxed conditions that most candidates apply when they "take" these exams (i.e., "I'm getting a little tired, I think I'll go to the refrigerator and get a snack"), you should adjust your score downward by 10–15% to get a more accurate measure of the score you would have received on exam day. Also, you must be honest with yourself for your score on this exam to have any meaning. Don't assume, for example, that if your answer is close, the graders will be generous with points.

PRACTICE EXAM 1
MORNING SESSION

Questions 1, 2, and 3 relate to Joe and Sara Finnegan. A total of 43 minutes is allocated to these questions. *Candidates should answer these questions in the order presented.*

Joe and Sara Finnegan are both 62 years old and live in Kerrville, Texas. They are retired and have a combined investable net worth of $2 million, the bulk of which was inherited from Sara's father's estate. Included in their total wealth is Joe's $500,000 defined-contribution retirement plan that is managed separately in a 401(k) retirement plan. Joe makes the investment decisions for his 401(k) plan, but Sara makes the investment decisions for their other portfolio. Joe will not begin withdrawing funds from his retirement plan until he reaches age 70.

The Finnegans have no children, but they have agreed to pay the nursing home expenses for Joe's 86-year-old father, who is in very poor health. These expenses are projected to be $130,000 per year, and are expected to last for at least three years. The Finnegans home in Kerrville is valued at $750,000. The Finnegans do not have a mortgage on their home. They enjoy traveling around the world and project living expenses to total $115,000 per year. The Finnegans' entire income is generated from their portfolio and is taxed at 15%. The Finnegans would like to exclude inflation from any and all projections related to their account, so that they can evaluate their position based on current dollar amounts.

Mr. Finnegan's 401(k) plan is administered by a local bank trust department. The trust department offers its clients a range of portfolio allocations from aggressive to conservative as shown in Exhibit 1. Without regard for asset class characteristics or his own risk and return objectives, Mr. Finnegan has selected a portfolio that is equally weighted in each asset class and instructed his trust manager to rebalance the portfolio at the end of each year to maintain the equal weighting. Mr. Finnegan is concerned about potential losses in his account but prefers not to make any investment decisions beyond maintaining his initial allocation.

Exhibit 1: Alternative Portfolios

Asset Class	Current Yield	Aggressive Asset Mix	Conservative Asset Mix
Domestic Equity Stocks—Income	4.0%	40%	15%
International Stocks	3.0%	25%	5%
Domestic Bonds	4.0%	5%	50%
International Bonds	4.0%	5%	25%
Alternative Investments	2.0%	25%	5%

QUESTION 1 HAS TWO PARTS FOR A TOTAL OF 7 MINUTES

A.   **Identify** and **explain** *two* behavioral characteristics that are evident in Joe Finnegan's allocation of his 401(k) retirement account.

(4 minutes)

B.   Based solely on the way in which he designed his 401(k) investment portfolio, **select** the investor personality type *most likely* exhibited by Joe and **justify** your selection with two reasons.

(3 minutes)

Answer Question 1B in the template provided.

Template for Question 1B

Personality Type (circle one)	Comments
Methodical Investor	
Cautious Investor	
Spontaneous Investor	

QUESTION 2 HAS THREE PARTS FOR A TOTAL OF 20 MINUTES

The local bank trust department also custodies the Finnegans' taxable $1.5 million inheritance account, but for this account Sara Finnegan directs all the trades. Sara expresses her social priorities through her financial investments. She deliberately excludes tobacco, defense, oil and gas, and chemical companies from her universe of potential investments and she is obsessed with tax minimization. Sara's portfolio allocation is shown in Exhibit 2.

Exhibit 2: Finnegan's Portfolio

Investments	Weight	Cost Basis	Current Price	Current Yield	Expected Capital Appreciation	Expected Standard Deviation
Cash	1%			1.0%	0%	1%
Municipal Bond Fund	50%	$12.40	$12.40	5.0%	0%	5%
Domestic Equity Income	4%	$18.00	$22.00	4.0%	12%	13%
Individual domestic stocks:						
Solar Power	7%	$10.00	$35.00	0.0%	35%	40%
Biotech Inc.	7%	$30.00	$13.00	0.0%	30%	36%
The Drug Company	7%	$75.00	$80.00	2.0%	20%	28%
Chip Design	7%	$58.00	$20.00	1.0%	22%	22%
Conglomerate Inc.	7%	$28.00	$70.00	4.0%	10%	13%
International Stock Fund	10%	$14.00	$30.00	3.0%	8%	18%

Sara is also passionate about animals. Her activism has led the Finnegans to become involved with the Spay Neuter Action Project (SNAP), and it is their intention to bequest the stock of Conglomerate Inc. to the organization. They also hope to use the growth in the portfolio's assets to make additional contributions of similar size as often as possible.

A.   From the information provided, **indicate** one item that would affect Sara's ability to tolerate risk and one item that would affect her willingness to tolerate risk and **explain** each with one reason.

Answer Question 2A in the template provided.

(6 minutes)

Template for Question 2A

	One item that would affect Sara's risk tolerance
Ability to tolerate risk	
Willingness to tolerate risk	

B.   In the template provided, **formulate** the constraints portion of an investment policy statement for Sara, addressing *each* of the following.

(12 minutes)

Template for Question 2B

Constraints	Comments
i. Liquidity Requirements	
ii. Taxes	
iii. Time Horizon	
iv. Unique Circumstances	

C.   **Describe** the tax consequences if the Finnegans make an immediate charitable bequest of their Conglomerate Inc. holdings to SNAP.

    i.   **Determine** how the Finnegans will *most likely* be allowed to value the donation.

    ii.   **Determine** how the donation would *most likely* be treated on their personal federal tax return.

(2 minutes)

QUESTION 3 HAS ONE PART FOR A TOTAL OF 16 MINUTES

Using the data provided in Question 2, Exhibit 2, **recommend** the most appropriate asset allocation adjustments for the Finnegans' $1.5 million portfolio to meet their goal of funding charities and Joe's father's nursing home care. Sara has indicated that she does not want to alter her current allocation to the international stock fund. **Indicate** how the allocation to each asset class listed below should be changed from the current allocation, and **justify** your responses. Your answer should address the risk-adjusted returns of the non-cash asset categories.

Answer Question 3 in the template provided.

(16 minutes)

Template for Question 3

Asset Class	Allocation	Justification
Cash	higher same lower	
Municipal Bonds	higher same lower	
Domestic Equity Income Fund	higher same lower	
Individual Domestic Stocks	higher same lower	

QUESTION 4 HAS ONE PART FOR A TOTAL OF 9 MINUTES

Martina Edwards is retiring and stepping down from her position as portfolio manager at the Huron Foundation, which funds undergraduate and graduate environmental science research. She is currently training her replacement, Greg Matlock, who previously worked as the portfolio manager for the defined benefit pension plan of a large corporation.

During training, Edwards tries to relate the role of a foundation portfolio manager to the role of a portfolio manager for a defined benefit pension plan by making the following statements:

> "The objectives and constraints for defined benefit pension plans and foundations are very similar. Since, unless specifically directed otherwise, the lives of both are infinite, for example, their primary return objective is to cover the effects of inflation and thereby preserve the purchasing power of the investment portfolio."

> "Huron Foundation does not need to be concerned about the correlation between the plan sponsor financial performance and performance of the portfolio. For defined benefit plans, however, this is a significant concern."

> "Payouts are typically based on the quality of the funding applications and proposals received each year, so Huron's liquidity needs tend to fluctuate over time. Since they are based on reasonably easily determined pension obligations, however, the liquidity needs of defined benefit pension plans do not fluctuate."

Determine whether you agree or disagree with *each* statement made by Edwards. If you disagree, **support** your decision with *one* reason related to portfolio management. *Note: supporting your opinion by simply reversing an incorrect statement will receive no credit.*

Answer Question 4 in the template provided.

(9 minutes)

Template for Question 4

Statement	Determine whether you agree or disagree with *each* statement made by Edwards (circle one)	If you disagree, support your opinion with *one* reason related to portfolio management
"The objectives and constraints for defined benefit pension plans and foundations are very similar. Since, unless specifically directed otherwise, the lives of both are infinite, for example, their primary return objective is to cover the effects of inflation and thereby preserve the purchasing power of the investment portfolio."	Agree Disagree	
"Huron Foundation does not need to be concerned about the correlation between the plan sponsor financial performance and performance of the portfolio. For defined benefit plans, however, this is a significant concern."	Agree Disagree	
"Payouts are typically based on the quality of the funding applications and proposals received each year, so Huron's liquidity needs tend to fluctuate over time. Since they are based on reasonably easily determined pension obligations, however, the liquidity needs of defined benefit pension plans do not fluctuate."	Agree Disagree	

©2010 Kaplan, Inc.

QUESTION 5 HAS TWO PARTS FOR A TOTAL OF 15 MINUTES

Jacque Claude is an analyst for Lafayette Portfolio Managers, a French firm. Lafayette provides investment advice regarding stocks and bonds for wealthy individuals. Claude is discussing the characteristics of international investments before a group of clients, during which he makes the following comments:

> "Although withholding taxes are frequently assessed by foreign governments on dividends and interest, the presence of domestic tax credits means that they are no longer a significant obstacle to international investing."

> "I would recommend that the return on a stock be compared to global sector benchmarks, because industry factors have increased in importance for explaining stock returns. In fact, I believe that diversifying across borders is no longer necessary as long as the investor has adequate industry representation."

> "Differing governmental monetary and fiscal policies cause bond market correlations to be low, often lower than that between equity markets. As a result, adding global bonds to global equity portfolios can improve the performance of a global efficient frontier, especially for lower risk portfolios."

A.   **State** whether or not *each* of these comments is correct. If incorrect, **explain** why.

Answer Question 5A in the template provided.

(9 minutes)

Template for Question 5A

Comment	Correct or incorrect? (circle one)	Explanation, if incorrect
"Although withholding taxes are frequently assessed by foreign governments on dividends and interest, the presence of domestic tax credits means that they are no longer a significant obstacle to international investing."	Correct Incorrect	
"I would recommend that the return on a stock be compared to global sector benchmarks because industry factors have increased in importance for explaining stock returns. In fact, I believe that diversifying across borders is no longer necessary as long as the investor has adequate industry representation."	Correct Incorrect	
"Differing governmental monetary and fiscal policies cause bond market correlations to be low, often lower than that between global equity markets. As a result, adding global bonds to global equity portfolios can improve the performance of a global efficient frontier, especially for lower risk portfolios."	Correct Incorrect	

Claude is examining the risk and returns for an investment in a Japanese stock and has collected the following statistics.

- The return on the stock in yen was 12%.
- The yen has appreciated by 5% relative to the euro.
- The standard deviation of stock returns was 29%.
- The standard deviation of the yen-euro exchange rate was 14%.
- The correlation between the stock returns and the yen is 0.30.

B.   **Calculate** the return on the stock in euros and the contribution of currency risk.

(6 minutes)

QUESTION 6 HAS FOUR PARTS FOR A TOTAL OF 25 MINUTES

In 1955, David Peebles, founder of the successful California-based Peebles Winery, established the Tokay Endowment to fund research on producing globally competitive California wine grapes. Since Peebles's initial contribution of $1 million, the fund has grown to its $75 million current value.

Peebles's grandson, Vincent Scavuzzo, a graduate of a globally recognized private business school and holder of the CFA Charter, was recently given responsibility for managing the endowment's portfolio. He believes the endowment's asset mix, currently 60% equities ($45 million) and 40% bonds ($30 million), needs to be updated to include alternative investments. He has gathered the historical data in Exhibits 1 and 2 on the Tokay portfolio, managed futures, hedge funds, and buyout funds (a form of private equity). He is suggesting the fund invest 10% of total assets in managed futures by selling a portion of the bonds held.

Exhibit 1: Returns and Standard Deviation for the Most Recent 10-Year Period

	Annualized Return	Standard Deviation
Tokay equities	9.8%	14.9%
Tokay bonds	6.9%	4.3%
Buyout funds	13.9%	15.2%
Hedge funds	14.6%	10.1%
Managed futures	12.5%	11.9%
Risk-free asset	3.0%	—

Exhibit 2: Correlations for the Most Recent 10-Year Period

	Tokay Equities	Tokay Bonds	Buyout Funds	Hedge Funds	Managed Futures
Tokay equities	1.00				
Tokay bonds	0.37	1.00			
Buyout funds	0.86	0.28	1.00		
Hedge funds	0.85	0.10	0.45	1.00	
Managed futures	−0.12	0.10	−0.04	−0.14	1.00

Mario Rudd, a trusted friend and financial analyst, offers Scavuzzo some advice:

"I agree that adding alternatives to your portfolio will improve its return performance from a risk-adjusted perspective. If I was making the decision, however, I would invest in hedge funds instead of managed futures. Their historical Sharpe ratios have been consistently higher than those of managed futures."

A.   In the template provided, **discuss** *six* major due diligence criteria that the Tokay Endowment should consider when selecting an active manager for its alternative investments.

(6 minutes)

Template for Question 6A

Due diligence discussion
1.
2.
3.
4.
5.
6.

B.   Using the data in Exhibits 1 and 2, **determine** whether you agree with Rudd's recommendation and **support** your decision with one reason. *Note: Using Rudd's statement in its current form or reworded is insufficient support of your answer.*

(4 minutes)

C.   **Discuss** *two* reasons managed futures should be added to Tokay's Endowment portfolio.

(6 minutes)

D.   **Discuss** the criteria Tokay Endowment should consider when evaluating a potential investment in middle-market buyout funds. Specifically, **comment** on the following:
- Benchmarks.
- Investment characteristics.
- Impact on the overall portfolio's risk/return profile.

(9 minutes)

Template for Question 6D

Benchmarks	
Investment characteristics	
Impact on the overall portfolio's risk/return profile	

QUESTION 7 HAS TWO PARTS FOR A TOTAL OF 8 MINUTES

Tom Amato is an analyst for Orthogonal Research and specializes in commodities markets. Amato is discussing the pricing of commodities in the spot and futures markets and makes the following comments:

"To derive the futures contract price using the cost of carry model, an investor would add the periodic financing and storage costs to the spot rate. For assets that have a convenience yield, the convenience yield would then be subtracted to obtain the no arbitrage price for a futures contract."

"The financing and storage costs for corn are substantial and can be greater than the convenience yield, and futures contracts save the investor the cost of holding spot corn. Therefore, considering both long term contracts of two to three years as well as short term contracts of a few months, the futures price curve will be continually upward sloping."

A.   **State** whether or not *each* of these comments is correct. If incorrect, **explain** why.

Answer Question 7A in the template provided.

(6 minutes)

Amato is examining the following futures prices for crude oil, gasoline, and heating oil.

One-month crude oil futures price	$70.29 per barrel[1]
Two-month gasoline futures price	$1.7500 per gallon
Two-month heating oil futures price	$1.8200 per gallon

[1]There are 42 gallons of crude oil in a barrel.

B.   **Calculate** the value of a 5-3-2 crack spread.

(2 minutes)

Template for Question 7A

Comment	Is the statement correct or incorrect? (circle one)	If incorrect, explain why
"To derive the futures contract price using the cost of carry model, an investor would add the periodic financing and storage costs to the spot rate. From this, the convenience yield would be subtracted to obtain the no arbitrage price for a futures contract."	**Correct** **Incorrect**	
"The financing and storage costs for corn are substantial and are greater than the convenience yield. Futures contracts save the investor the costs of holding the spot. Therefore, using short-term contracts of a few months to long-term contracts of two to three years, the futures price curve will be upward sloping."	**Correct** **Incorrect**	

QUESTION 8 HAS THREE PARTS FOR A TOTAL OF 32 MINUTES

Johan and Andrea Kraus are both 85 years old. Their current annual spending rate is €125,000, and they anticipate that the real rate of spending will grow at 3% annually. Their current portfolio contains €600,000 of cash equivalents, a €300,000 position in a diversified bond fund, and a €300,000 position in a diversified equity fund.

The Krauses have decided that they would like to gift a substantial portion of their wealth, so they are going to meet with financial planner, Jens Schultz, CFA, to update their investment policy statement. Schultz has constructed the mortality table in Exhibit 1 for the Krauses given a three-year planning horizon.

Exhibit 1: Mortality Table

Years	Johan		Andrea	
	Age	Prob.	Age	Prob.
1	86	0.8882	86	0.9171
2	87	0.7645	87	0.8244
3	88	0.6277	88	0.7208

Schultz plans on computing the Kraus's core capital and excess capital based on the probabilities in Exhibit 1. He estimates inflation will be 2%, and the real risk-free rate is 4%.

A.   Fill in all *non-shaded* areas of the template provided.

(19 minutes)

Template for 8A

Year	Combined Probability	Real Annual Spending	Expected Real Spending	Present Value
1				
2				
3				
Core Capital				
Excess Capital				

Show your calculations for Question 8A in the space provided.

©2010 Kaplan, Inc.

Use this page to show your calculations for Question 8A.

Schultz believes the Krauses have not been taking advantage of available methods to avoid double taxation on their U.S. income. He has determined that the appropriate tax rates are 40% in the United States and 45% in Germany. Schultz estimates the Krauses will receive income of $60,000 from their U.S. assets next year.

B.   In the template provided, **indicate** the *most likely* tax jurisdiction claimed on the Krauses' income by the United States and by Germany.

(4 minutes)

Template for Question 8B

Country	Tax Jurisdiction (circle one)
United States	Source Jurisdiction Residence Jurisdiction
Germany	Source Jurisdiction Residence Jurisdiction

C.   **Determine** the Kraus's *total* income tax liability on the income received from U.S. assets under the credit method, the exemption method, and the deduction method.

Answer Question 8C in the template provided. Show your calculations.

(9 minutes)

Template for Question 8C

Credit Method	
Exemption Method	
Deduction Method	

QUESTION 9 HAS THREE PARTS FOR A TOTAL OF 14 MINUTES

Helen Baker, CFA, invests in distressed securities. Specifically, she creates an arbitrage position by shorting the underlying company equity and purchasing a long position in the company's distressed debt. Baker's strategy is to capitalize on her knowledge of, and patience for, particular situations. To this end, she takes advantage of creditors who want to liquidate securities of companies that are in or near bankruptcy. In addition, Baker exploits the fact that distressed companies lack adequate research coverage. Baker buys the distressed debt for 50 cents or less on the dollar.

A.   i.   **Explain** the distressed debt arbitrage strategy *most likely* utilized by Baker.

        ii. Assuming the company's prospects improve, **explain** how the strategy will perform with respect to prices of the stocks and bonds as well as coupon interest and dividends paid and/or received.

(6 minutes)

B.   **Describe** the following three sources of risk in distressed debt investing, and **comment** on the relative importance of each.

    i.   Event risk.
    ii. Market liquidity risk.
    iii. Market risk.

(6 minutes)

C.   **Describe** J factor risk as it relates to distressed debt investing.

(2 minutes)

QUESTION 10 HAS TWO PARTS FOR A TOTAL OF 12 MINUTES

Heather Ramberg, a consultant to the board of directors of Reins Foundation, has been asked to analyze and recommend an asset allocation for Reins. Ramberg has read Reins's investment policy statement and found the following information:

Return objective: 8.5%.

Risk objective: Maximum standard deviation 10%.

To analyze the appropriate asset allocation, Ramberg produced data on the 5 corner portfolios shown in Exhibit 1.

Exhibit 1: Data on Five Corner Portfolios

Corner Portfolio	Expected Return (%)	Expected Standard Deviation (%)	Sharpe Ratio	Portfolio Weights, in %			
				U.S. Equities	Foreign Equities	Global Bonds	U.S. Real Estate
1	10.2	14.1	0.5106	0.0	100.0	0.0	0.0
2	10.1	13.6	0.5221	100.0	0.0	0.0	0.0
3	9.3	12.1	0.5207	35.6	25.4	20.0	19.0
4	8.2	9.0	0.5778	38.4	12.9	36.7	12.0
5	7.8	8.9	0.5506	31.4	15.9	39.7	13.0

Risk-free rate = 3.0%

A.   **Select** the two adjacent corner portfolios to be used in finding the *most* appropriate strategic asset allocation for Reins's portfolio, assuming that short selling or other borrowing (margin) is not allowed.

(2 minutes)

B.   **Determine** the *most* appropriate combination (percentage weights of the final combination) of the two corner portfolios selected in Part A.

(3 minutes)

C.   Assuming the two corner portfolios have been combined according to the weights in Part B, **determine** the percentage of the final combination that will be invested in foreign equities.

(3 minutes)

D.   Using data from Exhibit 1 and assuming that short selling (leverage) is permitted: (1) **determine** which corner portfolio or portfolios would *most likely* be selected and provide one reason to support your selection; and (2) **describe**, without calculations, the *most likely* portfolio allocation (i.e., weights of the assets that are combined).

(4 minutes)

QUESTION 11 HAS ONE PART FOR A TOTAL OF 12 MINUTES

Nick Richards is a pension consultant and is asked to evaluate the following portfolios:

- Portfolio 1 is highly concentrated, with five stocks representing 75% of the total portfolio.
- Portfolio 2 is highly diversified with over 400 stocks, none of which represents more than 1% of the total portfolio.
- Portfolio 3 is a diversified portfolio of 70 stocks, with the top ten names representing 30% of the total portfolio.

The following investment results were recorded during 2010:

	Portfolio 1	Portfolio 2	Portfolio 3	S&P 500
Return	42.0%	25.0%	16.0%	20.0%
Standard deviation	1.20	0.40	0.20	0.50
Beta	1.80	1.20	0.50	1.00

Risk-free rate: 6%

Compute the Sharpe, Treynor, M^2, and Jensen measures for each portfolio.

Answer Question 11 in the template provided.

(12 minutes)

Template for Question 11

Performance Measure	Portfolio	Calculation	Value
Sharpe	1		
	2		
	3		
Treynor	1		
	2		
	3		
M^2	1		
	2		
	3		

Jensen	1		
	2		
	3		

QUESTION 12 HAS TWO PARTS FOR A TOTAL OF 10 MINUTES

Beaver Dam Lumber (BDL) is one of the largest lumber companies in the United States, and the Beaver Dam Lumber Defined Benefit Pension Plan (BDLP) currently has a funding surplus. Slumping building starts in both the residential and commercial sectors, however, have led to declining sales. In response, BDL has offered early retirement to some employees, and the BDLP investment committee has decided to restructure the plan's portfolio more conservatively.

As a result of the early retirement offer, BDLP will have to make lump-sum payments totaling $20,000,000 over the next year. The BDLP investment committee has met and adopted a required return objective for their portfolio of 8.5% with a minimum acceptable return of –8.0%, coinciding with a Roy's Safety First ratio of 2.0.

The BDLP investment committee instructs Stephen Shamley, CFA, to evaluate the plan's $200,000,000 portfolio allocation and recommend changes. Shamley presents the five alternative allocations shown in Exhibit 1 for the committee's consideration.

Exhibit 1: Alternative Asset Allocations and Return/Risk Measures

Asset Class	Allocations (%)				
	A	B	C	D	E
Cash & equivalents	5	5	10	4	10
Global fixed income	35	30	30	40	35
Domestic fixed income	15	5	5	20	10
U.S. equities	30	30	30	16	35
Non-U.S. equities	15	15	13	20	10
Lumber industry equities	0	15	12	0	0
	Risk and Return (%)				
Expected total return	8.65	9.25	9.06	8.29	9.04
Expected standard deviation	8.53	8.43	8.83	8.35	8.19

A.   Of the allocations shown in Exhibit 1, **select** the *most* appropriate allocation for BDLP. **Support** your decision with *two* reasons, other than meeting the return requirement.

(6 minutes)

B.   For each of the four portfolios *not* selected, **state** *one* reason why it is not the *most* appropriate.

(4 minutes)

END OF MORNING SESSION

©2010 Kaplan, Inc.

Exam 1 Afternoon Session
Topic Breakdown

Question	Topic	Minutes
13	Ethics and Standards	18
14	Ethics and Standards	18
15	Economic Concepts	18
16	Risk Management Applications of Derivatives	18
17	Fixed Income Portfolio Management	18
18	Fixed Income Portfolio Management	18
19	Execution of Portfolio Decisions	18
20	Risk Management Applications of Derivatives	18
21	Risk Management	18
22	Global Investing/GIPS	18
	Total	180

EXAM 1 SELECTED RESPONSE ITEM SET ANSWER SHEET

The afternoon session of the Level III exam contains 10 Selected Response Item Sets, each with six questions, and you must answer them by filling in a bubble sheet with a number 2 or HB pencil. For realism, we suggest that you use this answer sheet and darken the bubbles corresponding to your answers. This sheet will also facilitate entering your answers into our online Performance Tracker. You have 180 minutes for this session of the exam. That equates to 3 minutes per item set question, so budget your time well.

13.1.	Ⓐ Ⓑ Ⓒ			18.1.	Ⓐ Ⓑ Ⓒ	
13.2.	Ⓐ Ⓑ Ⓒ			18.2.	Ⓐ Ⓑ Ⓒ	
13.3.	Ⓐ Ⓑ Ⓒ			18.3.	Ⓐ Ⓑ Ⓒ	
13.4.	Ⓐ Ⓑ Ⓒ			18.4.	Ⓐ Ⓑ Ⓒ	
13.5.	Ⓐ Ⓑ Ⓒ			18.5.	Ⓐ Ⓑ Ⓒ	
13.6.	Ⓐ Ⓑ Ⓒ			18.6.	Ⓐ Ⓑ Ⓒ	
14.1.	Ⓐ Ⓑ Ⓒ			19.1.	Ⓐ Ⓑ Ⓒ	
14.2.	Ⓐ Ⓑ Ⓒ			19.2.	Ⓐ Ⓑ Ⓒ	
14.3.	Ⓐ Ⓑ Ⓒ			19.3.	Ⓐ Ⓑ Ⓒ	
14.4.	Ⓐ Ⓑ Ⓒ			19.4.	Ⓐ Ⓑ Ⓒ	
14.5.	Ⓐ Ⓑ Ⓒ			19.5.	Ⓐ Ⓑ Ⓒ	
14.6.	Ⓐ Ⓑ Ⓒ			19.6.	Ⓐ Ⓑ Ⓒ	
15.1.	Ⓐ Ⓑ Ⓒ			20.1.	Ⓐ Ⓑ Ⓒ	
15.2.	Ⓐ Ⓑ Ⓒ			20.2.	Ⓐ Ⓑ Ⓒ	
15.3.	Ⓐ Ⓑ Ⓒ			20.3.	Ⓐ Ⓑ Ⓒ	
15.4.	Ⓐ Ⓑ Ⓒ			20.4.	Ⓐ Ⓑ Ⓒ	
15.5.	Ⓐ Ⓑ Ⓒ			20.5.	Ⓐ Ⓑ Ⓒ	
15.6.	Ⓐ Ⓑ Ⓒ			20.6.	Ⓐ Ⓑ Ⓒ	
16.1.	Ⓐ Ⓑ Ⓒ			21.1.	Ⓐ Ⓑ Ⓒ	
16.2.	Ⓐ Ⓑ Ⓒ			21.2.	Ⓐ Ⓑ Ⓒ	
16.3.	Ⓐ Ⓑ Ⓒ			21.3.	Ⓐ Ⓑ Ⓒ	
16.4.	Ⓐ Ⓑ Ⓒ			21.4.	Ⓐ Ⓑ Ⓒ	
16.5.	Ⓐ Ⓑ Ⓒ			21.5.	Ⓐ Ⓑ Ⓒ	
16.6.	Ⓐ Ⓑ Ⓒ			21.6.	Ⓐ Ⓑ Ⓒ	
17.1.	Ⓐ Ⓑ Ⓒ			22.1.	Ⓐ Ⓑ Ⓒ	
17.2.	Ⓐ Ⓑ Ⓒ			22.2.	Ⓐ Ⓑ Ⓒ	
17.3.	Ⓐ Ⓑ Ⓒ			22.3.	Ⓐ Ⓑ Ⓒ	
17.4.	Ⓐ Ⓑ Ⓒ			22.4.	Ⓐ Ⓑ Ⓒ	
17.5.	Ⓐ Ⓑ Ⓒ			22.5.	Ⓐ Ⓑ Ⓒ	
17.6.	Ⓐ Ⓑ Ⓒ			22.6.	Ⓐ Ⓑ Ⓒ	

PRACTICE EXAM 1
AFTERNOON SESSION

Questions 13.1–13.6 relate to Dynamic Investment Services.

Dynamic Investment Services (DIS) is a global, full-service investment advisory firm based in the United States. Although the firm provides numerous investment services, DIS specializes in portfolio management for individual and institutional clients and only deals in publicly traded debt, equity, and derivative instruments. Walter Fried, CFA, is a portfolio manager and the director of DIS's offices in Austria. For several years, Fried has maintained a relationship with a local tax consultant. The consultant provides a DIS marketing brochure with Fried's contact information to his clients seeking investment advisory services, and in return, Fried manages the consultant's personal portfolio and informs the consultant of potential tax issues in the referred clients' portfolios as they occur. Because he cannot personally manage all of the inquiring clients' assets, Fried generally passes the client information along to one of his employees but never discloses his relationship with the tax accountant. Fried recently forwarded information on the prospective Jones Family Trust account to Beverly Ulster, CFA, one of his newly hired portfolio managers.

Upon receiving the information, Ulster immediately set up a meeting with Terrence Phillips, the trustee of the Jones Family Trust. Ulster began the meeting by explaining DIS's investment services as detailed in the firm's approved marketing and public relations literature. Ulster also had Phillips complete a very detailed questionnaire regarding the risk and return objectives, investment constraints, and other information related to the trust beneficiaries. While reading the questionnaire, Ulster learned that Phillips heard about DIS's services through a referral from his tax consultant. Upon further investigation, Ulster discovered the agreement set up between Fried and the tax consultant, which is legal according to Austrian law but was not disclosed by either party. Ulster took a break from the meeting to get more details from Fried. With full information on the referral arrangement, Ulster immediately makes full disclosure to Phillips. Before the meeting with Phillips concluded, Ulster began formalizing the investment policy statement (IPS) for the Jones Family Trust and agreed to Phillips's request that the IPS should explicitly forbid derivatives positions in the Trust portfolio.

A few hours after meeting with the Jones Family Trust representative, Ulster accepted another new referral client, Steven West, from Fried. Following DIS policy, Ulster met with West to address his investment objectives and constraints and explain the firm's services. During the meeting, Ulster informed West that DIS offers three levels of account status, each with an increasing fee based on the account's asset value. The first level has the lowest account fees but receives oversubscribed domestic IPO allocations only after the other two levels receive IPO allocations. The second-level clients have the same priority as third-level clients with respect to oversubscribed domestic IPO allocations and receive research with significantly greater detail than first-level clients. Clients who subscribe to the third level of DIS services receive the most detailed research reports and are allowed to participate in both domestic and international IPOs. All clients receive research and recommendations at approximately the same time. West decided to engage DIS's services as a second-level client. While signing the enrollment papers, West told Ulster, "If you can give me the kind of performance I am looking for, I may move the rest of my assets to DIS." When Ulster inquired about the other accounts, West would not specify how much or what type of assets he held in other accounts. West also noted that a portion of the existing assets to be transferred to Ulster's control were private equity investments in small start-up companies, which DIS would need to manage. Ulster assured him that DIS would have no problem managing the private equity investments.

After her meeting with West, Ulster attended a weekly strategy session held by DIS. All managers were required to attend this particular meeting since the focus was on a new strategy designed to reduce portfolio volatility while slightly enhancing return using a combination of futures and options on various asset classes. Intrigued by the idea, Ulster implemented the strategy for all of her clients and achieved positive results for all portfolios. Ulster's average performance results after one year of using the new strategy are presented in Figure 1. For comparative purposes, performance figures without the new strategy are also presented.

Figure 1

	Average Sharpe Ratio	
	Without Strategy	*With Strategy*
Individual portfolios	0.80	0.89
Institutional portfolios	0.63	0.71

At the latest strategy meeting, DIS economists were extremely pessimistic about emerging market economies and suggested that the firm's portfolio managers consider selling emerging market securities out of their portfolios and avoid these investments for the next 12 to 15 months. Fried placed a limit order to sell his personal holdings of an emerging market fund at a price 5% higher than the market price at the time. He then began selling his clients' (all of whom have discretionary accounts with DIS) holdings of the same emerging market fund using market orders. All of his clients' trade orders were completed just before the price of the fund declined sharply by 13%, causing Fried's order to remain unfilled.

13.1. Did Ulster violate CFA Institute Standards of Professional Conduct by accepting either Phillips or West as new clients?
   A. Standards were violated in accepting both Phillips and West as clients.
   B. There was no violation in accepting Phillips, but there was a violation in accepting West.
   C. There were no Standards violations in accepting either client.

13.2. Does the referral agreement between Fried and the tax consultant violate any CFA Institute Standards of Professional Conduct?
   A. No.
   B. Yes, because client confidentiality is being undermined by the arrangement.
   C. Yes, because it involves non-monetary compensation with no observable cost.

13.3. During her initial meeting with West, did Ulster violate any CFA Institute Standards of Professional Conduct?
   A. Yes.
   B. No, because she developed a detailed investment policy to ensure the suitability of investment choices for the client's account.
   C. No, because she ensured that all conflicts of interest were disclosed to the client before the investment policy statement was created.

13.4. According to CFA Institute Standards of Professional Conduct, which of the following statements regarding Ulster's meeting with West is *most* accurate? Ulster may:
   A. offer the different service levels and may accept the account without full knowledge of West's other accounts.
   B. not offer the different service levels but may accept the account without full knowledge of West's other accounts.
   C. not offer the different service levels and may not accept the account without full knowledge of West's other accounts.

13.5. By utilizing the futures and options strategy as suggested by DIS's economists, did Ulster violate any CFA Institute Standards of Professional Conduct?
   A. Yes.
   B. No, because she acted in her clients' best interest by reducing portfolio risk while increasing portfolio return.
   C. No, because she treated all clients fairly by applying the strategy to both individual and institutional clients.

13.6. According to CFA Institute Standards of Professional Conduct, should Fried have taken a different course of action with respect to the limit order on the emerging market fund?
A. No.
B. Yes, Fried should not have sold any shares of the emerging market fund.
C. Yes, Fried should have waited to place the limit order until after the market orders were filled.

Questions 14.1–14.6 relate to Crane & Associates.

Shirley Riley, CFA, has just been promoted from vice president of trading to chief investment officer (CIO) at Crane & Associates, LLC (CA), a large investment management firm. Riley has been with CA for eight years, but she has much to learn as she assumes her new duties as CIO. Riley has decided to hire Denny Simpson, CFA, as the new compliance officer for CA. Riley and Simpson have been reviewing procedures and policies throughout the firm and have discovered several potential issues.

Communications with Clients

Portfolio managers are encouraged to communicate with clients on a regular basis. At a minimum, managers are expected to contact clients on a quarterly basis to review portfolio performance. Each client must have an investment policy statement (IPS) created when their account is opened, specifying the objectives and constraints for their portfolio. IPSs are reviewed at client request at any time. When market conditions or client circumstances dictate a change in the investment style or strategy of a client portfolio, the client is notified immediately by phone or email and the client's IPS is revised as necessary before any changes are made.

Employee Incentive Program

CA offers several incentive programs to employees. One of the most popular of these programs is the CA IPO program. Whenever CA is involved in an initial public offering (IPO), portfolio managers are allowed to participate. The structure is simple—for every 100 shares purchased on behalf of a client, the manager is awarded five shares for his own account. The manager is thus rewarded for getting an IPO sold and at the same time is able to share in the results of the IPO. Any time shares are remaining 72 hours before the IPO goes public, other employees are allowed to participate on a first-come, first-serve basis. Employees seem to appreciate this opportunity, but CA does not have exact numbers on employee participation in the program.

Private Equity Fund

CA has a private equity fund that is internally managed. This fund is made available only to clients with more than $5 million in assets managed by CA, a policy that is fully disclosed in CA's marketing materials. Roughly one-third of the fund's assets are invested in companies that are either very small capitalization or thinly traded (or both). The pricing of these securities for monthly account statements is often difficult. CA support staff get information from different sources—sometimes using third party services, sometimes using CA valuation models. In some instances, a manager of the private equity fund will enter an order during the last trading hour of the month to purchase 100 shares of one of these small securities at a modest premium to the last trade price. If the trade gets executed, that price can then be used on the account statements. The small size of these trades does not significantly affect the fund's overall position in any particular company holding, which is typically several thousand shares.

Soft Dollar Usage

Several different managers at CA use independent research in developing investment ideas. One of the more popular research services among CA managers is "Beneath the Numbers (BTN)," which focuses on potential accounting abuses at prominent companies. This service often provides early warnings of problems with a stock, allowing CA managers the opportunity to sell their clients' positions before a negative surprise lowers the price. Stocks covered by BTN are typically widely held in CA client accounts. Managers at CA have been so happy with BTN that they have also subscribed to a new research product provided by the same authors—"Beneath the Radar (BTR)." BTR recommends small capitalization securities that are not large enough to attract much attention from large institutional investors. The results of BTR's recommendations are mixed thus far, but CA managers are willing to be patient.

As they discuss these issues, Riley informs Simpson that she is determined to bring CA into full compliance with the CFA Institute's "Asset Manager Code of Professional Conduct." The following questions should be answered with the Asset Manager Code as a guide.

14.1. Indicate whether CA's policies related to investment policy statement (IPS) reviews and notification of changes in investment style/strategy are consistent with the Asset Manager Code of Professional Conduct.
A. Both policies are inadequate.
B. Both policies are consistent with the Asset Manager Code of Professional Conduct.
C. The IPS review policy is inadequate, but the policy on communicating changes in style/strategy is adequate.

14.2. Indicate whether CA's policies related to its IPO program, specifically allowing portfolio manager participation and employee participation, are consistent with the Asset Manager Code of Professional Conduct.
A. Policies on both portfolio manager and employee participation in IPOs are not consistent with the Asset Manager Code of Professional Conduct.
B. The employee participation in IPOs policy is consistent with the Asset Manager Code, as is the portfolio manager's policy on participation in IPOs.
C. The portfolio manager's policy on IPOs is not consistent with the Asset Manager Cod; however, the employee policy on IPOs is consistent with the Asset Manager Code.

14.3. Participation in CA's private equity fund is limited to clients with $5 million under management. This policy:
   A. does not violate the Asset Manager Code of Professional Conduct.
   B. would be acceptable so long as a similar investment vehicle was made available to all clients.
   C. is not consistent with the Asset Manager Code of Professional Conduct.

14.4. In discussing the pricing of thinly traded securities in the private equity fund, Riley suggested that CA should choose one pricing method and apply it consistently, thus avoiding the need to disclose specific pricing methods to clients. Simpson responded that using third party sources or internal valuation models was acceptable, so long as the pricing sources are fully disclosed to clients. Indicate whether Riley's comment and/or Simpson's responses are *correct* or *incorrect*.
   A. Both Riley's comment and Simpson's response are correct.
   B. Riley's comment is not correct; however, Simpson's response is correct.
   C. Riley is correct, while Simpson is not correct.

14.5. Trading stocks during the last trading hour of a month to establish a fair market price:
   A. does not violate the Asset Manager Code of Professional Conduct.
   B. is acceptable so long as the trade is not material relative to the overall CA position in the security.
   C. is not consistent with the Asset Manager Code of Professional Conduct.

14.6. Simpson has verified that CA has adequate disclosures of its soft dollar usage. Given that full disclosure is made to clients, indicate whether CA's use of soft dollars for BTN and BTR are consistent with the Asset Manager Code of Professional Conduct.
   A. Given the adequate disclosures, use of soft dollars for both BTN and BTR is acceptable.
   B. Use of soft dollars for BTN is acceptable, but not for BTR.
   C. Neither of these publications provide direct benefit to the client; thus, neither may be paid for with soft dollars.

Questions 15.1–15.6 relate to GloboFunds.

Joe Lipscomb is a junior economist for GloboFunds, a large investment management company. He has been asked to develop economic forecasts for several developing and developed markets to support a few of the global funds that the firm manages.

Lipscomb is aware that many of his colleagues use the Cobb-Douglas production function to forecast real GDP growth, but he is not familiar with it. He asks Donald Prater, one of his senior colleagues, to explain the function. While discussing the Cobb-Douglas production function, Prater makes the following statements:

Statement 1:   By assuming constant returns to scale in the Cobb-Douglas production function, we assume that the percentage change in total factor productivity is some constant, positive value.

Statement 2:   The Solow residual is the portion of the percentage change in real output that is not explained by the percentage change in total factor productivity, the percentage change in capital stock, and the percentage change in labor.

After gaining a basic understanding of the Cobb-Douglas production function, Lipscomb is ready to evaluate the growth of a few countries. Prater asks Lipscomb to analyze three countries and determine which has the highest expected real GDP growth rate. Lipscomb has gathered the estimates for the three countries in Figure 1:

Figure 1: Growth Expectations for Countries 1, 2, and 3				
Country	Growth in Total Factor Productivity	Growth in Capital Stock	Growth in Labor Input	Output Elasticity of Capital (α)
1	2.0%	4.0%	9.0%	0.7
2	4.0%	4.5%	7.5%	0.4
3	3.0%	8.5%	5.5%	0.3

After determining which country has the highest expected growth rate, Prater asks Lipscomb to assist him by determining the intrinsic value of the equity market for a fourth developing country. The country is expected to have high growth next year that will then decline linearly over the next 20 years to a sustainable growth rate. The estimated real required rate of return is 12%, and the most recent dividend was $15. Data regarding country four are shown in Figure 2:

Figure 2: Growth Expectations for Country 4				
Year	Growth in Total Factor Productivity	Growth in Capital Stock	Growth in Labor Input	Output Elasticity of Capital(α)
1	5.2%	6.9%	8.9%	0.4
21	0.5%	1.7%	2.0%	0.7

GloboFunds has placed a significant bet on a developed country (Country 5) in Western Europe. There is some fear internally that this equity market is becoming overvalued. Lipscomb decides to evaluate the intrinsic value of this market using the Yardeni model. The yield on A-rated corporate bonds is 7.5%, the long-term earnings growth rate is estimated to be 5%, and the current P/E ratio is 15. Lipscomb has estimated that the weighting factor for the importance of earnings growth is 0.15 for this country.

GloboFunds is looking at expanding into alternative investments by managing a global macro hedge fund, but the portfolio managers are unsure as to the best forecasting approach to implement. They have asked Lipscomb to identify the best method. The fund will place bets on the direction of equity markets and currencies using exchange traded funds, forwards, and futures.

15.1.   Is Prater's first statement regarding constant returns to scale and the percentage change in total factor productivity correct?
A. Yes.
B. No, the percentage change in total factor productivity is assumed to be zero when assuming constant returns to scale.
C. No, the percentage change in total factor productivity can be any real number when assuming constant returns to scale.

15.2.   Is Prater's second statement regarding the Solow residual correct?
A. Yes.
B. No, the Solow residual is equal to the percentage change in capital stock.
C. No, the Solow residual is equal to the percentage change in total factor productivity.

15.3.   Based on the growth and elasticity data compiled by Lipscomb, which country has the highest expected real GDP growth rate?
A. Country 1.
B. Country 2.
C. Country 3.

15.4. The intrinsic value of the equity market in Country 4 is *closest* to:
A. 154.
B. 328.
C. 345.

15.5. Based on the Yardeni Model, Lipscomb would *most likely* conclude that the equity index is:
A. overvalued.
B. undervalued.
C. fairly valued.

15.6. Regarding the forecasting approach that would be *best* suited for the global macro hedge fund, Lipscomb would *most likely* select:
A. the top-down approach.
B. the bottom-up approach.
C. both the top-down and bottom-up approaches.

Questions 16.1–16.6 relate to Garrison Investments.

Garrison Investments is a money management firm focusing on endowment management for small colleges and universities. Over the past 20 years, the firm has primarily invested in U.S. securities with small allocations to high quality long-term foreign government bonds. Garrison's largest account, Point University, has a market value of $800 million and an asset allocation as detailed in Figure 1.

Figure 1: Point University Asset Allocation

Asset Class	Allocation	Dividend/Coupon*	Beta
Large cap equities	40%	2.0%	1.0
Mid cap equities	25%	1.2%	1.3
Small cap equities	15%	0.9%	1.5
U.S. Bonds	10%	5.0%	0
U.K. Bonds	5%	4.7%	0
German Bonds	5%	4.0%	0
European Index	0%	1.8%	1.2

*Bond coupon payments are all semiannual.

Managers at Garrison are concerned that expectations for a strengthening U.S. dollar relative to the British pound could negatively impact returns to Point University's U.K. bond allocation. Therefore, managers have collected information on swap and exchange rates. Currently, the swap rates in the United States and the United Kingdom are 4.9% and 5.3%, respectively. The spot exchange rate is 0.45 GBP/USD. The U.K. bonds are currently trading at face value.

Garrison recently convinced the board of trustees at Point University that the endowment should allocate a portion of the portfolio to European equities. The board has agreed to the plan but wants the allocation to international equities to be a short-term tactical move. Managers at Garrison have put together the following proposal for the reallocation:

> To minimize trading costs while gaining exposure to international equities, the portfolio can use futures contracts on the domestic 12-month mid-cap equity index and on the 12-month European equity index. This strategy will temporarily exchange $80 million of U.S. mid-cap exposure for European equity index exposure. Relevant data on the futures contracts are provided in Figure 2.

Figure 2: Mid-cap Index and European Index Futures Data

Futures Contract	Price	Beta	Multiplier
Mid-cap Index	$908	1.10	250
European Index	$2,351	1.05	50

Three months after proposing the international diversification plan, Garrison was able to persuade Point University to make a direct short-term investment of $2 million in Haikuza International (HI), a Japanese electronics firm. HI exports its products primarily to the United States and Europe, selling only 30% of its production in Japan. In order to control the costs of its production inputs, HI uses currency futures to mitigate exchange rate fluctuations associated with contractual gold purchases from Australia. In its current contract, HI has one remaining purchase of Australian gold that will occur in nine months. The company has hedged the purchase with a long 12-month futures contract on the Australian dollar (AUD).

Managers at Garrison are expecting to sell the HI position in one year but have become nervous about the impact of an expected depreciation in the value of the Yen relative to the U.S. dollar. Thus, they have decided to use a currency futures hedge. Analysts at Garrison have estimated that the covariance between the local currency returns on HI and changes in the USD/Yen spot rate is –0.184 and that the variance of changes in the USD/Yen spot rate is 0.92.

16.1. Which of the following is *closest* to the notional principal on a swap that would allow Point University to hedge the currency risk of the interest payments from their U.K. bond holdings?
A. GBP 16,000,000.
B. USD 38,000,000.
C. GBP 18,000,000.

16.2. With regard to Garrison's proposal to generate temporary exposure to European equities in the Point University portfolio, **determine** the appropriate position in the mid-cap equity index futures.
A. Buy 416 contracts.
B. Sell 298 contracts.
C. Sell 416 contracts.

16.3. With regard to Garrison's proposal to generate temporary exposure to European equities in the Point University portfolio, **determine** the appropriate position in the European equity index futures.
A. Buy 778 contracts.
B. Sell 595 contracts.
C. Sell 778 contracts.

16.4. **Determine** the type(s) of exchange rate risk exposure Haikuza hedged using currency futures.
   A. Economic exposure.
   B. Translation exposure.
   C. Transaction exposure.

16.5. Of the following, **determine** which *best* describes the risks and costs associated with Haikuza's currency hedging strategy.
   A. Haikuza's strategy is subject to basis risk and will have lower transaction costs than a short-term contract strategy.
   B. Haikuza's strategy is subject to basis risk and will have higher transaction costs than a short-term contract strategy.
   C. Haikuza's strategy is not subject to basis risk and will have lower transaction costs than a short-term contract strategy.

16.6. **Determine** which of the following *best* describes the minimum variance hedge ratio for Garrison's currency futures hedge on the Haikuza investment.
   A. For every futures contract sold to hedge translation risk, 0.2 futures contracts must be purchased to hedge economic risk.
   B. For every futures contract sold to hedge translation risk, 0.8 futures contracts must be purchased to hedge economic risk.
   C. For every futures contract sold to hedge translation risk, 1.2 futures contracts must be purchased to hedge economic risk.

Questions 17.1–17.6 relate to Northern Capital Advisors.

Dakota Watson and Anthony Smith are bond portfolio managers with Northern Capital Investment Advisors (NCIA). NCIA is based in the United States and has $2,000 million under management, including $950 million in global bond markets. NCIA's clients are primarily institutional investors such as insurance companies, foundations, and endowments. Because most of their clients insist on margins over relevant fixed-income benchmarks, Watson and Smith actively manage their bond portfolios to generate excess returns while minimizing tracking error.

One of the funds that Northern Capital offers invests in emerging market bonds. An excerpt from its prospectus reveals the following fund objectives and strategies:

> "The fund generates a return by constructing a portfolio using all major fixed-income sectors within the Asian region (except Japan) with a bias toward non-government bonds. The fund makes opportunistic investments in both investment grade and high yield bonds. Northern Capital analysts seek bond issues that are expected to outperform U.S. bonds that have similar credit risk, interest rate risk, and liquidity risk. Value is added by finding bonds that have been overlooked by other developed world bond funds. The fund favors non-dollar, local currency-denominated securities to avoid the default risk associated with a lack of hard currency on the part of foreign issuers."

Although Northern Capital examines the availability of excess returns in foreign markets by investing outside the index in those markets, many of its strategies involve spread analysis on U.S. bonds. Discussing the analysis of spreads in the U.S. bond market, Watson makes the following statements about the option-adjusted and swap spreads:

Statement 1:   "Due to changes in the structure of the primary bond market in the U.S., the option-adjusted spread is becoming increasingly valuable for analyzing the attractiveness of bond investments."

Statement 2:   "One advantage of the swap spread framework is that it provides investors with the tools to compare the relative attractiveness of fixed- and floating-rate bonds."

Watson's view of the U.S. economy is somewhat bearish. She forecasts that interest rates in the U.S. could fall as a result of a decline in the demand for loanable funds. Although she feels yields might decline, she believes strongly that market uncertainty will drive up interest rate volatility and has reallocated a portion of her bond portfolio to investment grade bonds.

Smith is even less decided about the economy, but his bond trading strategy has been quite successful in the past. As one example, he recently sold at par a 20-year, AA-rated $50,000 Mahan Corporation bond with a 7.75% coupon that he also purchased at par. With the proceeds, he bought a newly issued A-rated Quincy Corporation bond with an 8.25% coupon. By swapping the first bond for the second, he enhanced his annual income, which he considers quite favorable if interest rates fall as he expects.

Watson has become quite interested in the mortgage-backed security (MBS) market lately. In addition to an increased allocation to investment grade bonds, she has reallocated a portion of the corporate bond portfolio to MBS. She argues that, although a moderate drop in rates could move their prices slightly higher, corporate bonds on net could fall in value because of increased uncertainty in yields. MBS, on the other hand, should experience a net increase in value. She identifies this strategy as a structure trade.

Smith is examining the liquidity of three bonds. Their characteristics are listed in the table below:

	Issue Size	Coupon Rate	Term	Market
Bond A	$720 million	5.85%	10 years	Public Market
Bond B	$1,600 million	6.13%	7 years	Public Market
Bond C	$380 million	5.95%	20 years	Private Placement

17.1. Which of the following *best* describes the relative value analysis used in the Northern Capital emerging market bond fund? It is a:
 A. top-down approach.
 B. bottom-up approach.
 C. combination of a top-down approach and a bottom-up approach.

17.2. Regarding the statements made by Watson on the usefulness of the option adjusted spread and the swap spread, are both statements correct?
 A. Yes.
 B. No, only statement 2 is correct.
 C. No, both statements are incorrect.

17.3. Which of the following *best* describes Watson's increased allocation to investment grade bonds?
 A. Credit-defense trade.
 B. Pure yield pickup trade.
 C. Yield curve adjustment trade.

17.4. Which of the following *best* describes a primary shortcoming of Smith's strategy?
   A. The yields on the Mahan Corporation bond could increase.
   B. The yields on the Quincy Corporation bond could increase.
   C. The liquidity of the Mahan Corporation bond is likely lower.

17.5. Based solely on Watson's expectations, determine whether she has properly identified and executed her strategy.
   A. It is executed correctly, but she identifies it incorrectly.
   B. It is executed incorrectly, but she identifies it correctly.
   C. It is executed correctly, and she identifies it correctly.

17.6. Regarding the bonds Smith is examining, which of the following is *most likely* to have the greatest liquidity?
   A. Bond A.
   B. Bond B.
   C. Bond C.

Questions 18.1–18.6 relate to Andre Hickock.

Andre Hickock, CFA, is a newly hired fixed income portfolio manager for Candlewood Investments, LLC. Hickock is reviewing the portfolios of several pension clients that have been assigned to him. The first portfolio, Montana Hardware, Inc., has the characteristics shown in Figure 1.

Figure 1: Asset Allocation of Montana Hardware, Inc.

Sector	% of Portfolio	Duration	
U.S. Treasury	14.6%	7.54	1.1
U.S. agencies	23.7%	9.02	2.14
U.S. corporates	31.8%	4.52	1.44
U.S. mortgages (MBS)	11.4%	1.33	.152
Non-U.S. governments	18.5%	3.22	.596
	100.0%		

Hickock is attempting to assess the risk of the Montana Hardware portfolio. The benchmark bond index that Candlewood uses for pension accounts similar to that of Montana Hardware has an effective duration of 5.25. His supervisor, Carla Mity, has discussed bond risk measurement with Hickock. Mity is most familiar with equity risk measures and is not convinced of the validity of duration as a portfolio risk measure. Mity told Hickock, "I have always believed that standard deviation is the best measure of bond portfolio risk. You want to know the volatility, and standard deviation is the most direct measure of volatility."

Hickock is also reviewing the bond portfolio of Buffalo Sports, Inc., which is comprised of the following assets shown in Figure 2.

Figure 2: Asset Allocation of Buffalo Sports, Inc.

Sector	% of Portfolio	Duration
U.S. Treasury	10.1%	6.15
U.S. agencies	14.5%	7.20
U.S. corporates	20.9%	5.80
U.S. mortgages (MBS)	33.7%	4.65
U.S. ABS	8.2%	3.67
Non-U.S. governments	12.6%	2.50
	100.0%	

The trustees of the Buffalo Sports pension plan have requested that Candlewood explore alternatives to reduce the risk of the MBS sector of their bond portfolio. Hickock responded to their request as follows:

"I believe that the current option-adjusted spread (OAS) on the MBS sector is quite high. In order to reduce your risk, I would suggest that we hedge the interest rate risk using a combination of 2-year and 10-year Treasury security futures. I would further suggest that we do not take any steps to hedge spread risk at this time."

18.1   Mity's comment regarding the use of standard deviation instead of duration to measure bond portfolio risk is:
   A. correct because duration does not directly address volatility.
   B. incorrect because standard deviation does not address interest rate risk.
   C. incorrect because historical variance measures for specific bonds are not meaningful predictors of future volatility.

18.2.   **Calculate** the duration of the Montana Hardware pension portfolio and assess the interest rate risk of the portfolio versus Hickock's benchmark index. The interest rate risk of the Montana Hardware portfolio is:
   A. less than the benchmark.
   B. greater than the benchmark.
   C. the same as the benchmark.

18.3.   Hickock is reviewing other risk measures for the Montana Hardware portfolio. He has estimated the static spread duration for the portfolio to be 6.25. Which of the following statements regarding the Montana Hardware pension bond portfolio is *most* accurate?
   A. The portfolio has higher sensitivity to changes in interest rate levels than to changes in the spread over Treasury securities.
   B. The portfolio spread duration could be decreased by adding Treasury securities to the portfolio.
   C. A 50 basis point change in the zero volatility spread would lead to an approximately 6.25% change in the value of the portfolio.

18.4.   **Evaluate** Hickock's suggestions concerning the appropriate strategy for hedging interest rate risk and his suggestion not to hedge spread risk. Hickock is correct:
   A. only with regard to hedging interest rate risk.
   B. only with regard to his suggestion not to hedge spread risk.
   C. with regard to both suggestions.

18.5. In assessing the risk of a portfolio containing both bullet maturity corporate bonds and MBS, Hickock should always consider that:
   A. the duration of MBS securities will increase as the level of interest rates declines.
   B. MBS values will benefit from higher convexity as interest rates decline.
   C. MBS values will be more sensitive to changes in the shape of the yield curve than bullet maturity corporate bonds.

18.6. Under most circumstances, the *most* effective means of hedging the risk of a portfolio of MBS is to take an offsetting position in a:
   A. single Treasury security with a duration similar to the average duration of the MBS portfolio.
   B. portfolio consisting of a 2-year Treasury security and a 10-year Treasury security.
   C. portfolio consisting of a T-bill and a 30-year Treasury security.

Questions 19.1–19.6 relate to Kim Simpson and Janet Long.

Kim Simpson, CFA, manages a $75 million multi-cap growth portfolio. Simpson follows a growth investment strategy and her investment universe consists of small, medium, and large capitalization stocks. She turns the entire portfolio over once each year. Simpson is concerned about the amount of trading costs she has generated through the implementation of her investment strategy and decides to conduct a trade cost analysis with the cooperation of her trader, Janet Long, CFA. The first trade they examine is a leveraged purchase of 2,000 shares of Technology Company that was completed in a single day using a market order. The order was split into two trades as shown in Figure 1.

Figure 1: Technology Company buy order for 2,000 shares

Shares Purchased	Purchase Price	Ask Size	Ask Price	Bid Size	Bid Price
700	$79.25	700	$79.25	900	$79.00
1,300	$80.00	800	$80.10	1,100	$79.75

In conducting a comprehensive analysis of the trading markets, Simpson states that she is most concerned about market liquidity. Simpson defines a market with good liquidity as one with diversity of opinion, many buyers/sellers, and relatively wide bid-ask spreads. In addition to reviewing market liquidity, Simpson believes that, in order to assess market quality, both the ease with which investors can obtain accurate information and the certainty that a trade will be completed must be evaluated.

Simpson and Long review their trade of Nano Corporation, a small biotechnology company. Simpson used a limit order because her analyst had established a specific buy target and she wanted to hold down transaction costs. To handle both explicit and implicit trading costs, Simpson measures execution costs using implementation shortfall. The buy order for 100,000 shares of Nano stock has the following timeline:

- Nano stock price closes at $35.00 per share.
- *Day one*: Simpson places a limit order for 100,000 shares of Nano stock at $34.75 per share or better at the opening of trading. Nano's stock never falls below $35.00 per share and closes at $36.50 per share.
- *Day two*: Simpson adjusts her limit order price to $37.00 per share or better. Long is able to fill 50,000 shares of the order at $36.75 per share. Nano's stock climbs to $38.00 per share during the day and Simpson moves the limit price to $40.00 per share or better. Long completes the purchase of the remaining 50,000 shares of Nano at $40.00 per share, which is also the closing price of Nano's stock.
- The commission paid for each block trade is $2,500.

Long suggests implementing the Best Execution concept as established by the CFA Institute in its Trade Management Guidelines. Long states best execution would accept a high portfolio turnover strategy provided the overall portfolio value is greater after trading costs. Long asserts that her professional relationships are integral to best execution.

19.1.   The buy order for the Technology Company shares has an average effective spread *closest* to:
   A. $0.10.
   B. $0.15.
   C. $0.20.

19.2.   Which one of the following trader motivations *best* describes the Technology Company trade?
   A. Information-motivated.
   B. Value-motivated.
   C. Liquidity-motivated.

19.3.   Simpson discusses both the definition of market liquidity and how to assess market quality. Are her statements *correct*?
   A. Only the market liquidity statement is correct.
   B. Only the market quality statement is correct.
   C. Both statements are correct.

19.4.   The explicit cost component of the total implementation shortfall for the Nano Corporation trade is *closest* to:
   A. 0.15%.
   B. 0.25%.
   C. 0.35%.

19.5.   The total implementation shortfall for the Nano Corporation trade is *closest* to:
   A. 4%.
   B. 7%.
   C. 10%.

19.6.   Regarding Long's statements on best execution, determine whether her mention of professional relationships and high portfolio turnover are *most likely* correct or incorrect.
   A. Only the statement about business relationships is correct.
   B. Only the statement about high portfolio turnover is correct.
   C. Both statements are correct.

Questions 20.1–20.6 relate to Donaghy Management Company.

Donaghy Management Company (DMC) manages several funds only available to high net worth individuals. In preparation for an upcoming meeting, the firm has circulated among its managers the information in Figure 1 on strategies and market expectations relevant to each of three funds.

Figure 1: Fund Strategies and Market Expectations

	Fund A	*Fund B*	*Fund C*
Strategy	Predict and profit from volatility in the equity market using options on a broad equity index.	Market neutral fund with offsetting long and short equity positions. The fund utilizes leverage to enhance returns.	Long-only international equity fund. Individual securities may be delta-hedged using call options to reduce exposure to the position without selling it.
Market Expectations	Volatility in the equity market is expected to increase in the near future. However, the direction of the volatility is uncertain.	Credit markets are expected to tighten in the near future. Increased interest rates are expected across all credit qualities.	International equity markets are forecast to rise in general. Certain securities are forecast to decline in value temporarily.

The manager of Fund A has collected data on put and call options on the broad market index underlying his strategy. The option data are presented in Figure 2. All options presented have the same expiration date.

Figure 2: Option Data for the Broad Market Index

Call Price	*Strike Price*	*Put Price*
35.40	1,475	6.80
18.10	1,500	17.00
7.90	1,515	24.60

During the meeting, the manager of Fund B states that in order to enhance returns for the fund, he intends to implement a box-spread strategy. The manager explains the strategy by stating, "The ending price of the asset underlying the box-spread strategy has no impact on the payoff of the strategy.

Thus, if the market price of the strategy implies a rate of return greater than the risk-free rate, an arbitrage opportunity exists."

Also during the meeting, DMC's president questioned the manager of Fund C about the mechanics of his hedging strategy. The manager explained the strategy with the following comments:

Comment 1:   "The hedge position is established to reduce the exposure to certain equity positions by writing call options on those equity positions. The necessary number of short option positions per share of stock held is calculated as the inverse of the option delta."

Comment 2:   "The hedge position only requires adjusting in the event of a price or volatility change in the underlying and is effective for small changes in the price of the underlying security."

20.1.   Which of the following option strategies would be *most* beneficial in terms of potential payoff for Fund A given its objectives and market expectations?
A. Long straddle.
B. Long bull spread.
C. Short butterfly spread.

20.2.   Using the data in Figure 2, **determine** which of the following is *closest* to the maximum profit from a long butterfly call strategy.
A. 7.1.
B. 13.0.
C. 17.9.

20.3.   In 110 days, the manager of Fund B expects to borrow $50,000,000 for 180 days at a rate of 180-day LIBOR plus 150 bp to pursue a leveraged strategy. LIBOR is currently 6.5%. The manager purchases an interest rate call on 180-day LIBOR that expires in 110 days with a premium of $120,000 and exercise rate of 6%. If LIBOR at the option expiration is 7.3%, **calculate** the effective annual rate on the loan.
A. 7.30%.
B. 8.29%.
C. 8.80%.

20.4.   **Evaluate** the comment made by the manager of Fund B with respect to the box-spread strategy. The manager is:
A. correct.
B. incorrect, because the payoff of the box-spread is sensitive to the ending price of the asset underlying the options.
C. incorrect, because an arbitrage opportunity only exists if the market price of the box-spread strategy implies a rate of return less than the risk-free rate.

20.5. **Determine** whether the comments made by the manager of Fund C with respect to determining the hedge position and adjusting the hedge position are *correct*.
   A. Only Comment 1 is correct.
   B. Only Comment 2 is correct.
   C. Both Comment 1 and Comment 2 are correct.

20.6. Under which of the following scenarios will Fund C be *most* exposed to the gamma effect resulting from delta hedged equity positions? When the option used to delta hedge is:
   A. at-the-money and close to expiration.
   B. at-the-money and not close to expiration.
   C. deep in-the-money and close to expiration.

Questions 21.1–21.6 relate to Joan Nicholson and Kim Fluellen.

Joan Nicholson, CFA, and Kim Fluellen, CFA, sit on the risk management committee for Thomasville Asset Management. Although Thomasville manages the majority of its investable assets, it also utilizes outside firms for special situations such as market neutral and convertible arbitrage strategies. Thomasville has hired a hedge fund manager, Boston Advisors, for both of these strategies. The managers for the Boston Advisors funds are Frank Amato, CFA, and Joseph Garvin, CFA. Amato uses a market neutral strategy and has generated a return of $20 million this year on the $100 million Thomasville has invested with him. Garvin uses a convertible arbitrage strategy and has lost $15 million this year on the $200 million Thomasville has invested with him, with most of the loss coming in the last quarter of the year. Thomasville pays each outside manager an incentive fee of 20% on profits. During the risk management committee meeting Nicholson evaluates the characteristics of the arrangement with Boston Advisors. Nicholson states that the asymmetric nature of Thomasville's contract with Boston Advisors creates adverse consequences for Thomasville's net profits and that the compensation contract resembles a put option owned by Boston Advisors.

Upon request, Fluellen provides a risk assessment for the firm's large cap growth portfolio using a monthly dollar VAR. To do so, Fluellen obtains the following statistics from the fund manager. The value of the fund is $80 million and has an annual expected return of 14.4%. The annual standard deviation of returns is 21.50%. Assuming a standard normal distribution, 5% of the potential portfolio values are 1.65 standard deviations below the expected return.

Thomasville periodically engages in options trading for hedging purposes or when they believe that options are mispriced. One of their positions is a long position in a call option for Moffett Corporation. The option is a European option with a 3-month maturity. The underlying stock price is $27 and the strike price of the option is $25. The option sells for $2.86. Thomasville has also sold a put on the stock of the McNeill Corporation. The option is an American option with a 2-month maturity. The underlying stock price is $52 and the strike price of the option is $55. The option sells for $3.82. Fluellen assesses the credit risk of these options to Thomasville and states that the current credit risk of the Moffett option is $2.86 and the current credit risk of the McNeill option is $3.82.

Thomasville also uses options quite heavily in their Special Strategies Portfolio. This portfolio seeks to exploit mispriced assets using the leverage provided by options contracts. Although this fund has achieved some spectacular returns, it has also produced some rather large losses on days of high market volatility. Nicholson has calculated a 5% 1-day VAR for the fund at $13.9 million. On average, the fund has produced losses exceeding $13.9 million in 13 of the 250 trading days in a year. Nicholson is concerned about the accuracy of the estimated VAR because when daily losses exceed $13.9 million, they are typically much greater than $13.9 million.

In addition to using options, Thomasville also uses swap contracts for hedging interest rate risk and currency exposures. Fluellen has been assigned the task of evaluating the credit risk of these contracts. The characteristics of the swap contracts Thomasville uses are shown in Figure 1.

Figure 1: Thomasville Swap Contracts

	Contract A	Contract B	Contract C
Swap Type	Currency	Interest Rate	Currency
Original maturity	3 years	4 years	4 years
Swap Terms	Yen-dollar	Plain vanilla	Euro-dollar
Time to Maturity	2.5 years	3.75 years	1.0 years

Fluellen later is asked to describe credit risk in general to the risk management committee. She states that cross-default provisions generally protect a creditor because they prevent a debtor from declaring immediate default on the obligation owed to the creditor when the debtor defaults on other obligations. Fluellen also states that credit risk and credit VAR can be quickly calculated because bond rating firms provide extensive data on the defaults for investment grade and junk grade corporate debt at reasonable prices.

21.1. **Evaluate** Nicholson's comments regarding Thomasville's compensation contract with Boston Advisors. Nicholson is:
A. correct.
B. incorrect, because Thomasville's contract is actually beneficial to the firm's net profits.
C. incorrect, because Thomasville's contract does not resemble a put option owned by Boston Advisors.

21.2. Which of the following is *closest* to the monthly VAR Fluellen will calculate for the large cap growth portfolio?
A. $4 million.
B. $7 million.
C. $17 million.

21.3. Regarding Fluellen's comments on the credit risk of the Moffett and McNeill options:
A. Fluellen is only correct regarding the Moffett option.
B. Fluellen is only correct regarding the McNeill option.
C. Fluellen is incorrect regarding both the Moffett and McNeill options.

21.4. Which of the following *best* describes the accuracy of the VAR measure calculated for the Special Strategies Portfolio?
A. It is accurate but should be supplemented with scenario analysis.
B. It is accurate and provides a complete measure of the fund's risk.
C. It is inaccurate and should be supplemented with comprehensive stress testing.

21.5. Which of the following swap contracts *likely* has the highest credit risk?
A. Contract A.
B. Contract B.
C. Contract C.

21.6. **Evaluate** Fluellen's comments to the risk management committee on credit risk in general. Fluellen is:
A. correct.
B. incorrect, because a lack of critical data makes the estimation of credit risk and credit VAR difficult.
C. incorrect, because cross-default provisions are intended to protect the debtor in the event of default.

Questions 22.1–22.6 relate to Barth Group.

Sue Gano and Tony Cismesia are performance analysts for the Barth Group (BG). BG provides consulting and compliance verification for investment firms wishing to adhere to the Global Investment Performance Standards (GIPS®). The firm also provides global performance evaluation and attribution services for portfolio managers. BG recommends the use of GIPS to its clients due to its prominence as the standard for investment performance presentation.

One of BG's clients, Nigel Investment Advisors (NIA), has a composite that specializes in exploiting trends in stock prices. This Contrarian composite goes long "loser" stocks and short "winner" stocks. The "loser" stocks are those that have experienced severe price declines over the past three years, while the "winner" stocks are those that have had a tremendous surge in price over the past three years. The Contrarian composite has a mixed record of success and is rather small. It contains only four portfolios. Gano and Cismesia debate the requirements for the Contrarian composite under the Global Investment Performance Standards.

NIA's Global Equity Growth composite invests in growth stocks internationally and is tilted when appropriate to small cap stocks. One of NIA's clients in the Global Equity Growth composite is Cypress University. The university has recently decided that it would like to implement ethical investing criteria in its endowment holdings. Specifically, Cypress does not want to hold the stocks from any countries that are deemed human rights violators. Cypress has notified NIA of the change, but NIA does not hold any stocks in these countries. Gano is concerned, however, that this restriction may limit investment manager freedom going forward.

Gano and Cismesia are discussing the valuation and return calculation principles for portfolios and composites, which they believe have changed over time. In order to standardize the manner in which investment firms calculate and present performance to clients, Gano states that the GIPS require the following:

Statement 1: "The valuation of portfolios must be based on market values and not book values or cost. Portfolio valuations must be performed quarterly for all periods prior to January 1, 2001. Monthly portfolio valuations and returns are required for periods between January 1, 2001 and January 1, 2010."

Statement 2: "Composites are groups of portfolios that represent a specific investment strategy or objective, and a definition must be made available upon request. Because composite values are based on portfolio valuation, the monthly requirement for return calculation also applies to composites for periods between January 1, 2001 and January 1, 2010."

The manager of the Global Equity Growth composite has a benchmark that is fully hedged against currency risk. Because the manager is confident in his forecasting of currency values, the manager does not hedge to the extent that the benchmark does. In addition to the Global Equity Growth composite, NIA has a second investment manager who specializes in global equity. The funds under her management constitute the Emerging Markets Equity composite. The benchmark for the Emerging Markets Equity composite is not hedged against currency risk. The manager of the Emerging Markets Equity composite does not hedge due to the difficulty in finding currency hedges for thinly traded emerging market currencies. The manager focuses on security selection in these markets and does not weight the country markets differently from the benchmark.

The managers of the Emerging Markets Equity composite would like to add frontier markets such as Bulgaria, Kenya, Oman, and Vietnam to their composite, with a 20% weight. They are attracted to frontier markets because, compared to emerging markets, frontier markets have much higher expected returns and lower correlations with each other and with developed markets. Frontier markets, however, also have lower liquidity and higher risk. As a result, the manager proposes that the benchmark be changed from one reflecting only emerging markets to one that reflects both emerging and frontier markets. The date of the change and the reason for the change will be provided in the footnotes to the performance presentation. The manager reasons that by doing so, the potential investor can accurately assess the relative performance of the composite over time.

Cismesia would like to explore the performance of the Emerging Markets Equity composite over the past two years. To do so, he determines the excess return each period and then compounds the excess return over the two years to arrive at a total two-year excess return. For the attribution analysis, he calculates the security selection effect, the market allocation effect, and the currency allocation effect each year. He then adds all the yearly security selection effects together to arrive at the total security selection effect. He repeats this process for the market allocation effect and the currency allocation effect.

22.1.   What are the GIPS requirements for the Contrarian composite of Nigel Investment Advisors?
   A.   The composite can be formed and the composite must report all performance statistics.
   B.   The composite can be formed; however, the number of portfolios and dispersion does not have to be reported.
   C.   The composite cannot be formed because it has less than six portfolios in it, so there are no presentation requirements.

22.2. What are the GIPS requirements for the Cypress University portfolio in the Global Equity Growth composite of Nigel Investment Advisors?
   A. The historical and future record of performance of the Cypress University portfolio should be kept in the Global Equity Growth composite.
   B. Because the Cypress University portfolio is nondiscretionary, its future record of performance must be removed from the Global Equity Growth composite.
   C. Because the Cypress University portfolio is nondiscretionary, its historical and future record of performance must be removed from the Global Equity Growth composite.

22.3. Regarding the statements made by Gano on the GIPS requirements for portfolios and composites, are both statements *correct*?
   A. Yes.
   B. No, only statement 1 is correct.
   C. No, both statements are incorrect.

22.4. Which of the following *best* describes the currency management of the managers of the Global Equity Growth and the Emerging Markets Equity composites?
   A. Both managers are using active currency management.
   B. Both managers are using passive currency management.
   C. The manager of the Global Equity Growth composite is using active currency management and the manager of the Emerging Markets Equity composite is using passive currency management.

22.5. Regarding the Emerging Markets Equity composite, which of the following *best* describes the manager's incorporation of frontier markets?
   A. The treatment is consistent with GIPS requirements.
   B. The treatment is inconsistent with GIPS requirements because the benchmark should not be changed.
   C. The treatment is inconsistent with GIPS requirements because of the manner in which the composite is formed.

22.6. Which of the following *best* describes Cismesia's calculation of the two-year excess return and two-year attribution analysis for the Emerging Markets Equity composite?
   A. The calculations for both the excess return and attribution analysis are correct.
   B. The calculations for both the excess return and attribution analysis are incorrect.
   C. The calculations for the excess return are correct but the calculations for the attribution analysis are incorrect.

END OF AFTERNOON SESSION

PRACTICE EXAM 2 MORNING SESSION QUESTION BREAKDOWN

MORNING SESSION		
Topic	Question	Points
Monitoring/Rebalancing	1A	4
Risk Management	1B	6
Monitoring/Rebalancing	1C	3
GIPS	2A	6
GIPS	2B	6
Portfolio Management	3A	12
Portfolio Management	3B	12
Equity Portfolio Management	4	9
Performance Evaluation	5	12
Fixed Income Derivatives	6A	4
Fixed Income Derivatives	6B	3
Fixed Income Derivatives	6C	4
Equity Portfolio Management	7A	6
Equity Portfolio Management	7B	8
Performance Evaluation	8A	12
Performance Evaluation	8B	6
Portfolio Management	9A	10
Portfolio Management	9B	5
Portfolio Management	10A	4
Portfolio Management	10B	9
Portfolio Management	11A	2
Portfolio Management	11B	9
Portfolio Management	11C	6
Portfolio Management	11D	4
Alternative Investments	12A	12
Alternative Investments	12B	6
Total		180

PRACTICE EXAM 2 SCORE SHEET

MORNING SESSION		
Question	Maximum Points	Your Approximate Score
1A	4	
1B	6	
1C	3	
2A	6	
2B	6	
3A	12	
3B	12	
4	9	
5	12	
6A	4	
6B	3	
6C	4	
7A	6	
7B	8	
8A	12	
8B	6	
9A	10	
9B	5	
10A	4	
10B	9	
11A	2	
11B	9	
11C	6	
11D	4	
12A	12	
12B	6	
Total	180	

AFTERNOON SESSION		
Question	Maximum Points	Your Approximate Score
13	18	
14	18	
15	18	
16	18	
17	18	
18	18	
19	18	
20	18	
21	18	
22	18	
Total	180	

Certain Passing Score: 252 of 360 (70%)
Probable Passing Score: 234

Please note that we write these exams to be as representative of Level III exam questions as possible. However, due to the relaxed conditions that most candidates apply when they "take" these exams (i.e., "I'm getting a little tired, I think I'll go to the refrigerator and get a snack"), you should adjust your score downward by 10–15% to get a more accurate measure of the score you would have received on exam day. Also, you must be honest with yourself for your score on this exam to have any meaning. Don't assume, for example, that if your answer is close, the graders will be generous with points.

PRACTICE EXAM 2
MORNING SESSION

QUESTION 1 HAS THREE PARTS FOR A TOTAL OF 13 MINUTES

Lauren Shoemaker, CFA, is the director of equity trading for a large mutual fund group. Shoemaker oversees the execution of roughly 5 million shares of daily trading volume. Over the past several years, it has become more difficult to efficiently handle the mutual fund group's large trade volume because the average trade size on the New York Stock Exchange has fallen so dramatically. Based on a recent conference attended by Shoemaker, she believes the solution to the mutual fund group's problem is algorithmic trading. Shoemaker has told a colleague that, in the future, traders will become irrelevant and the job of the trader will be eliminated. Figure 1 provides a partial trade blotter for Shoemaker's mutual fund group.

Figure 1: Trade blotter

Stock	Trade	Size (shares)	Avg. Daily Volume	Last Price	Bid Price	Ask Price	Urgency
Star	Sell	700,000	11,500,000	$39.75	$39.74	$39.76	High
Moon	Buy	500,000	2,200,000	$150.00	$149.62	$150.37	Low
Sun	Buy	500,000	6,000,000	$80.00	$79.98	$80.02	Low

A.   **Describe** two primary characteristics of algorithmic trading.

(4 minutes)

B.   **State** the appropriate trading strategy for each stock listed in the trade blotter in Figure 1 and **justify** your selection.

(6 minutes)

Answer Question 1-B in the template provided.

Template for Question 1-B

Stock	Appropriate algorithmic trading strategy	Justification
1. Star		
2. Moon		
3. Sun		

C.   Shoemaker has expressed concern about the role of traders in the future. **State** whether Shoemaker's statement regarding the future of the trader function is correct or incorrect and **support** your decision with one reason.

(3 minutes)

Answer Question 1-C in the template provided.

Template for Question 1-C

Circle one	Defend your selection
Correct Incorrect	

QUESTION 2 HAS TWO PARTS FOR A TOTAL OF 12 MINUTES

Dennis Richardson is the chief investment officer for Delray Portfolio Managers. Delray provides investment management services for institutions and wealthy individuals. Richardson is discussing the requirements for compliance with the Global Investment Performance Standards (GIPS®) and makes the following comments:

> "We have not reported the performance for our real estate composite because we only have eight portfolios in it, which is less than the minimum number of portfolios required to form a composite. Once we have the required ten portfolios necessary for composite creation, we will begin reporting performance for the real estate composite."

> "We have different policies for when portfolios are added to a composite. The time period for inclusion of new portfolios is longer for the private equity composite than it is for the small cap equity composite."

A.   **State** whether or not *each* of these comments is consistent with the GIPS standards. If inconsistent, **recommend** the change necessary to bring the firm into compliance with the GIPS standards.

(6 minutes)

Answer Question 2-A in the template provided.

Template for Question 2-A

Comment	Is the comment consistent with the requirements of GIPS? (circle one)	If not, recommend the change that will bring the firm into GIPS compliance
"We have not reported the performance for our real estate composite because we only have eight portfolios in it, which is less than the minimum number of portfolios required to form a composite. Once we have the required ten portfolios necessary for composite creation, we will begin reporting performance for the real estate composite."	Yes No	
"We have different policies for when portfolios are added to a composite. The time period for inclusion of new portfolios is longer for the private equity composite than it is for the small cap equity composite."	Yes No	

Delray has a real estate portfolio that invests in apartment buildings. Richardson is using the following data to calculate and report quarterly returns to current and prospective investors. The capital contribution in the table came 43% of the way into the quarter and the capital disbursement came 87% of the way into the quarter.

Total capital as of	January 1	$15,000,000
Capital contribution on	February 9	$800,000
Capital disbursement on	March 19	$620,000
Capital expenditure		$510,000
Property taxes paid		$148,000
Property sales		$930,000
Total non-recoverable expenses		$125,000
Interest paid on borrowed funds		$78,000
Accrued investment income		$546,000
Market value—beg. of quarter	January 1	$16,300,000
Market value—end of quarter	March 31	$17,100,000

B.   **Calculate** the capital return and income return for the real estate portfolio.

(6 minutes)

QUESTION 3 HAS TWO PARTS FOR A TOTAL OF 24 MINUTES

Gordon Brown would like to update the return objective of the $500 million Shailor College endowment so that the return includes an adjustment for long-term inflation expectations and for the costs associated with managing the endowment. Brown believes that inflation will average 4% over the next several years. The endowment's investment management fees have averaged 0.35% of assets over the past five years. Brown would also like to generate a revised asset allocation reflecting more diversification across asset classes, while maintaining the endowment's 4.5% payout.

A. **Prepare** the objectives and constraints for Shailor College's endowment portfolio. **Calculate** the compound return requirement. **Show** your calculations.

(12 minutes)

Answer Question 3-A in the template provided.

Template for Question 3-A

Objectives	Comments
Return	
Risk	

Constraints	Comments
Liquidity	
Legal/Regulatory	
Taxes	
Time Horizon	
Unique	

Note: Your response should include appropriate content for each objective and constraint based on Shailor College's current situation.

B.   Brown has developed the all-domestic allocation for Shailor College endowment shown on Figure 1. **Suggest** *four* changes to the allocation that would make it better suited to an endowment's stated investment objectives and support each suggested change with one explanation. *Note: Each suggested change in allocation should address risk and/or return characteristics and can be considered separately (i.e., holding the other asset allocations constant).*

(12 minutes)

Figure 1: Proposed Asset Allocation for Shailor College Endowment

Asset Class	Expected Total Return (%)	Historical Standard Deviation (%)	Proposed Weight (%)
T-bills	1.5	0.2	10.0
T-notes	2.0	0.5	10.0
Corporate bonds	6.0	6.5	10.0
Large Cap stocks	9.0	9.0	5.0
REITs	9.5	9.8	5.0
Small cap stocks	11.0	15.9	30.0
Hedge funds	13.0	18.3	10.0
Venture capital funds	14.0	22.9	20.0

Answer Question 3-B in the template provided.

Template for Question 3-B

Recommended Change	Explanation
1.	
2.	
3.	
4.	

QUESTION 4 HAS ONE PART FOR A TOTAL OF 9 MINUTES

Jeff Stone, another trustee of the Shailor College endowment, has questioned Brown's recommendation to employ an active management strategy for the entire equity portion of the endowment portfolio. Specifically, Stone made the following three statements:

Statement 1:   "Active management is appropriate for large-cap stocks, where managers can take big enough positions to capitalize on pockets of inefficiency."

Statement 2:   "Because the S&P 500 Index is price-weighted, out-performing stocks tend to have more and more influence on its value."

Statement 3:   "The Shailor College endowment should employ a passive index vehicle, such as a Russell 2000 index fund, for our small-cap stock portfolio. The market for small-cap stocks tends to be more efficient than the market for large-cap stocks and would provide more opportunities for us to benefit from active management."

Indicate whether or not you agree or disagree with each of Stone's statements. **Support** each decision with one reason.

(9 minutes)

Answer Question 4 in the template provided.

Template for Question 4

Comment	Circle one	Supporting statement
"Active management is appropriate for large-cap stocks, where managers can take big enough positions to capitalize on pockets of inefficiency."	Correct Incorrect	
"Because the S&P 500 Index is price-weighted, out-performing stocks tend to have more and more influence on its value."	Correct Incorrect	
"The Shailor College endowment should employ a passive index vehicle, such as a Russell 2000 index fund, for our small-cap stock portfolio. The market for small-cap stocks tends to be more efficient than the market for large-cap stocks and would provide more opportunities for us to benefit from active management."	Correct Incorrect	

QUESTION 5 HAS ONE PART FOR A TOTAL OF 12 MINUTES

Amy Morgan manages a $4 billion global equity fund and has discretion to invest in the stocks of firms located in both developed and emerging markets as long as she maintains guideline weights in each. Partly due to a disagreement over her most recent performance appraisal, she has suggested changes to her benchmark. She makes the following statements:

"For a benchmark to be considered valid, it must be investable. To be investable, I should be able to recreate and hold the benchmark as a portfolio."

"Although I agree with you that market value-weighted benchmarks are generally considered the most valid, the benchmark you have applied in my performance appraisal is not truly market value-weighted because you have not included the total market capitalization of all the benchmark firms."

"Perhaps as an alternative we could use a multi-factor model-based benchmark. Factor model-based benchmarks are considered valid benchmarks and, since they are based on sound statistical methods, their results are irrefutable."

"If you do not like the idea of multi-factor-based benchmarks, we can always go back to comparing my performance to the average equity manager. At least that way I know exactly who I'm up against."

Indicate whether you agree or disagree with each of Morgan's statements. If you disagree, **support** your decision with one reason related to the characteristics of valid benchmarks.

(12 minutes)

Answer Question 5 in the template provided.

Template for Question 5

Comment	Agree or disagree (circle one)	If you disagree, support your decision with one reason related to the characteristics of valid benchmarks
"For a benchmark to be considered valid, it must be investable. To be investable, I should be able to recreate and hold the benchmark as a portfolio."	Agree Disagree	
"Although I agree with you that market value-weighted benchmarks are generally considered the most valid, the benchmark you have applied in my performance appraisal is not truly market value-weighted because you have not included the total market capitalization of all the benchmark firms."	Agree Disagree	
"Perhaps as an alternative we could use a multi-factor model-based benchmark. Factor model-based benchmarks are considered valid benchmarks and, since they are based on sound statistical methods, their results are irrefutable."	Agree Disagree	
"If you do not like the idea of multi-factor-based benchmarks, we can always go back to comparing my performance to the average equity manager. At least that way I know exactly who I'm up against."	Agree Disagree	

QUESTION 6 HAS THREE PARTS FOR A TOTAL OF 11 MINUTES

Sid Mulder, CFA, manages a $250 million fixed income portfolio. Currently, the weighted average duration for his portfolio is 6.8. Mulder is concerned about rising interest rates and has decided that he should adjust the duration of his portfolio to reduce the impact of rising interest rates. Mulder plans to use Treasury futures contracts to achieve his target duration of 5.0. The duration of the cheapest-to-deliver (CTD) bond is 6.5, and the total futures price is $100,000. The conversion factor for the CTD is 1.3.

Mulder is also concerned about credit risk in his portfolio. Specifically, he is worried that there is significant risk of a spread widening for his $10 million in Blum Development bonds. Currently, the Blum bonds trade at a spread of 250 basis points (bp) over comparable maturity U.S. Treasury securities. To protect against this risk, Mulder is considering purchasing a credit forward with a notional principal of $10 million, a contract spread of 250bp, and a risk factor of 3.0.

A.   **Describe** the futures transaction Mulder should execute in order to achieve his target duration. Your response should include the number of contracts and whether these contracts should be bought or sold.

(4 minutes)

B.   Mulder has chosen to modify his portfolio duration using futures, as opposed to buying/selling additional securities. **Identify** one advantage of using futures in this situation, and **describe** how basis risk might affect Mulder's strategy.

(3 minutes)

C.   For the credit derivative Mulder is considering, **determine** the following:

    i.   The maximum potential loss to Mulder on the credit forward.
   ii.   The payoff if the spread narrows to 200bp at the maturity of the derivative.

(4 minutes)

Answer Question 6-C in the template provided. Show your calculations.

Template for Question 6-C

	Credit forward at a contract spread of 250bp
i. The maximum potential loss to Mulder on the credit forward.	
ii. The payoff if the spread narrows to 200bp at the maturity of the derivative.	

QUESTION 7 HAS TWO PARTS FOR A TOTAL OF 14 MINUTES

Free Range, Inc. (FRI) is a communications technology company based in the United States. The company was formed through a merger between Freedom, Inc., a traditional wired network technology company, and North Range Technologies, a wireless technology company. Managers at the firm are compensated largely through stock options. Over the past several years, the communications technology industry has been rapidly moving towards inventing and improving wireless communications technologies, generally seen as the future of the network communication industry. FRI has been a true innovator in this area, on average introducing a new patented wireless technology product once every nine months. However, the firm has not been free from difficulties. Concerned that the firm may not have met its potential, FRI's board of directors has hired an outside consultant to assess its operations. The consultant's report included the following comments:

> "One of the top executives at FRI, James Baltus, is a former executive from Freedom, Inc. Because he has obtained the approval for several investment initiatives related to traditional wired network technologies, Baltus has managed to shift a significant amount of FRI investments away from wireless communications technology to increase his importance in the firm."

> "In addition, another top executive, Uri Korkov, a former executive with North Range Technologies, has convinced FRI's investment committee to invest in several media production ventures. The media companies FRI has invested in generally require long investment periods and have high levels of risk, making them relatively expensive capital projects that divert attention away from FRI's core operations."

> "I recommend increasing the level of short-term debt financing in the capital structure of FRI in order to impose discipline on the firm's management and better align the interests of the firm's management with its shareholders."

A.   **Identify** and **describe** the moral hazard implied by each of the first two comments.

(6 minutes)

Answer Question 7-A in the template provided.

©2010 Kaplan, Inc.

Template for Question 7-A

Comment	Moral Hazard	Description
"Because he has obtained the approval of several investment initiatives related to traditional wired network technologies, Baltus has managed to shift a significant amount of FRI investments away from wireless communications technology to increase his importance in the firm."		
"Korkov … has convinced FRI's investment committee to invest in several media production ventures. The media companies FRI has invested in generally require long investment periods and have high levels of risk, making them relatively expensive capital projects that divert attention away from FRI's core operations."		

B.　　**Explain** *two* ways in which debt would provide incentives for management at FRI to act in the best interest of the firm's shareholders, and **explain** *two* limitations to the use of debt to motivate FRI's management.

(8 minutes)

Questions 8, 9, and 10 relate to Jim Wilson. *Candidates should answer the questions in order.*

Jim Wilson, age 42, helped found Tides Technology about 20 years ago and took it public ten years later. Over the last ten years Wilson has had complete control of Tides. Destiny, Inc., will soon purchase Tides by paying two shares of Destiny stock, valued at $45 per share, for each share of Tides stock. In total, Wilson holds a total of 100,000 shares of Tides stock. He holds 12,500 shares in his $1.25 million defined contribution pension plan portfolio and 87,500 shares in a taxable investment portfolio. The cost basis of the Tides stock in his taxable investment portfolio is $2.00. Exhibit 1 shows the allocation of his pension portfolio prior to the buyout by Destiny.

Exhibit 1: J. Wilson Pension Portfolio Prior to Sale of Tides

Investments	Weight (%)	Cost Basis ($)	Current Share Value ($)
Tides equity	30	8.00	30.00
Equity fund	40	10.00	15.00
Balanced portfolio	10	34.00	44.00
Bond fund	15	12.50	13.75
Money market fund	5	1.00	1.00

After the sale to Destiny is completed, Wilson wants to enter law school, which should take three years and cost $45,000 the first year, increasing annually by the rate of inflation of 3%. Although he has no plans of marriage, Wilson will provide care for his autistic brother, Tom. Total after-tax current annual expenses, including care for his brother, will amount to $175,000.

With the help of a financial planner, Wilson has compiled risk and return characteristics for three asset classes as well as their correlations with one another and with Wilson's human capital. The data are shown in Exhibits 2 and 3.

Exhibit 2: Risk and Returns for Asset Classes

Asset Class	Expected Yield (%)	Expected Growth (%)	Expected Standard Deviation (%)
Cash	1.5	0.0	2.4
Bonds	5.0	0.0	8.3
Stock	3.0	6.0	15.4

Exhibit 3: Asset Class Correlations

Class	Cash	Bonds	Stock	Human Capital
Cash	1.00	0.65	0.27	0.41
Bonds	—	1.00	0.36	0.60
Stock	—	—	1.00	0.15
Human capital	—	—	—	1.00

QUESTION 8 HAS TWO PARTS FOR A TOTAL OF 18 MINUTES

A.   Explain, relative to Wilson's ownership of Tides stock, the three stages of the equity holding life including entrepreneur, executive, and investor. In your explanation, you should address the nature of the holding and the risk faced by Wilson (market and/or specific risk). **State** and **explain** Wilson's probable desire for diversification and emotional tie to the stock at each stage. In addressing this question, assume Wilson's taxable portfolio starts out as 100% Tides stock.

(12 minutes)

Answer Question 8-A in the template provided.

Template for Question 8-A

Stage	Nature of the position in Tides stock and type of risk faced (circle one)	State and explain Wilson's probable desire for diversification
Entrepreneur	Market risk Specific risk Both types of risk	
Executive	Market risk Specific risk Both types of risk	
Investor	Market risk Specific risk Both types of risk	

B. Post-sale, and assuming Wilson desires to diversify his taxable portfolio of Destiny stock, **explain** how he would utilize each of the following, how diversification is achieved, and the liquidity of the position:
i.   Public exchange fund.
ii. Completion portfolio.
iii. Equity collar.

(6 minutes)

Answer Question 8-B in the template provided.

Template for Question 8-B

Strategy	Description of strategy
Public exchange fund	
Completion portfolio	
Equity collar	

QUESTION 9 HAS TWO PARTS FOR A TOTAL OF 15 MINUTES

Wilson is meeting with his financial adviser, Drew Goebel, CFA, to review his financial situation. Wilson is particularly interested in establishing a law practice after graduation from law school. He estimates start-up costs for the practice, including reference books, furniture, and advertizing, will total $200,000. He expects his living expenses and care for his brother, which totaled $175,000 this year, to increase at the general rate of inflation of 3% per year.

A.   **Formulate** the return portion of Wilson's investment policy statement (IPS) for his taxable investment portfolio and **calculate** the total after-tax return that portfolio must earn next year, his first year in law school. Show your calculations. (You should ignore Wilson's pension assets.)

(10 minutes)

B.   **Determine** whether Wilson's ability to tolerate for risk would be considered above average, average, or below average. **Support** your decision with *two* reasons.

(5 minutes)

Answer Question 9-B in the template provided.

Template for Question 9-B

Wilson's ability to tolerate risk would be considered: (Circle one)	Support with *two* reasons
Above average Average Below average	

QUESTION 10 HAS TWO PARTS FOR A TOTAL OF 13 MINUTES

Jim Wilson has graduated from law school and opened his law office. Because of his popularity in the business community, his law business started out very well. Now that he is fairly certain of his future, he is meeting with his financial adviser, Drew Goebel, CFA, to determine the appropriate asset allocation for his investment portfolio. He has told Goebel that regardless of his asset allocation, how well his law practice does, or how long he (Jim) lives, he wants to be sure his brother Tom receives proper care for the rest of his life. Goebel has indicated that in determining a total asset allocation, Jim's human capital should be considered and, to care for Tom, he might consider purchasing life insurance.

A.   **Indicate** the *most likely* relationship between the discount rate used to calculate human capital and (1) the value of human capital, and (2) the optimal amount of life insurance. **Support** your decision on the amount of life insurance with one reason

(4 minutes)

Answer Question 10-A in the template provided.

Template for Question 10-A

Change in the discount rate on human capital (your choice)	Effect on the value of human capital (circle one)	Effect on the amount of life insurance (circle one)	Support your decision on the amount of life insurance with *one* reason
Increase Decrease	Increase No change Decrease	Increase No change Decrease	

B.   Based solely on the data in Exhibits 2 and 3, reproduced below, **indicate** the *best* allocation of stocks, bonds, and cash in Wilson's investment portfolio. **Support** each of your decisions with one reason.

(9 minutes)

Answer Question 10-B in the template provided.

Exhibit 2: Risk and Returns for Asset Classes

Asset Class	Expected Yield (%)	Expected Growth (%)	Expected Standard Deviation (%)
Cash	1.5	0.0	2.4
Bonds	5.0	0.0	8.3
Stock	3.0	6.0	15.4

Exhibit 3: Asset Class Correlations

Class	Cash	Bonds	Stock	Human Capital
Cash	1.00	0.65	0.27	0.41
Bonds	—	1.00	0.36	0.60
Stock	—	—	1.00	0.15
Human capital	—	—	—	1.00

Template for Question 10-B

Asset Class	Recommended allocation (circle one)	Support with *one* reason
Cash	0% to 5% 6% to 10% 11% to 20%	
Bonds	36% to 45% 46% to 55% 56% to 70%	
Stocks	41% to 50% 51% to 60% 61% to 70%	

QUESTION 11 HAS FOUR PARTS FOR A TOTAL OF 21 MINUTES

Paris Helicopter Leasing (PHL) is the largest corporate helicopter leasing company in Europe. PH has only a few competitors and a market capitalization of €5 billion. The PHL Defined Benefit Pension Plan (PHLP) has assets with a current market value of €125 million. Holly Rawlings, PHL's actuary, calculates the value of its Projected Benefit Obligation (PBO) using a 5% discount rate. She estimates the current PBO to be approximately €125 million with a duration of 17. Last year PHLP implemented an option for early retirement for long-term employees over 50 years of age, but so far no one has indicated a desire to take advantage of it. Should anyone elect to exercise the retirement option, they can elect to receive benefits in a lump-sum payout, a lifetime annuity, or a combination of the two.

A mostly independent investment committee manages PHLP. The committee recently hired Milton McCormick, CFA, as a consultant. After researching PHL, McCormick concluded that the company is financially sound and has a stable workforce. PHL has a low debt/equity ratio and a high return on equity compared to the rest of the corporate helicopter leasing industry. McCormick prepared Exhibit 1 to summarize the characteristics of the workforces for PHL and the corporate helicopter leasing industry.

Exhibit 1: Comparison of PHL and the Corporate Helicopter Leasing Industry

Workforce Characteristics	PHL	Industry Average
Average age of active employees	36 years	43 years
Active long-term employees over age 50	12%	16%
Active employees to retired employees	6 to 1	8 to 1

McCormick decides to discuss the PHLP's investments with PHL's President Brad Mauer. During the discussion, Mauer states, "Industry analysts are currently predicting an increase in leased transportation by corporate executives. With this increase in profitability and growth for this industry over the next decade, the PHLP should be able to see returns of at least 10% annually. The investment committee should increase PHLP's investment in transportation leasing industry equities from its current level of 15% of plan assets to at least 20%."

McCormick decides to also consult the investment committee, which states, "We have set a return objective that is 175 basis points above PHLP's minimum required return in order to meet our investment objective of building a fund surplus. This return objective is consistent with the current risk tolerance of PHLP."

A. **Determine** the required return for the Paris Helicopter Leasing Defined Benefit Pension Plan (PHLP). **Show** your calculations.

(2 minutes)

B. **Indicate** whether PHLP has a below-average, average, or above-average ability to take risk compared with the average for the corporate helicopter leasing industry with respect to sponsor financial status and profitability, workforce age, and retired employees and **justify** *each* response with *one* reason.

Answer Question 11-B in the template provided.

(9 minutes)

Template for Question 11-B

Risk factor	Indicate whether PHLP has below-average, average, or above average ability to tolerate risk compared with the average for the corporate helicopter leasing industry (circle one)	Justify *each* response with *one* reason
i. Sponsor financial status and profitability	Below average Average Above average	
ii. Workforce age	Below average Average Above average	
iii. Retired employees	Below average Average Above average	

C. **Indicate** whether *each* of the following factors increases, does not affect, or decreases PHLP's ability to tolerate risk and **justify** *each* response with *one* reason.

  i. Sponsor (PHL) and pension fund (PHLP) common risk exposures.
  ii. Retirement plan features.

Answer Question 11-C in the template provided.

(6 minutes)

Template for Question 11-C

Factor	Indicate whether the factor increases, does not affect, or decreases PHLP's ability to tolerate risk (circle one)	Justify *each* response with *one* reason
i. Sponsor (PHL) and pension fund (PHLP) common risk exposures	Increases Does not affect Decreases	
ii. Retirement plan features	Increases Does not affect Decreases	

D. **Formulate** *each* of the following constraints in PHLP's investment policy statement, and **justify** *each* response with *one* reason.

    i. Liquidity requirement.
    ii. Time horizon.

Answer Question 11-D in the template provided.

(4 minutes)

Template for Question 11-D

Constraint	Formulate *each* of the constraints in PHLP's investment policy statement and justify *each* response with *one* reason.
i. Liquidity requirement	
ii. Time horizon	

QUESTION 12 HAS TWO PARTS FOR A TOTAL OF 18 MINUTES

Harold Spare, CFA, is the chief financial officer (CFO) of Neptune Company. Neptune manufactures auto parts. In addition to his responsibilities as CFO, Spare oversees the company's defined benefit pension plan. The pension plan has assets of $3.5 billion. However, the plan is currently underfunded by $700 million. Spare is unhappy with the investment performance of the plan and believes the current asset allocation needs to be altered. To assist him in making a decision, Spare has hired an outside consultant.

The consultant recommends changing the asset mix from the current 60% stocks and 40% bonds (60/40) allocation to a 60% stocks, 30% bonds, and 10% hedge fund (60/30/10) allocation. The consultant justifies the recommendation by highlighting the fact that hedge funds would generate equity-like returns while reducing the portfolio's overall risk level. Thus, the 60/30/10 asset mix would produce higher returns with a risk level comparable to or less than the old asset mix. The consultant provides Figures 1 and 2 containing return, risk and correlation measures of four hedge fund strategies.

Figure 1: Performance of Hedge Fund Strategies

Strategy or Index	Annual Return	Annual Standard Deviation	Sharpe Ratio
Convertible arbitrage	13.46%	5.59%	1.64
Equity market neutral	15.90%	9.34%	1.24
Hedged equity	15.28%	6.07%	1.81
Global macro	16.98%	8.38%	1.51

Figure 2: Correlations Between Hedge Fund Strategies and Stocks and Bonds

	Stocks	Bonds	Event-Driven	Equity Hedge	Distressed Securities	Global Macro
Stocks	1.00					
Bonds	0.13	1.00				
Convertible arbitrage	0.59	0.07	1.00			
Equity market neutral	0.64	0.09	0.70	1.00		
Hedged equity	0.42	0.04	0.87	0.56	1.00	
Global macro	0.26	0.34	0.33	0.46	0.29	1.00

A.   **Describe** the primary strategy of each of the hedge fund styles proposed by the consultant. Include the structure of the strategy and how the strategy is expected to generate profits.

(12 minutes)

Answer Question 12-A in the template provided.

Template for Question 12-A

Hedge Fund Style	Description
Convertible arbitrage	
Equity market neutral	
Hedged equity	
Global macro	

B. **Name** and **describe** three special issues a manager should consider when recommending alternative investments to private wealth clients.

(6 minutes)

Answer Question 12-B in the template provided.

Template for Question 12-B

	Alternative investments special issues
1	
2	
3	

END OF MORNING SESSION

EXAM 2 AFTERNOON SESSION TOPIC BREAKDOWN

Question	Topic	Minutes
13	Ethics and Standards	18
14	Ethics and Standards	18
15	Economic Concepts	18
16	Equity Portfolio Management	18
17	Behavioral Finance	18
18	Fixed Income Portfolio Management	18
19	Risk Management Applications of Derivatives	18
20	Risk Management Applications of Derivatives	18
21	Asset Allocation; Alternative Investments	18
22	Capital Market Expectations	18
	Total	180

EXAM 2 SELECTED RESPONSE ITEM SET ANSWER SHEET

The afternoon session of the Level III exam contains 10 Selected Response Item Sets, each with six questions, and you must answer them by filling in a bubble sheet with a number 2 or HB pencil. For realism, we suggest that you use this answer sheet and darken the bubbles corresponding to your answers. This sheet will also facilitate entering your answers into our online Performance Tracker. You have 180 minutes for this session of the exam. That equates to 3 minutes per item set question, so budget your time well.

13.1. Ⓐ	Ⓑ	Ⓒ	
13.2. Ⓐ	Ⓑ	Ⓒ	
13.3. Ⓐ	Ⓑ	Ⓒ	
13.4. Ⓐ	Ⓑ	Ⓒ	
13.5. Ⓐ	Ⓑ	Ⓒ	
13.6. Ⓐ	Ⓑ	Ⓒ	

13.1. Ⓐ   Ⓑ   Ⓒ
13.2. Ⓐ   Ⓑ   Ⓒ
13.3. Ⓐ   Ⓑ   Ⓒ
13.4. Ⓐ   Ⓑ   Ⓒ
13.5. Ⓐ   Ⓑ   Ⓒ
13.6. Ⓐ   Ⓑ   Ⓒ

14.1. Ⓐ   Ⓑ   Ⓒ
14.2. Ⓐ   Ⓑ   Ⓒ
14.3. Ⓐ   Ⓑ   Ⓒ
14.4. Ⓐ   Ⓑ   Ⓒ
14.5. Ⓐ   Ⓑ   Ⓒ
14.6. Ⓐ   Ⓑ   Ⓒ

15.1. Ⓐ   Ⓑ   Ⓒ
15.2. Ⓐ   Ⓑ   Ⓒ
15.3. Ⓐ   Ⓑ   Ⓒ
15.4. Ⓐ   Ⓑ   Ⓒ
15.5. Ⓐ   Ⓑ   Ⓒ
15.6. Ⓐ   Ⓑ   Ⓒ

16.1. Ⓐ   Ⓑ   Ⓒ
16.2. Ⓐ   Ⓑ   Ⓒ
16.3. Ⓐ   Ⓑ   Ⓒ
16.4. Ⓐ   Ⓑ   Ⓒ
16.5. Ⓐ   Ⓑ   Ⓒ
16.6. Ⓐ   Ⓑ   Ⓒ

17.1. Ⓐ   Ⓑ   Ⓒ
17.2. Ⓐ   Ⓑ   Ⓒ
17.3. Ⓐ   Ⓑ   Ⓒ
17.4. Ⓐ   Ⓑ   Ⓒ
17.5. Ⓐ   Ⓑ   Ⓒ
17.6. Ⓐ   Ⓑ   Ⓒ

18.1. Ⓐ   Ⓑ   Ⓒ
18.2. Ⓐ   Ⓑ   Ⓒ
18.3. Ⓐ   Ⓑ   Ⓒ
18.4. Ⓐ   Ⓑ   Ⓒ
18.5. Ⓐ   Ⓑ   Ⓒ
18.6. Ⓐ   Ⓑ   Ⓒ

19.1. Ⓐ   Ⓑ   Ⓒ
19.2. Ⓐ   Ⓑ   Ⓒ
19.3. Ⓐ   Ⓑ   Ⓒ
19.4. Ⓐ   Ⓑ   Ⓒ
19.5. Ⓐ   Ⓑ   Ⓒ
19.6. Ⓐ   Ⓑ   Ⓒ

20.1. Ⓐ   Ⓑ   Ⓒ
20.2. Ⓐ   Ⓑ   Ⓒ
20.3. Ⓐ   Ⓑ   Ⓒ
20.4. Ⓐ   Ⓑ   Ⓒ
20.5. Ⓐ   Ⓑ   Ⓒ
20.6. Ⓐ   Ⓑ   Ⓒ

21.1. Ⓐ   Ⓑ   Ⓒ
21.2. Ⓐ   Ⓑ   Ⓒ
21.3. Ⓐ   Ⓑ   Ⓒ
21.4. Ⓐ   Ⓑ   Ⓒ
21.5. Ⓐ   Ⓑ   Ⓒ
21.6. Ⓐ   Ⓑ   Ⓒ

22.1. Ⓐ   Ⓑ   Ⓒ
22.2. Ⓐ   Ⓑ   Ⓒ
22.3. Ⓐ   Ⓑ   Ⓒ
22.4. Ⓐ   Ⓑ   Ⓒ
22.5. Ⓐ   Ⓑ   Ⓒ
22.6. Ⓐ   Ⓑ   Ⓒ

PRACTICE EXAM 2
AFTERNOON SESSION

Questions 13.1–13.6 relate to John Green and Federal Securities.

John Green, CFA, is a sell-side technology analyst at Federal Securities, a large global investment banking and advisory firm. In many of his recent conversations with executives at the firms he researches, Green has heard disturbing news. Most of these firms are lowering sales estimates for the coming year. However, the stock prices have been stable despite management's widely disseminated sales warnings. Green is preparing his quarterly industry analysis and decides to seek further input. He calls Alan Volk, CFA, a close friend who runs the Initial Public Offering section of the investment banking department of Federal Securities.

Volk tells Green he has seen no slowing of demand for technology IPOs. "We've got three new issues due out next week, and two of them are well oversubscribed." Green knows that Volk's department handled over 200 IPOs last year, so he is confident that Volk's opinion is reliable. Green prepares his industry report, which is favorable. Among other conclusions, the report states that "the future is still bright, based on the fact that 67% of technology IPOs are oversubscribed." Privately, Green recommends to Federal portfolio managers that they begin selling all existing technology issues, which have "stagnated," and buy the IPOs in their place.

After carefully evaluating Federal's largest institutional client's portfolio, Green contacts the client and recommends selling all of his existing technology stocks and buying two of the upcoming IPOs, similar to the recommendation given to Federal's portfolio managers. Green's research has allowed him to conclude that only these two IPOs would be appropriate for this particular client's portfolio. Investing in these IPOs and selling the current technology holdings would, according to Green, "double the returns that your portfolio experienced last year."

Federal Securities has recently hired Gordon Bentley, a CFA candidate who has passed Level II and is currently preparing to take the Level III CFA® exam, to reorganize Federal's compliance department. Bentley tells Green that he may be subject to CFA Institute sanctions due to inappropriate contact between analysts and investment bankers within Federal Securities. Bentley has recommended that Green implement a firewall to rectify the situation and has outlined the key characteristics for such a system. Bentley's suggestions are as follows:

1. Any communication between the departments of Federal Securities must be channeled through the compliance department for review and eventual delivery. The firm must create and maintain watch, restricted, and rumor lists to be used in the review of employee trading.

2. All beneficial ownership, whether direct or indirect, of recommended securities must be disclosed in writing.

3. The firm must increase the level of review or restriction of proprietary trading activities during periods in which the firm has knowledge of information that is both material and nonpublic.

Bentley has identified two of Green's analysts, neither of whom have non-compete contracts, who are preparing to leave Federal Securities and go into competition. The first employee, James Ybarra, CFA, has agreed to take a position with one of Federal's direct competitors. Ybarra has contacted existing Federal clients using a client list he created with public records. None of the contacted clients have agreed to move their accounts as Ybarra has requested. The second employee, Martha Cliff, CFA, has registered the name Cliff Investment Consulting (CIC), which she plans to use for her independent consulting business. For the new business venture, Cliff has developed and professionally printed marketing literature that compares the new firm's services to that of Federal Securities and highlights the significant cost savings that will be realized by switching to CIC. After she leaves Federal, Cliff plans to target many of the same prospects that Federal Securities is targeting, using an address list she purchased from a third-party vendor. Bentley decides to call a meeting with Green to discuss his findings.

After discussing the departing analysts, Green asks Bentley how to best handle the disclosure of the following items: (1) although not currently a board member, Green has served in the past on the board of directors of a company he researches and expects that he will do so again in the near future; and (2) Green recently inherited put options on a company for which he has an outstanding buy recommendation. Bentley is contemplating his response to Green.

13.1. According to Standard II(A) Material Nonpublic Information, when Green contacted Volk, he:
   A. violated CFA Institute Standards.
   B. violated of CFA Institute Standards unless the contact was disclosed to his clients.
   C. did not violate CFA Institute Standards since he was conducting a legitimate research activity.

13.2.   According to CFA Institute Standards of Professional Conduct, which of the following statements regarding Green's recommendation to Federal Securities' clients is *most* accurate?
   A. Green violated the Standards by making a material misrepresentation in his report to Federal Securities' clients.
   B. Green violated the Standards by failing to preserve the confidentiality of Federal Securities' investment banking clients.
   C. Green did not violate the Standards since he made a suitable recommendation in the best interest of Federal Securities' clients.

13.3.   According to CFA Institute Standards of Professional Conduct, which of the following statements related to Green's investment recommendation to the large institutional client is *most* accurate?
   A. Green has misrepresented the expected performance of the IPOs, but has dealt fairly with clients.
   B. Green has misrepresented the expected performance of the IPOs and has not dealt fairly with clients.
   C. Green has not misrepresented the expected performance of the IPOs, but he has not dealt fairly with clients.

13.4.   Which of Bentley's recommendations regarding the key characteristics of a firewall are inconsistent with those recommended by CFA Institute Standards of Professional Conduct?
   A. Characteristic 1.
   B. Characteristic 2.
   C. Characteristic 3.

13.5.   With respect to their plans to go into competition with Federal Securities, have Ybarra or Cliff violated any CFA Institute Standards of Professional Conduct?
   A. Both Ybarra and Cliff have violated CFA Institute Standards.
   B. Neither has violated CFA Institute Standards.
   C. Ybarra has violated CFA Institute Standards, while Cliff has not.

13.6.   Assess whether, in light of CFA Institute Standards of Professional Conduct, Bentley's disclosure recommendations are correct or incorrect with respect to the two items noted by Green. How should Bentley respond to Green regarding disclosure requirements on Item 1—Green's prior Board participation, and Item 2—Green's inherited put options?
   A. Green's Board position issue need not be disclosed, but the inherited put options must be disclosed to Green's employer, clients, and prospects.
   B. Both of Green's items must be fully disclosed to his employer, clients, and prospects.
   C. Since Green is not a current Board member, no disclosure is needed and the put options need not be disclosed since the buy recommendation has already been completed and is in place.

Questions 14.1–14.6 relate to CMT Investments.

Robert Keith, CFA, has begun a new job at CMT Investments as Head of Compliance. Keith has just completed a review of all of CMT's operations, and has interviewed all the firm's portfolio managers. Many are CFA charterholders, but some are not. Keith intends to use the CFA Institute Code and Standards, as well as the Asset Manager Code of Professional Conduct, as ethical guidelines for CMT to follow.

In the course of Keith's review of the firm's overall practices, he has noted a few situations which potentially need to be addressed.

Situation 1:

CMT Investments' policy regarding acceptance of gifts and entertainment is not entirely clear. There is general confusion within the firm regarding what is and is not acceptable practice regarding gifts, entertainment, and additional compensation.

Situation 2:

Keith sees inconsistency regarding fee disclosures to clients. In some cases, information related to fees paid to investment managers for investment services provided are properly disclosed. However, a few of the periodic costs, which will affect investment return, are not disclosed to the clients. Most managers are providing clients with investment returns net of fees, but a few are just providing the gross returns. One of the managers stated "providing gross returns is acceptable, as long as I show the fees such that the client can make their own simple calculation of the returns net of fees."

Situation 3:

Keith has noticed a few gaps in CMT's procedure regarding use of soft dollars. There have been cases where "directed brokerage" has resulted in less than prompt execution of trades. He also found a few cases where a manager paid a higher commission than normal, in order to obtain goods or services. Keith is considering adding two statements to CMT's policy and procedures manual specifically addressing the primary issues he noted.

Statement 1: "Commissions paid, and any corresponding benefits received, are the property of the client. The benefit(s) must directly benefit the client. If a manager's client directs the manager to purchase goods or services that do not provide research services that benefit the client, this violates the duty of loyalty to the client."

Statement 2: "In cases of 'directed brokerage,' if there is concern that the client is not receiving the best execution, it is acceptable to utilize a less than ideal broker, but it must be disclosed to the client that they may not be obtaining the best execution."

Situation 4:

Keith is still evaluating his data, but it appears that there may be situations where proxies were not voted. After completing his analysis of proxy voting procedures at CMT, Keith wants to insert the proper language into the procedures manual to address proxy voting.

Situation 5:

Keith is putting into place a "disaster recovery plan," in order to ensure business continuity in the event of a localized disaster, and also to protect against any type of disruption in the financial markets. This plan includes the following provisions:

- Procedures for communicating with clients, especially in the event of extended disruption of services provided.
- Alternate arrangement for monitoring and analyzing investments in the event that primary systems become unavailable.
- Plans for internal communication and coverage of crucial business functions in the event of disruption at the primary place of business, or a communications breakdown.

Keith is considering adding the following provisions to the disaster recovery plan in order to properly comply with the CFA Institute Asset Manager Code of Professional Conduct:

Provision 1: "A provision needs to be added incorporating off-site backup for all pertinent account information."

Provision 2: "A provision mandating testing of the plan on a company-wide basis, at periodical intervals, should be added."

Situation 6:

Keith is spending an incredible amount of time on detailed procedures and company policies that are in compliance with the CFA Institute Code and Standards, and also in compliance with the CFA Institute Asset Manager Code of Professional Conduct. As part of this process, he has had several meetings with

CMT senior management, and is second-guessing the process. One of the senior managers is indicating that it might be a better idea to just formally adopt both the Code and Standards and the Asset Manager Code of Conduct, which would make a detailed policy and procedure manual redundant.

14.1.   In response to Situation 1, Keith is redrafting the language outlining acceptable behavior regarding gifts and entertainment. Which statement would be the most accurate, or comply best with CFA Institute Code and Standards, and the Asset Manager Code of Professional Conduct?

A. Any gifts with a value under U.S. $100 are acceptable. All gifts and/or entertainment with a value in excess of U.S. $100 are to be accepted only after receipt of written consent from all parties involved.

B. Managers must refuse to accept any gifts, other than those of minimal value, from those that provide a service to the firm, business partners, or prospective investment targets. Gifts from clients are acceptable, as long as consent from CMT is received.

C. Gifts of reasonable value from clients and prospective investment targets are permitted. Managers must refuse to accept any gifts, other than those with a token value, from any parties who provide a service to the firm.

14.2.   Which of the following statements *most* accurately describes the obligations of investment managers related to disclosure of fees under the CFA Institute Asset Manager Code of Professional Conduct?

A. A general statement concerning certain fees and costs is acceptable, as long as the majority of the fees paid to the firm are disclosed to the client. Both gross- and net-of-fees returns must be disclosed.

B. All fees must be disclosed to the client, including any periodic account costs. Both gross- and net-of-fees returns must be disclosed.

C. All fees, including periodic costs, must be reported to the client. Either gross- or net-of-fees results are acceptable, as long as the client can make the simple "net" calculation from the information provided.

14.3.   Indicate whether Keith's statements in Situation 3 involving soft dollars/client brokerage are correct or incorrect.

A. Statements 1 and 2 are both correct.

B. Only Statement 1 is correct.

C. Only Statement 2 is correct.

14.4. Which of the following statements *most* accurately describes the obligations of investment managers related to the voting of proxies under the CFA Institute Asset Manager Code of Professional Conduct?

   A. Proxies, since they have economic value to the client, must always be voted on, whether on routine or non-routine issues.

   B. Managers may exercise discretion, and especially in the case of index funds, they do not have to vote proxies.

   C. Proxy issues that are not routine will require more analysis. Also, there may be cases in which all proxies do not have to be voted, if a cost-benefit analysis determines that the client would be better served to let some proxies go.

14.5. Are Keith's suggested additional provisions to the disaster recovery plan correct or incorrect, according to the CFA Institute Asset Manager Code of Professional Conduct?

   A. Both Provisions are correct.

   B. Only Provision 1 is correct.

   C. Only Provision 2 is correct.

14.6. Keith wants to assure CMT's compliance with the requirements of the CFA Institute Code and Standards of Professional Conduct. Which of the following statements *most* accurately describes CMT's responsibilities in order to assure compliance?

   A. CMT must adopt the Asset Manager Code of Conduct, as required by the CFA Institute Code and Standards. The policy manual is acceptable, but not necessary.

   B. Although adoption of the CFA Institute Asset Manager Code of Conduct is not a requirement, the Standards of Practice encourage firms to adopt this Code. CMT must adopt supplemental policies and procedures as part of a policy manual in order to properly implement the CFA Institute guidelines.

   C. The Standards of Practice do not require CMT to adopt the Asset Manager Code of Conduct, nor is there a requirement to publish a detailed procedural manual. Disclosure of policies is required, and any changes or updates to policies must be immediately disseminated.

Questions 15.1–15.6 relate to Monica Garza.

Monica Garza is a portfolio manager for Southwood Group, a large investment management firm, where she is in charge of economic and capital market forecasting. Brett Crosby, director of research at Southwood, has asked Garza to assist him in identifying the forecasting approach that would best suit an equity long-short hedge fund the company would like to open. The fund will purchase securities from its investment universe that are considered to have the highest forecasted alphas and sell short securities with negative forecasted alphas. The overall long-short exposure will vary based on the number of securities with positive and negative forecasted alphas.

After reviewing the forecasting method to be used by the new hedge fund, Crosby asks Garza to forecast GDP growth. To do this, Garza obtains predictions for changes in several underlying macroeconomic factors, including those listed Exhibit 1 with their predicted changes.

Exhibit 1: Predicted Changes in Economic Factors

Factor	Predicted Change
Savings rate	Decrease
Pollution controls	Increase
Retirement age	Increase

Garza then gathers the data in Exhibit 2 for the periods 1991–2000 and 2001–2010.

Exhibit 2: Historical Economic Data

	Growth in Total Factor Productivity	Growth in Capital Stock	Growth in Labor Input	Output Elasticity of Capital (α)
1991–2000	1.25%	−0.50%	2.50%	0.6
2001–2010	2.35%	1.25%	0.42%	0.6

Using the data she gathered, Garza will calculate the implied price of the market index. She notes that the major equity market index value is currently 1600 and the last dividend was $75. She believes the required rate of return for the market is 8.0%.

Crosby then asks Garza to review the major relative valuation models and provide short descriptions of each. Garza reviews the Fed model, the Yardeni model, and the 10-year moving average price/earnings ratio model, P/10-year MA(E), and makes the following comments:

Comment 1: The Fed model compares the earnings yield for the S&P 500 index to the yield on U.S. Treasury securities. When the earnings yield for the S&P 500 is greater than the yield on Treasury securities, equities are said to be over-valued and should fall.

Comment 2: The Yardeni model is used to estimate earnings yield for a market index and is computed as the yield on A-rated corporate bonds less the long-term growth rate forecast multiplied by a weighting factor. Although the Yardeni model incorporates a risk premium above that of Treasuries, the premium is not a true measure of equity risk.

Comment 3: The 10-year moving average price/earnings ratio model is computed as the value of the S&P 500 index divided by the average of the previous 10-years' reported earnings. One of the major drawbacks of this model is that it does not consider the effects of inflation.

After completing a review of the relative valuation models, Garza turns back to evaluating the value of the market index. She now decides to employ the equity q ratio and gathers the information in Exhibit 3:

Exhibit 3: Valuation Data ($Billions)

Market value (replacement cost) of assets	50
Book value of assets	35
Market value of liabilities	26
Market value of equity	20

15.1. In response to Crosby's question regarding the forecasting approach that would be *best* suited for the hedge fund, Garza should suggest using a:
A. top-down approach.
B. bottom-up approach.
C. combination of top-down and bottom-up approaches.

15.2. Which of the following is *most likely* correct regarding the predicted changes in the underlying factors? All else equal, the predicted change in:
A. the savings rate will lead to an increase in GDP growth.
B. the retirement age will lead to an increase in GDP growth.
C. pollution controls will lead to an increase in GDP growth.

15.3. The component of economic growth that contributed the *most* to real GDP growth during 1991–2000 is:
A. labor input.
B. capital stock.
C. total factor productivity.

15.4. If Garza assumes that the sustainable economic growth rate will be the same as the growth rate realized over the period 2001–2010, the intrinsic value of the market index would be *closest* to:
A. 1578.
B. 1586.
C. 1637.

15.5. Which of Garza's comments regarding relative equity market valuation models is correct?
A. Comment 1.
B. Comment 2.
C. Comment 3.

15.6. Based on the equity *q* ratio, Garza would *most likely* conclude that the equity index is:
A. overvalued.
B. undervalued.
C. fairly valued.

Questions 16.1–16.6 relate to Geneva Management, Marcus Reinhart, and Jamison Kiley.

Geneva Management (GenM) selects long-only and long-short portfolio managers to develop asset allocation recommendations for their institutional clients.

GenM Advisor Marcus Reinhart recently examined the holdings of one of GenM's long-only portfolios actively managed by Jamison Kiley. Reinhart compiled the holdings for two consecutive non-overlapping 5-year periods. The Morningstar Style Boxes for the two periods for Kiley's portfolio are provided in Exhibits 1 and 2.

Exhibit 1: Morningstar Style Box: Long-Only Manager for 5-Year Period 1

	Value	*Blend*	*Growth*
Large-cap	20	30	40
Mid-cap	2	3	5
Small-cap	0	0	0

Exhibit 2: Morningstar Style Box: Long-Only Manager for 5-Year Period 2

	Value	*Blend*	*Growth*
Large-cap	45	30	20
Mid-cap	1	2	2
Small-cap	0	0	0

Reinhart contends that the holdings-based analysis might be flawed because Kiley's portfolio holdings are known only at the end of each quarter. Portfolio holdings at the end of the reporting period might misrepresent the portfolio's average composition. To compliment his holdings-based analysis, Reinhart also conducts a returns-based style analysis on Kiley's portfolio. Reinhart selects four benchmarks:

1. SCV: a small-cap value index.

2. SCG: a small-cap growth index.

3. LCV: a large-cap value index.

4. LCG: a large-cap growth index.

Using the benchmarks, Reinhart obtains the following regression results:

Period 1: $R_P = 0.02 + 0.01(SCV) + 0.02(SCG) + 0.36(LCV) + 0.61(LCG)$

Period 2: $R_P = 0.02 + 0.01(SCV) + 0.02(SCG) + 0.60(LCV) + 0.38(LCG)$

Kiley's long-only portfolio is benchmarked against the S&P 500 Index. The Index's current sector allocations are shown in Exhibit 3.

Exhibit 3: S&P 500 Index Sector Allocations

Sector	Percent Allocation
Energy	12
Materials	3
Industrials	11
Consumer Discretionary	9
Consumer Staples	10
Health Care	12
Financials	19
Information Technology	17
Telecommunications	4
Utilities	3

GenM strives to select managers whose correlation between forecast alphas and realized alphas has been fairly high, and to allocate funds across managers in order to achieve alpha and beta separation. GenM gives Reinhart a mandate to pursue a core-satellite strategy with a small number of satellites each focusing on a relatively few number of securities.

In response to the core-satellite mandate, Reinhart explains that a Completeness Fund approach offers two advantages:

Advantage 1: The Completeness Fund approach is designed to capture the stock selecting ability of the active manager, while matching the overall portfolio's risk to its benchmark.

Advantage 2: The Completeness Fund approach allows the Fund to fully capture the value added from active managers by eliminating misfit risk.

16.1. Which one of the following statements about Kiley's long-only portfolio is *most correct*? Kiley's portfolio:
   A. is only exposed to systematic risk.
   B. is only exposed to unsystematic risk.
   C. attempts to earn a positive alpha through security selection.

16.2.   Reinhart is concerned that the portfolio managed by Kiley has style drift. Is Reinhart's concern supported by either holdings-based style analysis or returns-based style analysis?
   A.   Only the holdings-based style analysis supports style drift.
   B.   Only the returns-based style analysis supports style drift.
   C.   Both approaches support style drift.

16.3.   Assuming Kiley feels that the Utilities Sector is overvalued now, the largest active weight that Kiley can apply to the Utilities sector is:
   A.   −3%.
   B.   0%.
   C.   3%.

16.4.   Reinhart is *more likely* to satisfy the GenM alpha and beta separation objective by:
   A.   allocating funds to his long-only active managers and to his passive market index fund manager.
   B.   allocating funds to his market-neutral long-short managers and to his passive market index fund manager.
   C.   allocating funds solely to his market-neutral long-short managers.

16.5.   Assuming no material change in the forecasting ability of GenM's managers and considering the core-satellite mandate faced by Reinhart, which of the following statements is *correct*?
   A.   The GenM information coefficient will be relatively low.
   B.   The GenM investor breadth will be relatively low.
   C.   The GenM information ratio will be relatively low.

16.6.   State whether the two advantages to the Completeness Fund approach explained by Reinhart are *correct*.
   A.   Only advantage 1 is correct.
   B.   Only advantage 2 is correct.
   C.   Both advantages 1 and 2 are correct.

Questions 17.1–17.6 relate to Pace Insurance.

Pace Insurance is a large, multi-line insurance company that also owns several proprietary mutual funds. The funds are managed individually, but Pace has an investment committee that oversees all of the funds. This committee is responsible for evaluating the performance of the funds relative to appropriate benchmarks and relative to the stated investment objectives of each individual fund. During a recent investment committee meeting, the poor performance of Pace's equity mutual funds was discussed. In particular, the inability of the portfolio managers to outperform their benchmarks was highlighted. The net conclusion of the committee was to review the performance of the manager responsible for each fund and dismiss those managers whose performance had lagged substantially behind the appropriate benchmark.

The fund with the worst relative performance is the Pace Mid-Cap Fund, which invests in stocks with a capitalization between $40 billion and $80 billion. A review of the operations of the fund found the following:

- The turnover of the fund was almost double that of other similar style mutual funds.
- The fund's portfolio manager solicited input from her entire staff prior to making any decision to sell an existing holding.
- The beta of the Pace Mid-Cap Fund's portfolio was 60% higher than the beta of other similar style mutual funds.
- No stock is considered for purchase in the Mid-Cap Fund unless the portfolio manager has 15 years of financial information on that company, plus independent research reports from at least three different analysts.
- The portfolio manager refuses to increase her technology sector weighting because of past losses the fund incurred in the sector.
- The portfolio manager sold all the fund's energy stocks as the price per barrel of oil rose above $80. She expects oil prices to fall back to the $40 to $50 per barrel range.

A committee member made the following two comments:

Comment 1: "One reason for the poor recent performance of the Mid-Cap Mutual Fund is that the portfolio lacks recognizable companies. I believe that good companies make good investments."

Comment 2: "The portfolio manager of the Mid-Cap Mutual Fund refuses to acknowledge her mistakes. She seems to sell stocks that appreciate, but she holds stocks that have declined in value."

The supervisor of the Mid-Cap Mutual Fund portfolio manager made the following statements:

Statement 1: "The portfolio manager of the Mid-Cap Mutual Fund has engaged in quarter-end window dressing to make her portfolio look better to investors. The portfolio manager's action is a behavioral trait known as over-reaction."

Statement 2: "Each time the portfolio manager of the Mid-Cap Mutual fund trades a stock, she executes the trade by buying or selling one-third of the position at a time, with the trades spread over three months. The portfolio manager's action is a behavioral trait known as anchoring."

17.1.   A committee member suggested that the portfolio manager of the Mid-Cap Fund may be overconfident about her abilities. Which of the following facts from the review of the Mid-Cap fund is *least likely* to suggest that the manager is overconfident?
A. The high turnover of the Mid-Cap Fund relative to similar style mutual funds.
B. The reliance of the manager on staff input before selling an existing holding.
C. Consideration only of stocks with 15 years of financial data and three independent research reports.

17.2.   The under-weighting of the technology sector by the Pace portfolio manager could be *best* described as an example of:
A. conservatism (anchoring-and-adjustment).
B. regret minimization.
C. gambler's fallacy.

17.3.   The Pace portfolio manager's sale of all the energy stocks could be *best* described as an example of:
A. conservatism (anchoring-and-adjustment).
B. regret minimization.
C. gambler's fallacy.

17.4.   The committee member's Comment 1 could be *best* described as an example of:
A. mental accounting.
B. representativeness.
C. hindsight bias.

17.5.   The committee member's Comment 2 suggests that the manager of the Pace Mid-Cap Fund suffers from:
A. loss aversion.
B. hindsight bias.
C. money illusion.

17.6. Indicate whether Statement 1 and Statement 2 made by the supervisor are correct.
- A. Only Statement 1 is correct.
- B. Only Statement 2 is correct.
- C. Neither Statement is correct.

Questions 18.1–18.6 relate to Integrated Analytics.

Jack Higgins, CFA, and Tim Tyler, CFA, are analysts for Integrated Analytics (IA), a U.S.-based investment analysis firm. IA provides bond analysis for both individual and institutional portfolio managers throughout the world. The firm specializes in the valuation of international bonds, with consideration of currency risk. IA typically uses forward contracts to hedge currency risk.

Higgins and Tyler are considering the purchase of a bond issued by a Norwegian petroleum products firm, Bergen Petroleum. They have concerns, however, regarding the strength of the Norwegian krone currency (NKr) in the near term, and they want to investigate the potential return from hedged strategies. Higgins suggests that they consider forward contracts with the same maturity as the investment holding period, which is estimated at one year. He states that if IA expects the Norwegian NKr to depreciate and that the Swedish krona (Sk) to appreciate, then IA should enter into a hedge where they sell Norwegian NKr and buy Swedish Sk via a 1-year forward contract. The Swedish Sk could then be converted to dollars at the spot rate in one year.

Tyler states that if an investor cannot obtain a forward contract denominated in Norwegian NKr and if the Norwegian NKr and euro are positively correlated, then a forward contract should be entered into where euros will be exchanged for dollars in one year. Tyler then provides Higgins the following data on risk-free rates and spot rates in Norway and the U.S., as well as the expected return on the Bergen Petroleum bond.

Return on Bergen Petroleum bond in Norwegian NKr	7.00%
Risk-free rate in Norway	4.80%
Expected change in the NKr relative to the U.S. dollar	–0.40%
Risk-free rate in United States	2.50%

Higgins and Tyler discuss the relationship between spot rates and forward rates and comment as follows.

- Higgins: "The relationship between spot rates and forward rates is referred to as interest rate parity, where higher forward rates imply that a country's spot rate will increase in the future."
- Tyler: "Interest rate parity depends on covered interest arbitrage which works as follows. Suppose the 1-year U.K. interest rate is 5.5%, the 1-year Japanese interest rate is 2.3%, the Japanese yen is at a one-year forward premium of 4.1%, and transactions costs are minimal. In this case, the international trader should borrow yen, invest in pound denominated bonds, and use a yen-pound forward contract to pay back the yen loan."

The following day, Higgins and Tyler discuss various emerging market bond strategies and make the following statements.

- Higgins: "Over time, the quality in emerging market sovereign bonds has declined, due in part to contagion and the competitive devaluations that often accompany crises in emerging markets. When one country devalues their currency, others often quickly follow and as a result the countries default on their external debt, which is usually denominated in a hard currency."
- Tyler: "Investing outside the index can provide excess returns. Because the most common emerging market bond index is concentrated in Latin America, the portfolio manager can earn an alpha by investing in emerging country bonds outside of this region."

Turning their attention to specific issues of bonds, Higgins and Tyler examine the characteristics of two bonds: a 6-year maturity bond issued by the Midlothian Corporation and a 12-year maturity bond issued by the Horgen Corporation. The Midlothian bond is a U.S. issue and the Horgen bond was issued by a firm based in Switzerland. The characteristics of each bond are shown in the table below. Higgins and Tyler discuss the relative attractiveness of each bond and, using a total return approach, which bond should be invested in, assuming a 1-year time horizon.

	Currency of Denomination	Annualized Bond Yield	Bond Modified Duration
Midlothian Bond	U.S. Dollars	8.00%	4.69
Horgen Bond	Swiss franc	9.00%	7.25

18.1. What are the currency hedge strategies for the Bergen Petroleum bond that Higgins and Tyler are referring to? Higgins is referring to:
A. a cross-hedge, and Tyler is referring to a proxy-hedge.
B. an indirect-hedge, and Tyler is referring to a proxy-hedge.
C. an indirect-hedge, and Tyler is referring to a correlation-hedge.

18.2. On the basis of expected return, should the Bergen Petroleum bond be hedged against currency risk and what is the hedged return?
A. No, the hedged return is 4.70%.
B. No, the hedged return is 6.60%.
C. Yes, the hedged return is 6.60%.

18.3. Regarding their statements concerning the relationship between spot rates and forward rates, determine whether Higgins and Tyler are *correct*.
A. Both Higgins's and Tyler's statements are correct.
B. Both Higgins's and Tyler's statements are incorrect.
C. Only Higgins's statement is correct.

18.4. Regarding their statements concerning the emerging market bond investments, determine whether Higgins and Tyler are *correct*.
A. Both Higgins and Tyler are correct.
B. Both Higgins and Tyler are incorrect.
C. Only Tyler is correct.

18.5. Assume that both the Midlothian and Horgen bonds are being considered for purchase. Determine which of the following statements provides the *best* description of the appropriate strategy using breakeven spread analysis. If the yield for the Horgen bond:
A. is expected to increase more than 14 basis points, invest in the Midlothian bond.
B. is expected to increase more than 7 basis points, invest in the Midlothian bond.
C. is expected to fall more than 21 basis points, invest in the Midlothian bond.

18.6. Which of the following statements provides the *best* description of the advantage of using breakeven spread analysis? Breakeven spread analysis:
A. provides an estimate of exchange rate risk.
B. quantifies the change in spread needed to offset a foreign yield advantage.
C. assesses the risk of a foreign bond investment independent of the bond's duration.

Questions 19.1–19.6 relate to United Global Group.

United Global Group (UGG) is a major property and casualty insurance company. UGG has a total investment portfolio of $25 billion. The portfolio is divided into $22 billion in bonds and $3 billion in equities. UGG's equity strategy employs enhanced indexing with the S&P 500 Index as the benchmark. UGG adjusts its equity portfolio by employing the 200-day moving average technical indicator. When more than 80% of the stocks are trading above their 200-day moving average, this indicator considers the equity market overbought—a bearish signal. In contrast, if less than 20% of the stocks are trading above their 200-day moving average, the market is considered oversold—a bullish signal that means investors should expect a positive correction. UGG management uses this indicator to move in and out of equities. Rather than actually selling their equities, UGG uses futures to create a synthetic cash position to execute any bearish trigger. Relevant data is shown in Figure 1.

Figure 1: Selected Data

S&P 500 Index futures contract	1058
S&P 500 Index dividend yield	1.60%
Time to expiration	5 months
Risk free rate (annual)	3.00%
UGG equity portfolio beta	1.00
S&P 500 Index futures contract beta	1.00
UGG bond portfolio modified duration	5.90
Treasury bond futures contract price	$150,000
Treasury bond futures modified duration	5.10
Cash equivalents modified duration	0.20
S&P 500 Index futures contract multiplier	$250

UGG's management applied its technical indicator to the Japanese market and discovered that it is in an oversold situation. Based on this factor, management allocated half of UGG's equity portfolio, or 162,225,000,000 yen, to the Japanese market. Relevant data are shown in Figure 2.

Figure 2: Selected Data

Nikkei 225 index futures contract	10,337
Nikkei 225 index dividend yield	1.00%
Time to expiration	6 months
Japanese risk-free rate (annual)	2.00%
Multiplier	$5.00
Nikkei 225 index futures contract beta	1.00
UGG's Japanese portfolio beta	0.90
Exchange rate	108.15 yen to $1

19.1.   The 200-day moving average is sending a bearish signal, so UGG management has decided to immediately neutralize its equity position. The number of futures contracts sold to create a synthetic cash position should be between:
   A. 7,001 and 9,000 contracts.
   B. 9,001 and 11,000 contracts.
   C. 11,001 and 13,000 contracts.

19.2.   Assume the S&P 500 Index is at 1,125 when the futures contract expires. The payoff of the futures position would be a loss:
   A. of less than $1 million.
   B. between $1 million and $100 million.
   C. greater than $100 million.

19.3.   Based on UGG's models, management intends to adjust its current asset allocation to 75% bonds and 25% stocks. Using the information provided in Figure 1, the strategy to adjust to the new bond and stock allocation is to sell bond futures contracts and buy approximately:
   A. 12,290 equity futures contracts.
   B. 13,387 equity futures contracts.
   C. 15,199 equity futures contracts.

19.4.   UGG would like to fully hedge against a possible decline in the Japanese market. Using the data in Figure 2, the number of (short) contracts needed to hedge the yen-denominated portion of the equity portfolio is between:
   A. 24,000 and 25,000 contracts.
   B. 25,000 and 26,000 contracts.
   C. 26,000 and 27,000 contracts.

19.5.   Which of the following statements is *most correct*?
   A. UGG can use yield beta to adjust their exposure to equities.
   B. UGG can fully hedge their foreign currency payment risk by selling the foreign currency forward.
   C. UGG can replicate a long stock position by buying equity futures and a risk-free bond.

19.6.   UGG is exposed to the U.S. bond market and both the U.S. and Japanese equity markets. Given these exposures, which of the following statements is *most correct*?
   A. UGG is likely to use a mixture of corporate and Treasury bond futures to hedge their U.S. bond portfolio.
   B. UGG is likely to manage exchange rate risk using forward contracts on the yen/USD exchange rate for liquidity reasons.
   C. UGG can lock in the Japanese risk-free rate by using futures to hedge the equity portfolio and using a forward to hedge yen/USD currency risk.

Questions 20.1–20.6 relate to Director Securities.

Walter Skinner, CFA, manages a bond portfolio for Director Securities. The bond portfolio is part of a pension plan trust set up to benefit retirees of Thomas Steel Inc. As part of the investment policy governing the plan and the bond portfolio, no foreign securities are to be held in the portfolio at any time and no bonds with a credit rating below investment grade are allowable for the bond portfolio. In addition, the bond portfolio must remain unleveraged. The bond portfolio is currently valued at $800 million and has a duration of 6.50. Skinner believes that interest rates are going to increase, so he wants to lower his portfolio's duration to 4.50. He has decided to achieve the reduction in duration by using swap contracts. He has two possible swaps to choose from:

1. Swap A: 4-year swap with quarterly payments.

2. Swap B: 5-year swap with semiannual payments.

Skinner plans to be the fixed-rate payer in the swap, receiving a floating-rate payment in exchange. For analysis, Skinner always assumes the duration of a fixed rate bond is 75% of its term to maturity.

Several years ago, Skinner decided to circumvent the policy restrictions on foreign securities by purchasing a dual currency bond issued by an American holding company with significant operations in Japan. The bond makes semiannual fixed interest payments in Japanese yen but will make the final principal payment in U.S. dollars five years from now. Skinner originally purchased the bond to take advantage of the strengthening relative position of the yen. The result was an above average return for the bond portfolio for several years. Now, however, he is concerned that the yen is going to begin a weakening trend, as he expects inflation in the Japanese economy to accelerate over the next few years. Knowing Skinner's situation, one of his colleagues, Bill Michaels, suggests the following strategy:

"You need to offset your exposure to the Japanese yen by establishing a short position in a synthetic dual currency bond that matches the terms of the dual currency bond you purchased for the Thomas Steel bond portfolio. As part of the strategy, you will have to enter into a currency swap as the fixed-rate yen payer. The swap will neutralize the dual-currency bond position but will unfortunately increase the credit risk exposure of the portfolio."

Skinner has also spoken to Orval Mann, the senior economist with Director Securities, about his expectations for the bond portfolio. Mann has also provided some advice to Skinner in the following comment:

"I know you expect a general increase in interest rates, but I disagree with your assessment of the interest rate shift. I believe interest rates are going to decrease. Therefore, you will want to synthetically remove the call features of any callable bonds in your portfolio by purchasing a payer interest rate swaption."

20.1. From Skinner's perspective, the duration of Swap A would be *closest* to:
  A. –2.50.
  B. –2.88.
  C. –3.00.

20.2. Determine the approximate notional principal required for Skinner to achieve a portfolio duration of 4.5 using Swap B.
  A. $320 million.
  B. $457 million.
  C. $492 million.

20.3. Evaluate the appropriateness of Michaels's suggested strategy to offset the bond portfolio exposure to the dual currency bond, and also evaluate Michaels's assessment of the swap portion of the transaction.
  A. Michael's suggested strategy is appropriate, but his assessment of the swap portion is incorrect.
  B. Michael's suggested strategy is inappropriate, but his assessment of the swap portion is correct.
  C. Michael's suggested strategy is appropriate, and his assessment of the swap portion is correct.

20.4. Critically evaluate Mann's suggested strategy in the event that interest rates move counter to Skinner's expectations.
  A. Mann's statement is correct.
  B. Mann is incorrect; callable bonds should be offset by selling a payer swaption.
  C. Mann is incorrect; callable bonds should be offset by purchasing a receiver swaption.

20.5. After his long conversation with Director Securities' senior economist, Orval Mann, Skinner has completely changed his outlook on interest rates and has decided to extend the duration of his portfolio. The *most* appropriate strategy to accomplish this objective using swaps would be to enter into a swap to pay:
  A. fixed and receive floating.
  B. floating and receive fixed.
  C. floating and receive floating.

20.6. Skinner has been consulting with Dwayne Barter, a client of Director Securities and CFO of a large corporation. Barter is interested in using interest rate swaps to convert his firm's floating rate debt to fixed rate debt. Barter is planning to enter into a swap to pay a fixed rate and receive a floating rate in exchange. Which of the following is the *most* accurate statement Skinner could make regarding such a transaction? The swap would:
  A. increase the market value risk of Barter's firm.
  B. reduce both the cash flow risk and market value risk of Barter's firm.
  C. increase both the cash flow risk and market value risk of Barter's firm.

Questions 21.1–21.6 relate to the Glendale Foundation.

Bartholomew Hope, CFA, is the chief investment officer of Children's Trust Foundation (CTF), a foundation that supports a wide variety of child-related causes. CTF's total assets total $2.3 billion. The foundation's current asset mix is 55% stocks, 35% bonds, and 10% cash (T-bills earn 3.5%). The foundation provides $126.5 million annually for a variety of programs for children, which is forecasted to remain more or less constant in real terms. Hope does not envision any major capital expenditures for the foreseeable future.

CTF's investment portfolio has underperformed its benchmark over the past three years. Hope believes corrective action is needed to address the issue of poor performance. Hope wants to evaluate the possibility the portfolio's risk to reward profile. Hope's staff generates Exhibit 1, which reviews the relevant necessary metrics to make the asset mix decision. The overall cost of investing the assets is 75 basis points.

Exhibit 1: Expected Returns, Risk, and Correlations for Asset under Consideration

	Mean Return	Standard Deviation	Correlation		
			1	2	3
Current portfolio	12.1%	10.0%	1.00		
Venture capital	11.4%	18.9%	0.50	1.00	
Hedge funds	13.5%	10.3%	0.75	0.25	1.00

One of the members of Hope's staff, Rene Meyer, includes a report on the key attributes of investing in venture capital funds. The report includes the following sections:

Structure: "Indirect venture capital investments are achieved by pooling the funds of multiple investors into a limited partnership (LP). The investors are limited partners who allow a general partner to control the investments for a period of 7 to 10 years. The general partner also invests capital, earning a management fee of 1.5% to 2.5% of invested capital and a carried interest fee, which is generally 20% of the fund profits, after the fund's hurdle rate has been met."

Strategy: "Because initial public offerings are a primary exit strategy of venture capital investing, the correlation between public equity markets and returns on venture capital investments are positive. Therefore, the primary focus of any venture capital investment undertaken by Glendale should be long-term return enhancement rather than significant diversification. In addition, Glendale must make sure that all of the committed capital is available for the required up front cash distribution to the general partner at the beginning of the investment period."

Hope recognizes there are several unique strategies within the hedge fund group that have very different risk to reward trade-offs. Hope identifies three hedge funds as potential investment opportunities for the CTF. Exhibit 2 lists the funds under consideration and their most recent securities transactions.

Exhibit 2: Hedge Fund Transactions

Fund X	Fund Y	Fund Z
Fund X purchased the stock of four companies within the chemical manufacturing industry while simultaneously selling short the stock of three companies in the transportation industry. The relative size of the trades left the fund with a net short exposure.	A long position was taken in Burg Inc., a grocery store chain. At the same time, a short position was taken in a second grocery store chain, TRE Corp. The overall beta of the trades was equal to 0.01 and the net investment was equal to zero.	Fund Z purchased a long position in an S&P 500 Index while simultaneously taking a short position in a broad based index tracking the Japanese market. Fund Z expected the S&P 500 to rise and the Japanese market to decline over the next year.

While Clark presents the hedge funds, Hope comments that he is concerned with the potential difficulties in measuring hedge fund manager performance. Glendale's charter has strict requirements regarding the performance assessment of investment managers who control the assets of the foundation. Hope believes the performance of alternative investments presented may be difficult to evaluate against a benchmark index as required by Glendale's charter.

21.1.   Which of the following approaches would be *most* appropriate for CTF?
    A. The asset-only approach.
    B. The asset-liability management approach.
    C. The liability-only approach.

21.2.   The following statements describe processes Hope has employed in identifying potential asset classes. Determine which is *least* appropriate.
    A. Considering the liquidity of all the asset classes under consideration.
    B. Grouping domestic and international equities together into one equity class.
    C. Considering all of relevant asset groups in developing the foundation's portfolio.

21.3.   Based on the data provided in Exhibit 1, determine whether adding venture capital or hedge funds to the CTF portfolio would allow the foundation to achieve a superior efficient frontier (Sharpe ratio calculations required).
    A. Add only the venture capital.
    B. Add only the hedge funds.
    C. Add both the venture capital and the hedge funds.

21.4.   One of Hope's staff members has written a report on the proposed private equity investment. State whether the comments in the report related to the structure and strategy of CTF's private equity investment are *correct*.
    A. Only the structure comment is correct.
    B. Only the strategy comment is correct.
    C. Neither of these comments is correct.

21.5.   State which of the following hedge funds identified by Hope and listed in Exhibit 2 *most likely* follows an equity market neutral strategy.
    A. Fund X.
    B. Fund Y.
    C. Fund Z.

21.6.   Which of the following is *least likely* to be a reason for Hope's concern over the ability to track hedge fund manager performance against a benchmark index as required by the Glendale Foundation charter?
    A. Values used to compute the hedge fund index returns typically suffer from stale pricing, which causes artificially low risk and correlation estimates.
    B. Indexes available for comparison remove the historical returns of hedge funds that have been dissolved.
    C. When a hedge fund is added to the available indexes, the fund's historical returns are added to the historical returns of the index, artificially improving overall performance.

Questions 22.1–22.6 relate to Otterbein forecasting.

Jimena Mora, CFA, and Jack Wieters, CFA, are economists for Otterbein Forecasting. Otterbein provides economic consulting and forecasting services for institutional investors, medium-sized investment banks, and corporations. In order to forecast the performance of asset classes and formulate strategic asset allocations, Mora and Wieters are currently examining the capital market expectations for four developed countries: Alzano, Lombardo, Bergamo, and Linden. Wieters was hired in 2009 and Mora is his supervisor.

Mora and Wieters use the Grinold and Kroner model to forecast equity market performance. Macroeconomic forecasts and capital market expectations for three countries are given below:

	Alzano	Bergamo	Lombardo
Change in Correlation with World Index	7.30%	12.20%	0.30%
Change in P/E ratio	0.70%	1.10%	−0.20%
Change in Shares Outstanding	−0.20%	1.20%	−0.80%
Dividend Yield	2.70%	0.60%	3.60%
Growth in Real Earnings	4.80%	5.70%	2.20%
Growth in Exports	3.70%	2.30%	1.70%
Growth in Imports	4.60%	7.20%	2.60%
Liquidity Risk Premium	2.00%	3.60%	0.70%
Long-Term Inflation Rate	2.80%	5.30%	1.90%

Mora is also examining the return on federal government bills and bonds of various maturities for the country of Linden. The data are provided below:

Maturity in Years	Yield
0.25	4.54
0.50	4.48
1.00	4.47
2.00	4.39
3.00	4.36
4.00	4.33
5.00	4.31
10.00	4.08
15.00	3.92
20.00	3.57

One of Otterbein Forecasting's largest clients is an institutional investor in Linden, the Balduvi Endowment. The current and potential asset allocations for the endowment are shown below:

Asset Class	Current and Potential Portfolios Asset Allocation Percentages (%)			
	Current	A	B	C
Cash Equivalents	3	3	3	3
Government Bonds	21	22	11	34
Investment Grade Bonds	21	22	11	33
High-Yield Bonds	10	17	26	5
Non-Cyclical Stocks	25	22	31	20
Cyclical Stocks	20	14	18	5

Mora asks Wieters for his opinion on the future of the economy in Linden and the appropriate investment for the Balduvi Endowment.

Mora has been asked by the Otterbein CEO to develop a model for explaining stock returns. In her master's degree training, Mora was instructed that the default risk premium has predictive power for stock returns; however, the CEO has asked her to include other macroeconomic variables. Mora examines the following data for the capital market history of Bergamo:

1. Default risk premiums, which she measures as the difference in yields between high-yield bonds and government bonds.

2. Maturity risk premiums, which she measures as the difference in yields between 10-year and 1-year government bonds.

3. Lagged changes in the stock market.

Mora uses these variables to explain stock returns in the following year. Using 40 years of data, she finds the following results for the significance of the variables in explaining stock returns:

Analysis	Variable		
	Default Risk Premium	Maturity Risk Premium	Lagged Changes in the Stock Market
Correlation	Significant	Insignificant	Significant
Regression	Significant	Insignificant	Significant

Mora concludes from the correlation analysis that, of the three variables studied, the default risk premium has the most predictive power for stock returns.

As the most recent hire at Otterbein Forecasting, Wieters is well versed on the latest evidence on asset pricing and financial engineering. However, Mora suspects that his limited experience results in erroneous forecasts.

For instance, during the credit crisis of 2007–2008, annual stock returns in Lombardo averaged –12.6%. However, using the 80-year history of its capital market, annual stock returns in Lombardo have averaged 13.6%. For his clients' strategic asset allocations in 2010 and onward, Wieters projects Lombardo stock returns of 6.5%. As his supervisor, Mora questions him about this, and she suggests that Wieters revise his projections upward.

Mora and Wieters are discussing the valuation and risk analysis of emerging market securities and economies. In their discussion, Mora makes the following comments:

Statement 1:   "Emerging countries are dependent on foreign financing of growth, but it is important that a country not take on too much debt. A financial crisis can lead to currency devaluations and capital flight. Foreign debt levels greater than 50% of GDP or debt greater than 200% of current account receipts may indicate that a country is over-levered."

Statement 2:   "In financial crises, emerging market debt is particularly susceptible, as currency devaluations will quickly reduce the principal and coupon value. Because most emerging debt is denominated in a domestic currency, the emerging government must have foreign currency reserves to defend its currency in the foreign exchange markets."

22.1.   Using the Grinold and Kroner model, which of the three countries has the highest expected return for its equity market?
A. Alzano.
B. Bergamo.
C. Lombardo.

22.2.   What does the bond data predict for the future of the economy in Linden?
A. The economy is likely to expand in the future.
B. The economy is likely to contract in the future.
C. The economy is likely to experience no growth in the future.

22.3.   Using only the forecast for the Linden economy, which of the following portfolios should Wieters recommend for the Balduvi Endowment?
A. Portfolio A.
B. Portfolio B.
C. Portfolio C.

22.4. Which of the following psychological traps is Mora *likely* susceptible to in her analysis of Bergamo stock returns?
   A. Status Quo trap.
   B. Recallability trap.
   C. Confirming Evidence trap.

22.5. Which of the following psychological traps is Wieters likely susceptible to in his forecast of Lombardo stock returns?
   A. Anchoring trap.
   B. Status Quo trap.
   C. Recallability trap.

22.6. Regarding the statements made by Mora on the analysis of emerging market securities and economies, are both statements *correct*?
   A. Yes.
   B. No, both statements are incorrect.
   C. No, only Statement 1 is correct.

END OF AFTERNOON SESSION

PRACTICE EXAM 3 MORNING SESSION QUESTION BREAKDOWN

MORNING SESSION		
Topic	Question	Points
Portfolio Management	1	17
Portfolio Management	2A	24
Portfolio Management	2B	8
Equity Portfolio Management	3A	8
Equity Portfolio Management	3B	9
Equity Portfolio Management	3C	6
Equity Portfolio Management	3D	6
Fixed Income/Risk Management	4A	4
Risk Management	4B	4
Risk Management	4C	12
Equity Portfolio Management	5A	4
Portfolio Management	5B	9
GIPS	6A	7
GIPS	6B	8
Portfolio Management	7A	3
Portfolio Management	7B	5
Asset Allocation	7C	4
Portfolio Management	7D	2
Monitoring/Rebalancing	7E	4
Portfolio Management	8A	4
Portfolio Management	8B	12
Fixed Income	9A	6
Fixed Income	9B	5
Fixed Income	9C	5
Fixed Income	9D	4
Total		180

PRACTICE EXAM 3 SCORE SHEET

MORNING SESSION		
Question	Maximum Points	Your Estimated Score
1	17	
2A	24	
2B	8	
3A	8	
3B	9	
3C	6	
3D	6	
4A	4	
4B	4	
4C	12	
5A	4	
5B	9	
6A	7	
6B	8	
7A	3	
7B	5	
7C	4	
7D	2	
7E	4	
8A	4	
8B	12	
9A	6	
9B	5	
9C	5	
9D	4	
Total	180	

AFTERNOON SESSION		
Question	Maximum Points	Your Score
10	18	
11	18	
12	18	
13	18	
14	18	
15	18	
16	18	
17	18	
18	18	
19	18	
Total	180	

Certain Passing Score: 252 of 360 (70%)
Probable Passing Score: 234 (65%)

Please note that we write these exams to be as challenging and representative as possible. However, due to the relaxed conditions that most candidates apply when they "take" these tests (e.g., "I need a break; I think I'll go to the refrigerator and get a snack"), you should adjust your score downward by 10–15 percentage points to get a more accurate measure of the score you would have actually received on exam day. Also, you must be honest with yourself for your score on this exam to have any meaning. Don't assume, for example, that if your essay answer is close, the graders will be generous with points.

PRACTICE EXAM 3
MORNING SESSION

QUESTION 1 HAS ONE PART FOR A TOTAL OF 17 MINUTES

Mary Middendorf, 52, is the current marketing director for MCTECH, a multinational supplier of computer and telecommunications equipment. Due to the recent acquisition of her firm by a larger organization, Middendorf has been informed that her position will be terminated in six months. Middendorf is visiting with Michelle Mightman, CFA, to discuss her financial situation. The following information is disclosed in her meeting.

- "My investment portfolio is currently valued close to $3,000,000. MCTECH had a fantastic profit sharing and incentive program. My current holding of MCTECH stock is close to $2,250,000. The rest of my portfolio is in a broad market stock index fund. I also have a money market checking account that carries a relatively constant balance of $10,000."

- "When my position is terminated with MCTECH in six months, I will receive a lump-sum after-tax cash payment of $750,000, which is approximately equal to three years salary. Additionally, the acquisition is an all-stock transaction, so my MCTECH position will be replaced by the stock of the acquiring firm."

- "The all-stock transaction will mean my portfolio will contain a much more stable security. The previous two years were substantially rocky for my investments, so I am happy the MCTECH stock will be replaced. My investment portfolio exhibited a substantial improvement with the news of the acquisition, and I look forward to the continued appreciation of my portfolio, due to the favorable performance of the acquiring company's stock. The new stock will also lower the volatility of my investments, which I will need over the next year or so."

- "Although various firms have given me employment offers commencing in six months, I would like to travel during the six months following my separation from MCTECH. I have worked diligently over the past 20 years, and I need a break before I begin working at another firm. Most employment offers I received are for amounts slightly higher than what I am currently making at MCTECH. I am confident I will be able to get other equivalent offers in a year's time."

- "I am not married, and I have no children. Although I like to travel, my living expenses are otherwise minimal, hence I do not require much in the way of current income."

Without calculations, **prepare** the objectives and constraints portion of an investment policy statement for Middendorf.

Answer Question 1 in the template provided.

(17 minutes)

Template for Question 1

Investment Policy Statement for Middendorf	
Objectives	Risk Tolerance
	Return Objectives
Constraints	Time Horizon
	Liquidity
	Legal/Regulatory
	Taxes
	Unique Circumstances

©2010 Kaplan, Inc.

QUESTION 2 HAS TWO PARTS FOR A TOTAL OF 32 MINUTES

John and Susan Tran are 81 and 74 years old, respectively, and they have one son, Jared, who is 45. Their current annual spending is $150,000, and they would like to maintain that level over their five-year planning horizon. Their current portfolio contains $200,000 of cash equivalents, a $500,000 position in a diversified bond fund, and a $300,000 position in a diversified equity fund.

The Trans have contacted a local financial planner, Mark Palmer, CFA, to assist them in their planning. Palmer has constructed the mortality table below for the Trans.

| Years | Husband | | Wife | |
	Age	Prob.	Age	Prob.
1	82	0.9248	75	0.9736
2	83	0.8418	76	0.9446
3	84	0.7501	77	0.9125
4	85	0.6489	78	0.8771
5	86	0.5371	79	0.8381

Additionally, Palmer has estimated the inflation rate at 3% and the real risk-free interest rate at 2%.

A.   Fill in all *non-shaded* areas of the following template. Show your calculations.

(24 minutes)

Template for Question 2-A

Year	Combined Probability	Real Annual Spending	Expected Real Spending	Present Value
1		150,000		
2		150,000		
3		150,000		
4		150,000		
5		150,000		
Core Capital				
Excess Capital				

The Trans are contemplating gifting their equity fund to Jared, and they would like to gift the remainder to a local charity. Palmer estimates that the equity fund will earn 7% per year. The Trans tax rate for investment returns is 25%, while their son's tax rate for investment returns is 35%. The inheritance tax rate on the Trans is estimated at 20%. If the Trans gift the equity fund to their son immediately, they can take advantage of a one-time tax-free gift provision in their tax code.

B. **Determine** whether it is more beneficial for the Trans to transfer the equity fund to their son immediately through a gifting arrangement or later as a bequest in five years by **calculating** the relative after-tax value of the two alternatives. (Show your calculations in the template provided.)

(8 minutes)

Template for Question Part 2-B

Is it more beneficial to gift or bequest the fund? (circle one)	Gift	Bequest
Value as Tax-Free Gift		
Value as Bequest		
Relative Value		

©2010 Kaplan, Inc.

QUESTION 3 HAS FOUR PARTS FOR A TOTAL OF 29 MINUTES

Royal Performance Verification provides independent analysis of portfolio manager performance and corporate governance effectiveness for investors worldwide. Carolyn Jensen and Vicki Miller are the senior analysts for Royal. Jensen and Miller are currently evaluating the performance for two portfolio managers, Sycamore Management and Malta Advisors. Both managers use active management. The figures for their most recent year's performance are provided below.

	Sycamore Management	Malta Advisors
Investor's benchmark	11.0%	18.0%
Manager return	12.0%	16.0%
Misfit active risk	2.8%	3.5%
Normal portfolio return	15.0%	14.0%
Total active risk	4.0%	4.1%

A.   Using the information provided, **assess** the performance of the two managers individually and **discuss** their relative performance.

(8 minutes)

Jensen and Miller also have responsibility for evaluating the investment style of portfolio managers. They are currently evaluating the style of two funds, one from the Rockford group and one from the Kishwaukee group. The Rockford fund trades as an exchange-traded fund (ETF) and the Kishwaukee fund trades as a mutual fund. Miller characterizes the style of portfolio managers by using a constrained regression where the manager's returns are regressed against various security indices. Jensen evaluates the manager's style by examining the characteristics of the securities in the manager's portfolio. The results of her examination of the broad market and the funds are provided below.

	Rockford Fund	Kishwaukee Fund	Broad Market
Dividend yield	1.2%	3.7%	2.8%
EPS growth for one year	17.3%	2.7%	5.9%
EPS growth for five years	19.7%	5.2%	12.1%
Median market cap (in billions)	$0.80	$47.90	$28.50
P/B ratio	3.27	2.11	2.97
P/E ratio	24.84	15.33	19.47

Industry weight			
Basic industries	7%	12%	14%
Business services	9%	6%	6%
Consumer goods	6%	4%	7%
Consumer services	14%	8%	9%
Energy	3%	4%	11%
Financials	10%	40%	20%
Information technology	27%	6%	16%
Health	18%	1%	12%
Media	5%	1%	1%
Utilities	1%	18%	4%
Total	100%	100%	100%

B.   Based on the information provided, **discuss** the following issues.

    i.   The relative earnings volatility for the two funds.

    ii. The relative abilities of Jensen's and Miller's style classifications to detect style drift.

    iii. The tax efficiency of the two funds.

(9 minutes)

The following week, Jensen and Miller evaluate the corporate governance structure of the PharmaScreen Corporation. PharmaScreen provides testing of drugs for pharmaceutical firms so that government approvals for the marketing of the drugs can be expedited. PharmaScreen began nine years ago, assisted with some seed capital from Cape Fear Capital, a large hedge fund located in the United States. PharmaScreen went public three years ago and Cape Fear has sold most of their original holdings. They are still PharmaScreen's single largest investor, however, holding 2.1% of PharmaScreen's outstanding stock.

Due to a series of management mistakes, PharmaScreen's stock has fallen to where it is now considered a small-cap value stock. Despite this, Jensen feels that PharmaScreen's niche within their industry provides the stock with tremendous upside potential. The firm's current market capitalization totals $53 million and its P/E ratio is 7.4.

As part of their investigation, Jensen and Miller examine PharmaScreen's ownership and compensation structures. During their discussion, Jensen makes the following comments:

- "I am encouraged that PharmaScreen has institutions that hold their stock. The institutions will help monitor management and will use their influence to effect the change needed in PharmaScreen's management."

- "PharmaScreen's management needs a compensation structure that more closely aligns the interests of management and shareholders. One possible solution would be to weight management's compensation more heavily towards out-of-the-money stock options so that they have a strong incentive to increase the stock price. The drawback of this form of compensation would be that management would have an incentive to undertake too much risk."

C.   **State** whether or not *each* of these comments is correct or incorrect and **explain** your selection.

Answer Question 3-C in the template provided.

(6 minutes)

Template for Question 3-C

Comment	Correct or incorrect? (circle one)	Explanation
"I am encouraged that PharmaScreen has institutions that hold their stock. The institutions will help monitor management and will use their influence to effect the change needed with PharmaScreen's management."	Correct Incorrect	
"PharmaScreen's management needs a compensation structure that more closely aligns the interests of management and shareholders. One possible solution would be to weight management's compensation more heavily toward out-of-the-money stock options so that they have a strong incentive to increase the stock price. The drawback of this form of compensation is that management would have an incentive to undertake too much risk."	Correct Incorrect	

D.   Regarding the role of debt as a corporate governance mechanism, **state** and **discuss**: *two* reasons why it is an effective mechanism and *one* limitation.

(6 minutes)

QUESTION 4 HAS THREE PARTS FOR A TOTAL OF 20 MINUTES

Tom Nicholson is the newly hired risk manager for Antelope Advisors. Antelope has approximately $1.7 billion under management for wealthy individuals. Antelope has teams of managers assigned to their specific asset classes. Antelope recommends investments in U.S. and developed country stocks and bonds, as well as nontraditional assets such as hedge funds, commodities, and emerging market stocks. Antelope also uses futures and options to hedge various positions when deemed appropriate.

During his review of Antelope's risk management policies, Nicholson makes the following comments:

- "Antelope must evaluate the risk of its bond positions and equity index option positions carefully, because of recent volatility in interest rates and in the stock markets. For bonds and options, standard deviation is not the preferred risk management tool. Necessary and sufficient risk measures for bonds and options are the duration of bonds and delta of options."

- "One risk management tool Antelope should consider is maximum loss optimization. This tool involves recognizing those factors with the greatest potential to damage the value of Antelope's portfolio. Antelope could then take steps to limit the damage from these factors."

A.   **State** whether or not *each* of these comments is correct or incorrect and **support** your decison.

Answer Question 4-A in the template provided.

(4 minutes)

Template for Question 4-A

Comment	Correct or incorrect? (circle one)	Explanation
"Antelope must evaluate the risk of its bond positions and equity index option positions carefully because of recent volatility in interest rates and in the stock markets. For bonds and options, standard deviation is not the preferred risk management tool. Necessary and sufficient risk measures for bonds and options are the duration of bonds and delta of options."	Correct Incorrect	
"One risk management tool Antelope should consider is maximum loss optimization. This tool involves recognizing those factors with the greatest potential to damage the value of Antelope's portfolio. Antelope could then take steps to limit the damage from these factors."	Correct Incorrect	

B.   Based on the information provided, **discuss** the following issues.

    i.   Whether Antelope should use a centralized or decentralized enterprise risk management system.

    ii.   Which of the three general VAR approaches is *least* appropriate for Antelope.

(4 minutes)

John Sims is the chief investment officer for Antelope. Antelope is considering using outside managers for a portion of their invested assets. The first manager is Andy Davis. Davis has had tremendous success during the past five years by investing in the sovereign debt of emerging market countries. He has consistently beaten his benchmark every year. The other manager under consideration is Bobby Brooks. Brooks invests in the equity of formerly government-owned companies in Eastern Europe.

Antelope specifies a minimum acceptable return of 5.3%, and the appropriate risk-free rate is 4.5%. The performance for both managers is provided in the following table. The returns and standard deviations are annualized using monthly returns.

Figure 1: Available Data for Davis and Brooks

	Davis	Brooks
Portfolio return	20.60%	21.30%
Maximum drawdown	15.20%	13.70%
Portfolio standard deviation	33.20%	31.20%
Portfolio downside deviation	15.05%	16.50%

C.   Using only the information provided in Figure 1, **evaluate** both managers using *three different* risk-adjusted return measures (i.e., ratios). **Show** your calculations. **Determine** which is the *most appropriate* for evaluation of the managers. **Justify** your choice.

(12 minutes)

QUESTION 5 HAS TWO PARTS FOR A TOTAL OF 13 MINUTES

Jeff Stovall is a consultant to the chief executive officer of a large bank, Capital City Bank. Stovall makes the following statements at a presentation to bank officers and regional money managers:

- "The trust officers at the bank may want to suggest an alpha-beta separation approach. This approach is particularly useful in less efficient markets such as small-cap markets."

- "Portfolio managers should be aware, however, that some institutions may not be able to use an alpha-beta separation approach because of institutional constraints."

A. **State** whether each of these comments is correct or incorrect and **explain** your decision.

Answer Question 5-A in the template provided.

(4 minutes)

Template for Question 5-A

Comment	Correct or incorrect? (circle one)	Explanation
"The trust officers at the bank may want to suggest an alpha-beta separation approach. This approach is particularly useful in less efficient markets such as small-cap markets."	Correct Incorrect	
"Portfolio managers should be aware, however, that some institutions may not be able to use an alpha-beta separation approach because of institutional constraints."	Correct Incorrect	

B.   Regarding banks, **discuss** the following issues.
      i.   The maturity of assets in the bank's security portfolio.
      ii.   The liquidity of assets in the bank's security portfolio.
      iii. The legal and regulatory constraints for banks.

(9 minutes)

©2010 Kaplan, Inc.

QUESTION 6 HAS TWO PARTS FOR A TOTAL OF 17 MINUTES

Tim Brewer, CFA, is vice president for Wealth Managers, Inc. (WMI). WMI has been asked by a pension board to make a presentation on the ability of the firm to manage assets and consistently generate successful results.

During the presentation, Brewer makes the following statements:

- "Since most of our investments are made in fixed income securities, our performance reflects accrual accounting for bond interest, but not for the interest income of non-fixed income securities."
- "As you can see from all the various countries in which we invest, we have to pay close attention to exchange rate effects. Since some of our investments are in countries where exchange rate information is difficult to retrieve, we use a multitude of sources to calculate the exchange rate effects for our composites and benchmarks. These differential sources of information allow us to find the most accurate exchange rate data and are disclosed in performance presentations."
- "Return performance is presented gross of all fees, expenses, and loads."

A.   **State** whether or not *each* of these comments is consistent with the Global Investment Performance Standards® (GIPS). If not consistent, **explain** why.

   Answer Question 6-A in the template provided.

   (7 minutes)

Template for Question 6-A

Comment	Does statement comply with GIPS requirements? (circle one)	Explanation
"Since most of our investments are made in fixed income securities, our performance reflects accrual accounting for bond interest, but not for the interest income of non-fixed income securities."	Yes No	
"As you can see from all the various countries in which we invest, we have to pay close attention to exchange rate effects. Since some of our investments are in countries where exchange rate information is difficult to retrieve, we use a multitude of sources to calculate the exchange rate effects for our composites and benchmarks. These differential sources of information allow us to find the most accurate exchange rate data and are disclosed in performance presentations."	Yes No	
"Return performance is presented gross of all fees, expenses, and loads."	Yes No	

B.   Brewer produces a performance presentation as representative of his firm's work (reproduced below). In the template provided, **list** and **discuss** a combination of four items in the presentation (other than omissions) that are not compliant with GIPS® and would prevent the presentation from being in compliance.

Answer Question 6-B in the template provided.

(8 minutes)

**Investment Opportunity Investors
Equity Composite
January 1, 2003 through March 31, 2009**

Year	Total Return (%)	Benchmark Return (%)	Number of Portfolios	Composite Dispersion (%)	Total Assets at End of Period (€ millions)	% of Total Firm Assets
2003*	18.71	14.34	28	4.1	189	66
2004	19.54	18.23	29	4.8	183	65
2005	12.81	11.75	34	5.9	329	75
2006	17.30	18.56	37	8.5	346	72
2007	11.86	11.20	36	1.7	333	68
2008	7.59	8.50	42	3.5	284	63
1st Quarter 2009 (annualized)	14.25	9.14	38	6.1	279	60

* 2003 results are not in compliance with GIPS® and accordingly have not been certified.

Investment Opportunity Investors has prepared and presented this report in compliance with the Global Investment Performance Standards (GIPS®).

Notes:

1. The benchmark composition is 100% DAX 100.
2. All values are based on market valuations.
3. Performance results are presented before management and custodial fees but after estimated trading expenses. The management fee schedule is contained in the appendix to this report.
4. This composite was created in January 2003. No modifications to the composites as presented here have occurred as a result of changes in personnel or for any other reason at any time. A complete list and description of firm composites and performance results is available upon request.

5. The dispersion of annual returns is measured by the standard deviation among asset-weighted portfolio returns for portfolios that were in the composite over the entire year.
6. Several non-fee paying accounts are included.
7. All accounts of at least €5,000,000 are included in the composite as of the first quarter under management.
8. All return calculations are geometrically linked and performed as prescribed by the Global Investment Performance Standards (GIPS®).
9. Percentage of total firm assets is calculated using discretionary accounts.

Template for Question 6-B

Four non-compliant items
1.
2.
3.
4.

QUESTION 7 HAS FIVE PARTS FOR A TOTAL OF 18 MINUTES

Within the past year, Ural Industries (UI) of Russia has acquired an American competitor, Peak Metals (PM). As a part of the acquisition, UI was required to assume the pension liabilities and assets accumulated by PM. Coming from a country where the concept of privately funded pensions is relatively new, UI has sought the advice of First Chicago Pension Advisors to help formulate a strategy for dealing with the plan.

Meagan Skalmoski, CFA, and Germaine Wilson, CFA, have been assigned to lead the project for First Chicago. Viktor Yushkinsky has assembled a team from the UI finance department to meet with Skalmoski and Wilson to discuss a variety of issues that will need to be addressed going forward. Yushkinsky's first two questions concern the evaluation of risk tolerance and how pension funds differ from other types of institutional investors.

A.   **List** *three* of the five principal characteristics that should be considered when evaluating pension fund risk tolerance.

(3 minutes)

B.   **List** *three* of the five constraints that require consideration for all institutional investors, and **identify** the key difference between the return requirements of a defined-benefit pension plan compared with an endowment.

(5 minutes)

In his next question, Yushkinsky asked for clarification on the role of the strategic allocation. One member of his team asked why it was necessary to specify such an allocation at all, given that the portfolio manager might need to be able to make adjustments to take advantage of market conditions. Another member asked how the key issues involved in setting an institutional asset allocation differ from those for individual investors.

C.   **Summarize** the role of the strategic asset allocation in terms of specifying the client's risk objectives, and its importance to the determination of long-term returns.

(4 minutes)

D.   **Contrast** and **discuss** the principal difference regarding asset allocation for institutions as compared with individual investors.

(2 minutes)

©2010 Kaplan, Inc.

The final questions from UI's team concerned the responsibilities of the portfolio's investment advisor: What are the advisor's key responsibilities, and what underlying factors are likely to dictate that the pension plan's fundamental investment objectives need to be reviewed and/or altered?

E.   **Describe** the institutional portfolio manager's two principal responsibilities. **Identify** the *two* primary factors that change through time and **indicate** the potential need to rebalance a client's portfolio.

(4 minutes)

QUESTION 8 HAS TWO PARTS FOR A TOTAL OF 16 MINUTES

Jack Easterling is a portfolio manager for Reed Management. Two of Easterling's clients are Mary Fisher and Tom Pollard. He is working with them on determining an asset allocation and the appropriate level of life insurance.

Fisher lives in Washington, D.C. and has been working for the federal government for over 15 years. She has good health care benefits and receives steady raises each year, thanks to the strong employee's union that represents her. She has never been married and lives alone with her two cats and two dogs.

Pollard lives in Northern Virginia and is married with two children. His wife stays at home to care for and home school the two children. Pollard works as a sales representative for a firm that provides pharmaceuticals and medical supplies to hospitals on a competitive bid basis. Although he is quite happy in his job and usually has substantial compensation, he is concerned about his future sales commissions due to declining reimbursements and increasing competition in the health care industry.

During separate meetings in Easterling's office, Fisher and Pollard make the following statements:

- Fisher: "I grew up in a family of four. My parents are deceased and I am estranged from my brother. Thus I will not have any heirs, except for my pets. If possible, I would like to leave a modest amount of funds to the local animal shelter upon my death and make sure my pets are cared for. I am in good health and, given my family's medical history, I expect to live another 30 years."

- Pollard: "I want to be sure my family is financially secure. My wife has never worked and has few professional job prospects. My parents died destitute and I had to pay for both their funerals. My father died at an early age due to a heart attack and my mother died of lung cancer. Although I am very conscious of my health, I do fear that I may be susceptible to the same health issues as my parents."

A. **Characterize** the *likely* asset allocation as to whether it should be weighted towards stocks or bonds for *each* investor. **Justify** your response with *one* reason for *each* investor. Use only the information previously provided.

(4 minutes)

B. **Characterize** the *likely* term life insurance requirement as high or low demand for *each* investor using the following factors:
    i.   Probability of death.
    ii. Human capital.
    iii. Bequest preferences.

    Justify your responses with *one* reason for *each* investor. Consider each factor *independently* of the others. Use only the information previously provided.

(12 minutes)

QUESTION 9 HAS FOUR PARTS FOR A TOTAL OF 20 MINUTES

Consolidated Trust Company, headquartered in Sydney, Australia, is evaluating some international bond investments. Colin Greystone, CFA, is the portfolio manager. He has identified and is evaluating two bonds in countries X and Y for purchase. Greystone believes that international bonds must be evaluated in terms of their potential for excess returns. He wants to identify the sources of excess returns, and the risks associated with these investments, and has gathered the data in Figure 1:

Figure 1: Data on Bond X, Bond Y, and the Domestic Economy

Bond X	Bond Y	Domestic Economy
$r_x = 4.55\%$	$r_y = 7.05\%$	
$c_x = 3.05\%$	$c_y = 5.65\%$	$c_d = 4.55\%$
Duration = 7	Duration = 6	

Notes: r = return on the bond in its currency
c_i = the cash return in country i

A.   **List** *six* sources of excess return from international bond investing.

(6 minutes)

B.   Suppose that the country beta for Bond X is 1.3, and that Australian domestic interest rates are expected to increase by 80 basis points. **Analyze** the effect on the yield change and value of Bond X.

(5 minutes)

C.   The investment horizon is one year. Greystone expects Currency Y to depreciate 0.95% against the domestic currency during this time. **Recommend** and **justify** whether or not the currency risk of the position should be hedged if he purchases Bond Y.

(5 minutes)

D.   Greystone feels that the yield on Bond X will increase about 15 bps over the coming year while the yield on Bond Y will remain more or less the same. **Determine**, based only on the data provided for Bonds X and Y in Figure 1 and Greystone's yield predictions, whether Bond X or Bond Y should produce the higher return for the coming six months.

(4 minutes)

END OF MORNING SESSION

Exam 3 Afternoon Session Topic Breakdown

Question	Topic	Minutes
10	Ethics and Standards	18
11	Ethics and Standards	18
12	Execution of Portfolio Decisions; Monitoring and Rebalancing	18
13	Equity Portfolio Management	18
14	Fixed Income Portfolio Management	18
15	Fixed Income Portfolio Management	18
16	Risk Management/Risk Management Applications of Derivatives	18
17	Risk Management Applications of Derivatives	18
18	Global Investment Performance Standards	18
19	Private Wealth Management	18
	Total	180

EXAM 3 SELECTED RESPONSE ITEM SET ANSWER SHEET

The afternoon session of the Level III exam contains 10 Selected Response Item Sets, each with six questions, and you must answer them by filling in a bubble sheet with a number 2 or HB pencil. For realism, we suggest that you use this answer sheet and darken the bubbles corresponding to your answers. This sheet will also facilitate entering your answers into our online Performance Tracker. You have 180 minutes for this session of the exam. That equates to 3 minutes per item set question, so budget your time well.

10.1. (A) (B) (C)   15.1. (A) (B) (C)
10.2. (A) (B) (C)   15.2. (A) (B) (C)
10.3. (A) (B) (C)   15.3. (A) (B) (C)
10.4. (A) (B) (C)   15.4. (A) (B) (C)
10.5. (A) (B) (C)   15.5. (A) (B) (C)
10.6. (A) (B) (C)   15.6. (A) (B) (C)

11.1. (A) (B) (C)   16.1. (A) (B) (C)
11.2. (A) (B) (C)   16.2. (A) (B) (C)
11.3. (A) (B) (C)   16.3. (A) (B) (C)
11.4. (A) (B) (C)   16.4. (A) (B) (C)
11.5. (A) (B) (C)   16.5. (A) (B) (C)
11.6. (A) (B) (C)   16.6. (A) (B) (C)

12.1. (A) (B) (C)   17.1. (A) (B) (C)
12.2. (A) (B) (C)   17.2. (A) (B) (C)
12.3. (A) (B) (C)   17.3. (A) (B) (C)
12.4. (A) (B) (C)   17.4. (A) (B) (C)
12.5. (A) (B) (C)   17.5. (A) (B) (C)
12.6. (A) (B) (C)   17.6. (A) (B) (C)

13.1. (A) (B) (C)   18.1. (A) (B) (C)
13.2. (A) (B) (C)   18.2. (A) (B) (C)
13.3. (A) (B) (C)   18.3. (A) (B) (C)
13.4. (A) (B) (C)   18.4. (A) (B) (C)
13.5. (A) (B) (C)   18.5. (A) (B) (C)
13.6. (A) (B) (C)   18.6. (A) (B) (C)

14.1. (A) (B) (C)   19.1. (A) (B) (C)
14.2. (A) (B) (C)   19.2. (A) (B) (C)
14.3. (A) (B) (C)   19.3. (A) (B) (C)
14.4. (A) (B) (C)   19.4. (A) (B) (C)
14.5. (A) (B) (C)   19.5. (A) (B) (C)
14.6. (A) (B) (C)   19.6. (A) (B) (C)

PRACTICE EXAM 3
AFTERNOON SESSION

Questions 10.1–10.6 relate to Cindy Hatcher and Bernhardt Capital.

Cindy Hatcher, CFA, has spent the last ten years as a portfolio manager with Bernhardt Capital. While working for Bernhardt, Hatcher was responsible for maintaining and improving the company's code of ethics and guidelines for ethical money management. As a result of Hatcher's efforts, Bernhardt saw a dramatic decline in the number of complaints received from their individual and institutional customers.

One of Bernhardt's direct competitors, Smith Investments, is keenly aware of Hatcher's reputation for ethical business practices and has offered her a job as their compliance officer. Hatcher has been apprised of several potential ethical problems at Smith that she will be directly responsible for fixing through implementation of policies and procedures that will prevent ethical dilemmas. The management at Smith is willing to grant Hatcher the authority to construct and implement policies to eliminate the ethical problems at the company.

Hatcher agrees to accept the position with Smith and resigns from employment with Bernhardt. As her first initiative with the company, Hatcher distributes to all employees at Smith a survey intended to acquaint her with the company's common business practices. Her goal is to identify those factors that are most likely to interfere with Smith's compliance with the CFA Institute's Code of Ethics and Standards of Practice. After collecting and analyzing the anonymous responses to the survey, Hatcher has identified the following four issues as the most frequently cited questionable business practices:

1. Many Smith employees have relatives who are clients of the firm. For relatives' accounts where the Smith employee does not have beneficial ownership, trades are generally executed in conjunction with trades for other discretionary accounts held at the firm. Only in accounts where the Smith employee has beneficial ownership are trades delayed until all discretionary account trading is completed.

2. Many of Smith's employees either personally own or maintain, through a family member, beneficial ownership of stocks that are also held in accounts for many of the firm's clients. While the company maintains a strict disclosure policy to the firm of such beneficial ownership and an "at will" disclosure policy to its clients, employees are not barred from trading these securities for their personal benefit even if their clients also own or have a direct or indirect financial interest in the same securities.

3. Account managers meet weekly to discuss the issues and concerns of the client portfolios managed at the firm. During the meetings, it is not unusual for individual clients to be identified and discussed. Information regarding the client's holdings and investment strategy is discussed as well as personal needs related to the client's portfolio. The meetings are held in order to provide guidance and continuing education to all of the firm's account managers.

4. At the suggestion of fixed-income analysts at the firm, most of the portfolio managers working for Smith have been adding B-rated corporate fixed-income securities to their portfolios. Analysts originally made (and continue to make) the suggestion due to the attractive yield potential offered by this class of investments. Smith's portfolio managers were thrilled with the idea since the returns on many of the portfolios' equity positions have been stifled by high profile accounting scandals.

Management at Smith Investments has been pleased with Hatcher's efforts so far but is concerned about the firm's ability to maintain compliance with the CFA Institute's Global Investment Performance Standards (GIPS®). The managing director of the firm, Erich Prince, has made the following comments to Hatcher:

> "I am concerned that we will not be able to claim compliance with GIPS at the end of the year since our new information system has inhibited our ability to include terminated portfolios in the historical record up to the last full measurement period before they were terminated. Also, we are unable to regroup portfolios that utilize hedging into separate composites from those that do not utilize hedging. These portfolios are currently grouped according to traditional value and growth strategies based on the capitalization of portfolio holdings (i.e., large vs. small)."

Hatcher eases Prince's mind by telling him she will "ensure full compliance with GIPS by the end of the quarter."

10.1. Which of the following *best* describes a policy that Hatcher could implement to eliminate violations of the CFA Institute Code and Standards in conjunction with trades placed for relatives of the employees of Smith Investments?
A. Implement a policy prohibiting trades in accounts belonging to relatives of Smith employees.
B. Restrict trades on relatives' accounts until all other trades have been placed for Smith's other clients.
C. No new policy is necessary since the current policy doesn't violate the Code and Standards.

10.2. Hatcher is concerned about Smith's policies related to disclosure of beneficial ownership of securities. Determine if Smith's disclosure policies are in violation of the CFA Institute Code and Standards and suggest a strategy to eliminate the violation if one exists.

A. The policy violates the Code and Standards and can be fixed by barring employees from trading the conflicting securities.

B. The policy violates the Code and Standards and can be fixed by requiring written disclosure to clients regarding Smith employees with beneficial ownership of conflicting securities.

C. This particular policy does not violate the Code and Standards.

10.3. Which of the following actions should Hatcher take to ensure that Smith Investments is in compliance with Standard IV(B.5) Preservation of Confidentiality? She should prohibit:

A. discussion of clients' individual needs at the weekly meetings of account managers.

B. discussion of clients' holdings and investment strategy at the weekly meetings of account managers.

C. identification of clients being discussed at the weekly meetings of account managers.

10.4. Smith's portfolio managers have been adding B-rated corporate fixed-income securities to their portfolios at the recommendation of the firm's fixed-income analysts. With regard to this situation, Smith's employees have violated the CFA Institute's Code and Standards for which of the following reasons?

A. Fixed-income analysts are recommending debt securities that are below an investment grade credit rating.

B. Portfolio managers have failed to consider the investment policy statement of each portfolio before adding the fixed-income securities to the portfolios.

C. Fixed-income analysts have failed to provide a detailed description of the investment characteristics of the corporate fixed-income securities to the portfolio managers.

10.5. Has Hatcher violated, either directly or indirectly, the CFA Institute Code of Ethics and Standards of Practice?

A. Hatcher violated Standard III(E) Responsibilities of Supervisors by accepting the position with the knowledge that violations were occurring at Smith.

B. Hatcher violated Standard III(E) Responsibilities of Supervisors by failing to make an adequate effort to uncover potential violations at Smith Investments.

C. Hatcher has not violated the Code or Standards.

10.6. Determine whether Smith Investments' treatment of terminated portfolios and/or their inability to separate hedged and non-hedged portfolios into separate composites could potentially jeopardize their ability to claim GIPS compliance.

A. Only their treatment of terminated portfolios could jeopardize Smith Investments' ability to claim compliance with the GIPS.

B. Only their inability to separate hedged and unhedged portfolios could jeopardize Smith Investments' ability to claim compliance with the GIPS.

C. Both their treatment of terminated portfolios and their inability to separate hedged and unhedged portfolios could jeopardize Smith Investments' ability to claim compliance with the GIPS.

Questions 11.1–11.6 relate to Harold Chang and Woodlock Management Group.

Harold Chang, CFA, has been the lead portfolio manager for the Woodlock Management Group (WMG) for the last five years. WMG runs several equity and fixed income portfolios, all of which are authorized to use derivatives as long as such positions are consistent with the portfolio's strategy. The WMG Equity Opportunities Fund takes advantage of long and short profit opportunities in equity securities. The fund's positions are often a relatively large percentage of the issuer's outstanding shares and fund trades frequently move securities prices. Chang runs the Equity Opportunities Fund and is concerned that his performance for the last three quarters has put his position as lead manager in jeopardy. Over the last three quarters, Chang has been underperforming his benchmark by an increasing margin and is determined to reduce the degree of underperformance before the end of the next quarter. Accordingly, Chang makes the following transactions for the fund:

Transaction 1: Chang discovers that the implied volatility of call options on GreenCo is too high. As a result, Chang shorts a large position in the stock options while simultaneously taking a long position in GreenCo stock, using the funds from the short position to partially pay for the long stock. The GreenCo purchase caused the share price to move up slightly. After several months, the GreenCo stock position has accumulated a large unrealized gain. Chang sells a portion of the GreenCo position to rebalance the portfolio.

Richard Stirr, CFA, who is also a portfolio manager for WMG, runs the firm's Fixed Income Fund. Stirr is known for his ability to generate excess returns above his benchmark, even in declining markets. Stirr is convinced that even though he has only been with WMG for two and a half years, he will be named lead portfolio manager if he can keep his performance figures strong through the next quarter. To achieve this positive performance, Stirr enters into the following transactions for the fund:

Transaction 2: Stirr decides to take a short forward position on the senior bonds of ONB Corporation, which Stirr currently owns in his Fixed Income Fund. Stirr made his decision after overhearing two of his firm's investment bankers discussing an unannounced bond offering for ONB that will subordinate all of its outstanding debt. As expected, the price of the ONB bonds falls when the upcoming offering is announced. Stirr delivers the bonds to settle the forward contract, preventing large losses for his investors.

Transaction 3: Stirr has noticed that in a foreign bond market, participants are slow to react to new information relevant to the value of their country's sovereign debt securities. Stirr, along with other investors, knows that an announcement from his firm regarding the sovereign bonds will be made the following day. Stirr doesn't know for sure, but expects the news to be positive, and prepares to enter a purchase order. When the positive news is released, Stirr is the first to act, making a large purchase before other investors and selling the position after other market participants react and move the sovereign bond price higher.

Because of their experience with derivatives instruments, Chang and Stirr are asked to provide investment advice for Cherry Creek, LLC, a commodities trading advisor. Cherry Creek uses managed futures strategies that incorporate long and short positions in commodity futures to generate returns uncorrelated with securities markets. The firm has asked Chang and Stirr to help extend their reach to include equity and fixed income derivatives strategies. Chang has been investing with Cherry Creek since its inception and has accepted increased shares in his Cherry Creek account as compensation for his advice. Chang has not disclosed his arrangement with Cherry Creek since he meets with the firm only during his personal time. Stirr declines any formal compensation but instead requests that Cherry Creek refer their clients requesting traditional investment services to WMG. Cherry Creek agrees to the arrangement.

Three months have passed since the transactions made by Chang and Stirr occurred. Both managers met their performance goals and are preparing to present their results to clients via an electronic newsletter published every quarter. The managers want to ensure their newsletters are in compliance with CFA Institute Standards of Professional Conduct. Chang states, "in order to comply with the Standards, we are required to disclose the process used to analyze and select portfolio holdings, the method used to construct our portfolios, and any changes that have been made to the overall investment process. In addition, we must include in the newsletter all factors used to make each portfolio decision over the last quarter and an assessment of the portfolio's risks." Stirr responds by claiming, "we must also clearly indicate that projections included in our report are not factual evidence but rather conjecture based on our own statistical analysis. However, I believe we can reduce the amount of information included in the report from what you have suggested and instead issue more of a summary report as long as we maintain a full report in our internal records."

11.1.   Determine whether Chang has violated any CFA Institute Standards of Professional Conduct with respect to Transaction 1.
   A. This is a violation of CFA Institute Standards due to use of the funds from the short position being used to partially pay for the long position.
   B. This is a violation of CFA Institute Standards since the immediate upward movement in GreenCo stock price was a result of the transaction artificially manipulating the market.
   C. No violation of CFA Institute Standards has occurred.

11.2.   Determine whether Stirr has violated any CFA Institute Standards of Professional Conduct with respect to Transaction 2 and Transaction 3.
   A. Both Transactions 2 and 3 violate CFA Institute Standards.
   B. Neither transaction is a violation of CFA Institute Standards.
   C. Transaction 2 is a violation of CFA Institute, while Transaction 3 is not.

11.3.   According to CFA Institute Standards of Professional Conduct, which of the following statements regarding Chang's arrangement with Cherry Creek, LLC is *most* accurate? Chang's arrangement:
   A. does not violate any Standards.
   B. violates the Standards because he has not obtained written consent from WMG to enter into the agreement.
   C. violates the Standards because he has misrepresented his ability to provide professional advice to Cherry Creek.

11.4.   According to CFA Institute Standards of Professional Conduct, which of the following statements regarding Stirr's arrangement with Cherry Creek, LLC is *most* accurate? Stirr's arrangement:
   A. does not violate any Standards.
 ✓ B. need only be disclosed to WMG to be acceptable.
   C. is acceptable only if disclosed to WMG and to clients and prospective clients.

11.5.   Determine whether Chang's comments regarding the disclosure of investment processes used to manage WMG's portfolios and the disclosure of factors used to make portfolio decisions over the last quarter are correct.
   A. Both of Chang's comments are correct.
   B. Neither of Chang's comments is correct.
 ✓ C. Only Chang's comment regarding disclosure of investment processes is correct.

11.6.   Determine whether Stirr's comments regarding the use of projections in the report and the length of the report are correct.
 ✓ A. Both of Stirr's comments regarding the projections in the report, and the length of the report, are correct.
   B. Only Stirr's comment about the projections in the report is correct.
   C. Only Stirr's comment regarding the length of the report is correct.

Questions 12.1–12.6 relate to Dan Draper.

Dan Draper, CFA, is a portfolio manager at Madison Securities. Draper is analyzing several portfolios which have just been assigned to him. In each case, there is a clear statement of portfolio objectives and constraints, as well as an initial strategic asset allocation. However, Draper has found that all of the portfolios have experienced changes in asset values. As a result, the current allocations have drifted away from the initial allocation. Draper is considering various rebalancing strategies that would keep the portfolios in line with their proposed asset allocation targets.

Draper spoke to Peter Sterling, a colleague at Madison, about calendar rebalancing. During their conversation, Sterling made the following comments:

Comment 1:   "Calendar rebalancing will be most efficient when the rebalancing frequency considers the volatility of the asset classes in the portfolio."

Comment 2:   "Calendar rebalancing on an annual basis will typically minimize market impact relative to more frequent rebalancing."

Draper believes that a percentage-of-portfolio rebalancing strategy will be preferable to calendar rebalancing, but he is uncertain as to how to set the corridor widths to trigger rebalancing for each asset class. As an example, Draper is evaluating the Rogers Corp. pension plan, whose portfolio is described in Exhibit 1.

Exhibit 1: Rogers Corp Pension Plan

Asset Class	Expected Return	Standard Deviation	Average Transaction Cost	Correlation With Other Assets in Portfolio
U.S. small-cap stocks	10%	15%	0.30%	0.21
Emerging market stocks	14%	22%	0.40%	0.10
Real estate limited partnership	16%	10%	3.00%	0.16
U.S. government bonds	6%	2%	0.05%	0.14

Draper has been reviewing Madison files on four high net worth individuals, each of whom has a $1 million portfolio. He hopes to gain insight as to appropriate rebalancing strategies for these clients. His research so far shows:

Client A is 60 years old, and wants to be sure of having at least $800,000 upon his retirement. His risk tolerance drops dramatically whenever his portfolio declines in value. He agrees with the Madison stock market outlook, which is for a long-term bull market with few reversals.

Client B is 35 years old and wants to hold stocks regardless of the value of her portfolio. She also agrees with the Madison stock market outlook.

Client C is 40 years old, and her absolute risk tolerance varies proportionately with the value of her portfolio. She does not agree with the Madison stock market outlook, but expects a volatile stock market, marked by numerous reversals, over the coming months.

12.1. Indicate whether Sterling's comments related to calendar rebalancing are correct or incorrect.
   A. Only comment 1 is correct.
   B. Only comment 2 is correct.
   C. Both comments are correct.

12.2. Draper believes that the risk tolerance for tracking error relative to the target asset mix and the volatility of any other asset classes in a portfolio are important factors in determining an appropriate rebalancing corridor. Assuming all other factors are equal, the optimal rebalancing corridor will be wider when:
   A. the risk tolerance for tracking error is high and the volatility of other asset classes is low.
   B. the risk tolerance for tracking error is high and the volatility of other asset classes is high.
   C. the risk tolerance for tracking error is low and the volatility of other asset classes is high.

12.3. Based on the information provided in Exhibit 1, which asset class of the Rogers pension plan should have the narrowest rebalancing corridor width?
   A. U.S. small cap stocks.
   B. Emerging market stocks.
   C. U.S. government bonds.

12.4. In selecting a rebalancing strategy for his clients, Draper would *most likely* select a constant mix strategy for:
   A. Client A.
   B. Client B.
   C. Client C.

12.5. A buy and hold strategy:
   A. would be appropriate for Client C.
   B. is an example of a concave strategy.
   C. is a linear strategy with a floor greater than zero and a multiplier equal to 1.

12.6. Which of the following statements is *most* accurate regarding rebalancing strategies? The constant:
   A. proportion strategy has a concave payoff curve and a multiplier greater than 1.
   B. proportion strategy has a convex payoff curve and a multiplier less than 1.
   C. mix strategy has a concave payoff curve and a multiplier less than 1.

Questions 13.1–13.6 relate to the Murray Funds.

Lucy Sakata, CFA, and Gary Lowenstein, CFA, are portfolio managers for Murray Funds, a provider of investment funds to institutional and wealthy individual investors. Murray frequently indexes in developed markets but uses full blown active management in less efficient markets and when they think their analysts have a particular expertise. The vast majority of Murray's clients attempt to minimize tracking error.

One of the Murray's funds invests in a Hong Kong index and is marketed as a way for investors to participate in the growth of the Asian economies. The index represents the best known Hong Kong stocks and Murray uses a full replication strategy for the fund. The index is a market cap-weighted index and ten firms represent over 70% of the index's total market cap. Sakata would like to market the Hong Kong fund to institutions with a required minimum investment of $50 million. Many potential clients are institutions who outsource their foreign equity management and are subject to maximum holdings on individual stocks.

Murray also has a Canada fund that invests in an index which represents the 25 largest cap stocks in Canada. It is marketed as a way for investors to exploit the growth in demand for commodities. The index adjusts for stock splits and repurchases as necessary. Most of the index's return has come from capital gains, rather than dividends, due to the tremendous increase in global demand for commodities. To encourage long-term holding, Murray places a back-end load of 3% on fund redemptions that are made within two years of initial investment.

Sakata and Lowenstein discuss the fundamental law of active management and how it applies to three hypothetical managers who invest against the broad large-cap U.S. market, as represented by the S&P 500 index.

- **Manager A** under-weights and over-weights the 500 individual stocks of the S&P 500 index as she sees appropriate, keeping industry exposures similar to those of the index. She has an information coefficient of 0.05 and is restricted to long-only positions.
- **Manager B** holds cash and long S&P 500 futures. He tries to generate excess returns by altering the duration of the cash position and has an information coefficient of 0.05.
- **Manager C** has an information coefficient of 0.07, and she uses a long-short strategy for the 500 stocks in the S&P 500 index.

Sakata is consulting with the trustees of the Powell Foundation. The foundation has a position in the three Murray funds described in Exhibit 1.

Exhibit 1: Powell Foundation Holdings

	Fund 1	Fund 2	Fund 3
Active return	3.30%	1.20%	4.50%
Active risk	5.30%	3.60%	6.70%
Fund size (in millions)	73.1	115.0	89.4
% of Powell Foundation Portfolio	20%	45%	35%
Current manager's tenure	11 years	4 years	16 years
EPS growth for 1 year	–2.3%	2.7%	5.9%
Median market cap (in billions)	$29.8	$17.2	$28.1
P/B ratio	0.87	3.01	4.88
Management fees (% of assets)	0.55%	0.41%	0.79%

Murray has a value fund that invests in stocks in the United States. Lowenstein is considering several equity style index providers as a benchmark for the fund. The characteristics of the index providers and the methodologies they use to construct equity style indices are described in Exhibit 2 below.

Exhibit 2: Comparison of Index Providers

	Provider A	Provider B
Licensing fee charged to ETF Funds	fixed rate	% of assets under management
Number of variables used to characterize value/growth	seven	three
Value/Growth categories	strong value, value, neutral, growth, strong growth	value and growth

In regard to the index providers, Lowenstein makes the following statements:

Statement 1: "I would like to use the indices from either provider in a returns-based style analysis. Based on the information in the table, I believe that if I regress a value manager's returns against Provider B's indices, the manager's selection return will appear artificially large."

Statement 2: "If an index provider uses buffering rules, a fund tracking that index will experience lower transactions costs."

13.1. Determine which of the following is the *most likely* reason that the Hong Kong fund will be inappropriate for the institutional investors.
   A. Illiquid stocks comprising the index.
   B. The weighting scheme of the index.
   C. The lack of potential excess returns.

13.2. Determine which of the following strategies would be the *most* appropriate for constructing the Canada fund.
   A. Optimization.
   B. Full replication.
   C. Stratified sampling.

13.3. Determine which of the three managers will *most likely* have the highest information ratio.
   A. Manager A.
   B. Manager B.
   C. Manager C.

13.4. Of the following strategies, determine which strategy is *most likely* pursued by Fund 1.
   A. Value.
   B. Growth.
   C. Market-oriented.

13.5. Assuming that the correlations between the equity managers' active returns are zero, determine which of the following is *closest* to the information ratio for the Powell Foundation.
   A. 0.74.
   B. 0.91.
   C. 1.09.

13.6. Determine whether the statements made by Lowenstein on the construction of equity style indices are correct or incorrect.
   A. Both statements are correct.
   B. Only Statement 1 is correct.
   C. Only Statement 2 is correct.

Questions 14.1–14.6 relate to Cardinal Fixed Income Management.

Joan Weaver, CFA, and Kim McNally, CFA, are analysts for Cardinal Fixed Income Management. Cardinal provides investment advisory services to pension funds, endowments, and other institutions in the United States and Canada. Cardinal recommends positions in investment-grade corporate and government bonds.

Cardinal has largely advocated the use of passive approaches to bond investments, where the predominant holding consists of an indexed or enhanced indexed bond portfolio. They are exploring, however, the possibility of using a greater degree of active management to increase excess returns. The analysts have made the following statements.

- Weaver: "An advantage of both enhanced indexing by matching primary risk factors and enhanced indexing by minor risk factor mismatching is that there is the potential for excess returns, but the duration of the portfolio is matched with that of the index, thereby limiting the portion of tracking error resulting from interest rate risk."
- McNally: "The use of active management by larger risk factor mismatches typically involves large duration mismatches from the index, in an effort to capitalize on interest rate forecasts."

As part of their increased emphasis on active bond management, Cardinal has retained the services of an economic consultant to provide expectations input on factors such as interest rate levels, interest rate volatility, and credit spreads. During his presentation, the economist states that he believes long-term interest rates should fall over the next year, but that short-term rates should gradually increase. Weaver and McNally are currently advising an institutional client that wishes to maintain the duration of its bond portfolio at 8.7. In light of the economic forecast, they are considering three portfolios that combine the following three bonds in varying amounts.

| | Annualized Bond Yield | Bond Maturity in years | Semiannual Coupon Payment | Portfolio | | |
				1	2	3
Bond A	6.2%	5.25	$3.10		50%	60%
Bond B	6.6%	8.50	$3.30	100%		10%
Bond C	7.1%	19.75	$3.55		50%	30%

Weaver and McNally next examine an investment in a semiannual coupon bond newly issued by the Manix Corporation, a firm with a credit rating of AA by Moody's. The specifics of the bond purchase are provided in the following given Weaver's projections. It is Cardinal's policy that bonds be evaluated for purchase on a total return basis.

Investment horizon	1 year
Cost of funds for Cardinal	9.00%
Bond maturity in years	20 years
Initial annualized bond yield	6.50%
Reinvestment rate for coupon	5.00%
Annual coupon rate paid semiannually	6.50%
Projected annualized yield to maturity at end of investment horizon	6.00%

One of Cardinal's clients, the Johnson Investment Fund (JIF), has instructed Weaver and McNally to recommend the appropriate debt investment for $125,000,000 in funds. JIF is willing to invest an additional 15% of the portfolio using leverage. JIF requires that the portfolio duration not exceed 5.5. Weaver recommends that JIF invest in bonds with a duration of 5.2. The maximum allowable leverage will be used and the borrowed funds will have a duration of 0.8. JIF is considering investing in bonds with options and has asked McNally to provide insight into these investments. McNally makes the following comments:

"Due to the increasing sophistication of bond issuers, the amount of bonds with put options is increasing, and these bonds sell at a discount relative to comparable bullets. Putables are quite attractive when interest rates rise, but, we should be careful if with them, because valuation models often fail to account for the credit risk of the issuer."

Another client, Blair Portfolio Managers, has asked Cardinal to provide advice on duration management. One year ago, their portfolio had a market value of $3,010,444 and a dollar duration of $108,000; current figures are provided below:

	Market Value	Duration	Dollar Duration
Bond 1	$940,000	3.8	$35,720
Bond 2	$820,000	2.8	$22,960
Bond 3	$780,000	4.7	$36,660
Bond 4	$621,000	3.5	$21,735

14.1. Regarding their statements on the relative duration positions of various approaches to enhanced index bond management, determine whether Weaver and McNally are correct or incorrect.
   A. Only Weaver is correct.
   B. Only McNally is correct.
   C. Both Weaver and McNally are correct.

14.2. Considering the economic consultant's forecast, determine the *most* appropriate portfolio for Weaver and McNally to recommend to their client.
   A. Portfolio 1.
   B. Portfolio 2.
   C. Portfolio 3.

14.3. The expected bond equivalent yield for the Manix Bond, using total return analysis, is *closest* to:
   A. 5.92%.
   B. 11.86%.
   C. 12.12%.

14.4. Does Weaver's recommended investment for the Johnson Investment Fund violate the investment guidelines?
   A. No, the duration of the portfolio is 5.2.
   B. Yes, the duration of the portfolio is 5.9.
   C. Yes, the duration of the portfolio is 6.1.

14.5. Evaluate McNally's comments to JIF regarding bonds with options. McNally is:
   A. correct.
   B. incorrect, because putable bonds command a premium price.
   C. incorrect, because valuation models for putable bonds incorporate credit risk.

14.6. To adjust the dollar duration of the Blair portfolio back to last year's level, Palmer should recommend that Blair rebalance each bond to approximately:
   A. 92% of its current value.
   B. 95% of its current value.
   C. 105% of its current value.

Questions 15.1–15.6 relate to Ethan Edwards and Searcher Securities.

Ethan Edwards, CFA, is a fixed income portfolio manager for Searcher Securities. Edwards has been reviewing the pension fund of Cicatrix Corp., a large account with $55 million in fixed income securities. He is considering proposing a contingent immunization strategy to the trustees of the Cicatrix pension fund. The average age of Cicatrix employees covered by the plan is 41. In a recent meeting, the trustees of the plan informed Edwards that a 6.0% return was an acceptable minimum for the next six years.

The Cicatrix pension bond portfolio was set up in a classical immunization strategy four years ago. At that time, the objective was to fund a $75 million liability in 10 years. The allocation was a barbell strategy using zero-coupon bonds with half of the bonds maturing in 4 years and half maturing in 15 years. The 4-year bonds are now maturing, and Edwards is hoping to use the proceeds to create a contingent immunized portfolio. Edwards plans to once again use a barbell structure, with half of the portfolio invested in maturities shorter than the 6-year time horizon set by the trustees and the other half in the original 15-year bonds.

One of the trustees of the Cicatrix pension fund asked Edwards whether rebalancing the portfolio was a concern when using classical immunization strategies. Edwards responded by claiming that as the yield curve shifts and time passes, the portfolio will need to be rebalanced. Edwards also stated that the costs to rebalance are high but can be mitigated by limiting the investment universe to highly liquid securities.

Another trustee asked Edwards to assess the feasibility of pursuing a multiple liability immunization strategy for the fund and report his findings. Among other items, Edwards's response contained the following information:

- Assuming parallel shifts in interest rates, multiple liability immunization is possible for the Cicatrix pension fund as long as the duration of the immunization portfolio is equal to the duration of the liability stream.

- As an alternative to multiple liability immunization, the Cicatrix pension fund could employ a cash flow matching strategy. A cash flow matching strategy would be free from immunization risk and typically would require less capital to fund the pension liabilities.

15.1. Select the most appropriate type of security to replace the maturing 4-year bonds to properly maintain a classical immunization strategy.
   A. 1-year zero coupon bond.
   B. 2-year zero coupon bond.
   C. 4-year zero coupon bond.

15.2. In order to minimize immunization risk in the event of a nonparallel interest rate shift, determine which of the following portfolio structures is preferable (assuming the entire portfolio will be restructured).
   A. Buying a series of 6-month T-bills.
   B. Buying zero coupon bonds maturing in 6 years.
   C. Buying high coupon bonds with a duration of 6.

15.3. Edwards estimates that the currently available immunized return for a 6-year time horizon is 7.25%. Assuming semiannual compounding, calculate the amount of assets needed today to achieve the required terminal value of the portfolio.
   A. $51.15 million.
   B. $55.00 million.
   C. $59.14 million.

15.4. Determine whether Edwards is correct with regard to his statement about the conditions requiring rebalancing to maintain an immunization strategy and his statement about reducing the costs of rebalancing.
   A. Only the statement on conditions requiring rebalancing is correct.
   B. Only the statement on reducing the costs of rebalancing is correct.
   C. Both of Edwards's statements are correct.

15.5. Evaluate Edwards's comment regarding the duration of the asset portfolio in multiple liability immunization. Edwards is:
   A. correct, because the immunization strategy requires that the duration of the asset portfolio is greater than the duration of the pension liabilities.
   B. incorrect, because the immunization strategy requires that the duration of the asset portfolio is less than the duration of the pension liabilities.
   C. correct, because the immunization strategy requires the duration of the asset portfolio to match the duration of the pension liabilities.

15.6. Determine whether Edwards's comments regarding the immunization risk and capital requirements for a cash flow matching strategy are correct.
   A. Only Edwards's comment regarding the immunization risk is correct.
   B. Only Edwards's comment regarding the capital requirements is correct.
   C. Both of Edwards's comments are correct.

Questions 16.1–16.6 relate to Upsala Asset Management.

Albert Wulf, CFA, is a portfolio manager with Upsala Asset Management, a regional financial services firm that handles investments for small businesses in Northern Germany. For the most part, Wulf has been handling locally concentrated investments in European securities. Due to a lack of expertise in currency management, he works closely with James Bauer, a foreign exchange expert who manages international exposure in some of Upsala's portfolios. Both individuals are committed to managing portfolio assets within the guidelines of client investment policy statements.

To achieve global diversification, Wulf's portfolio invests in securities from developed nations including the United States, Japan, and Great Britain. Due to recent currency market turmoil, translation risk has become a huge concern for Upsala's managers. The U.S. dollar has recently plummeted relative to the euro, while the Japanese yen and British pound have appreciated slightly relative to the euro. Wulf and Bauer meet to discuss hedging strategies that will hopefully mitigate some of the concerns regarding future currency fluctuations.

Wulf currently has a $1,000,000 investment in a U.S. oil and gas corporation. This position was taken with the expectation that demand for oil in the U.S. would increase sharply over the short-run. Wulf plans to exit this position 125 days from today. In order to hedge the currency exposure to the U.S. dollar, Bauer enters into a 90-day U.S. dollar futures contract, expiring in September. Bauer comments to Wulf that this futures contract guarantees that the portfolio will not take any unjustified risk in the volatile dollar.

Wulf recently started investing in securities from Japan. He has been particularly interested in the growth of technology firms in that country. Wulf decides to make an investment of ¥25,000,000 in a small technology enterprise that is in need of start-up capital. The spot exchange rate for the Japanese yen at the time of the investment is ¥135/€. The expected spot rate in 90 days is ¥132/€. Given the expected appreciation of the yen, Bauer purchases put options that provide insurance against any deprecation of the yen. While delta-hedging this position, Bauer discovers that current at-the-money yen put options sell for €1 with a delta of −0.85. He mentions to Wulf that, in general, put options will provide a cheaper alternative to hedging than with futures since put options are only exercised if the local currency depreciates.

The exposure of Wulf's portfolio to the British pound results from a 180-day pound-denominated investment of £5,000,000. The spot exchange rate for the British pound is £0.78/€. The value of the investment is expected to increase to £5,100,000 at the end of the180 day period. Bauer informs Wulf that due to the minimal expected exchange rate movement, it would be in the best interest of their clients, from a cost-benefit standpoint, to hedge only the principal of this investment.

Before entering into currency futures and options contracts, Wulf and Bauer discuss the possibility of also hedging market risk due to changes in the value of the assets. Bauer suggests that in order to hedge against a possible loss in the value of an asset Wulf should short a given foreign market index. Wulf is interested in executing index hedging strategies that are perfectly correlated with foreign investments. Bauer, however, cautions Wulf regarding the increase in trading costs that would result from these additional hedging activities.

16.1. Of the following cash management approaches, the one that best reflects Wulf and Bauer's currency management strategy is a:
   A. balanced mandate.
   B. currency overlay.
   C. separate asset allocation.

16.2. Regarding the U.S. investment in the oil and gas company, which of the following approaches would be best in eliminating potential basis risk?
   A. When the 90-day futures contract expires, Bauer should enter into another 90-day contract to further hedge against any changes in the dollar relative to the euro.
   B. Instead of the 90-day contract, Bauer should enter into a 180-day contract to cover the full 125-day period, which would eliminate additional transactions costs brought on by short-term contracts.
   C. Despite the large amount of transaction costs, Bauer should continually adjust the hedge until the futures maturity equals the desired holding period.

16.3. Regarding the Japanese investment in the technology company, determine the appropriate transaction in put options to adjust the current delta hedge, given that the delta changes to –0.92. Assume that each yen put allows the right to sell ¥1,000,000.
   A. Sell 2 yen put options.
   B. Sell 27 euro put options.
   C. Buy 29 yen put options.

16.4. Is Bauer correct in stating to Wulf that put options provide a cheaper means of hedging than futures?
   A. No, since Bauer is only concerned with unfavorable currency movements, futures would be cheaper.
   B. No, despite being less liquid, futures are less expensive to use.
   C. Yes, given that Bauer can choose to exercise the options or let them expire, options are cheaper since the payoff is only to one side.

16.5. Calculate the total rate of return that Wulf can expect from hedging the principal amount in the British denominated asset with currency futures. Assume that Bauer hedges the principal by selling £5,000,000 in pound futures at £0.79/€ and the value of the investment is £5,100,000. When this hedge is lifted the futures rate is £0.785/€ and the spot rate is £0.75/€.
   A. 6.08%.
   B. 5.45%.
   C. 2.00%.

16.6. Assuming Wulf and Bauer are successful in hedging both the foreign currency exposure and market risk exposure from the appreciation and depreciation of the asset, the expected return would be *closest* to:
   A. zero, since all risks have been hedged.
   B. the domestic risk-free rate.
   C. the foreign risk-free rate.

Questions 17.1–17.6 are related to Milson Investment Advisors.

Milson Investment Advisors (MIA) specializes in managing fixed income portfolios for institutional clients. Many of MIA's clients are able to take on substantial portfolio risk and therefore the firm's funds invest in all credit qualities and in international markets. Among its investments, MIA currently holds positions in the debt of Worth Inc., Enertech Company, and SBK Company.

Worth Inc. is a heavy equipment manufacturer in Germany. The company finances a significant amount of its fixed assets using bonds. Worth's current debt outstanding is in the form of non-callable bonds issued two years ago at a coupon rate of 7.2% and a maturity of 15 years. Worth expects German interest rates to decline by as much as 200 basis points (bps) over the next year and would like to take advantage of the decline. The company has decided to enter into a 2-year interest rate swap with semiannual payments, a swap rate of 5.8%, and a floating rate based on 6-month EURIBOR. The duration of the fixed side of the swap is 1.2. Analysts at MIA have made the following comments regarding Worth's swap plan:

> "The duration of the swap from the perspective of Worth is 0.95."

> "By entering into the swap, the duration of Worth's long-term liabilities will become smaller, causing the value of the firm's equity to become more sensitive to changes in interest rates."

Enertech Company is a U.S.-based provider of electricity and natural gas. The company uses a large proportion of floating rate notes to finance its operations. The current interest rate on Enertech's floating rate notes, based on 6-month LIBOR plus 150bp, is 5.5%. To hedge its interest rate risk, Enertech has decided to enter into a long interest rate collar. The cap and the floor of the collar have maturities of two years, with settlement dates (in arrears) every six months. The strike rate for the cap is 5.5% and for the floor is 4.5%, based on 6-month LIBOR, which is forecast to be 5.2%, 6.1%, 4.1%, and 3.8%, in 6, 12, 18, and 24 months, respectively. Each settlement period consists of 180 days. Analysts at MIA are interested in assessing the attributes of the collar.

SBK Company builds oil tankers and other large ships in Norway. The firm has several long-term bond issues outstanding with fixed interest rates ranging from 5.0% to 7.5% and maturities ranging from 5 to 12 years. Several years ago, SBK took the pay floating side of a semi-annual settlement swap with a rate of 6.0%, a floating rate based on LIBOR, and a tenor of eight years. The firm now believes interest rates may increase in 6 months, but is not 100% confident in this assumption. To hedge the risk of an interest rate increase, given its interest rate uncertainty, the firm has sold a payer interest rate swaption with a maturity of 6 months, an underlying swap rate of 6.0%, and a floating rate based on LIBOR.

MIA is considering investing in the debt of Rio Corp, a Brazilian energy company. The investment would be in Rio's floating rate notes, currently paying a coupon of 8.0%. MIA's economists are forecasting an interest rate decline in Brazil over the short term.

17.1.   Given Worth Inc.'s expectations regarding German interest rates, which of the following is *closest* to the effective interest rate the firm will pay on its liabilities after entering into the swap?
     A. Fixed rate of 5.8%.
     B. EURIBOR plus 140bp.
     C. EURIBOR less 140bp.

17.2.   Determine whether the MIA analysts' comments regarding the duration of the Worth Inc. swap and the effects of the swap on the company's balance sheet are correct or incorrect.
     A. Only the comment regarding the swap duration is correct.
     B. Only the comment regarding the swap balance sheet effects is correct.
     C. Both comments are correct.

17.3.   Which of the following is *closest* to the payoff on Enertech's collar 24 months from now? Enertech will:
     A. make a payment of $0.0020 per dollar of notional principal.
     B. make a payment of $0.0035 per dollar of notional principal.
     C. will receive a payment of $0.0035 per dollar of notional principal.

17.4.   Which of the following is *closest* to the effective interest rate that Enertech will pay 18 months from now assuming the notional principal of the collar is equal to the outstanding principal on the firm's floating rate notes?
     A. 2.8%.
     B. 3.5%.
     C. 3.8%.

17.5.   Which of the following statements correctly assesses SBK's swaption strategy to mitigate the risk of an interest rate increase? If interest rates increase, the strategy will:
     A. increase the market risk of SBK's debt.
     B. increase the cash flow risk of SBK's debt.
     C. effectively hedge the interest rate increase.

17.6.   Which of the following strategies would *best* hedge the risk of MIA's investment in the Rio Corp. floating rate notes?
     A. Sell an interest rate call with a strike rate of 8.0%.
     B. Sell an interest rate put with a strike rate of 7.0%.
     C. Purchase an interest rate put with a strike rate of 7.0%.

Questions 18.1–18.6 relate to Arthur Campbell and Campbell Asset Management.

Arthur Campbell, CFA, is the founder of Campbell Capital Management (CCM), a money management firm focused solely on high net worth individuals. Campbell started CCM two years ago after a 25-year career with a large bank trust department. CCM provides portfolios tailored to match the unique situation of each individual client. All of CCM's clientele have balanced portfolios. CCM does not use derivatives or exotic instruments to manage any of its portfolios. CCM's equity style is defined as growth at a reasonable price (GARP). Most of CCM's portfolios are managed under one of the following three approaches:

- Aggressive (10 accounts): 70% stocks and 30% bonds.
- Moderate (4 accounts): 50% stocks and 50% bonds.
- Conservative (25 accounts): 30% stocks and 70% bonds.

CCM has recently added the following two clients:

1. Harold Moss, a long-time acquaintance of Campbell. Campbell and Moss agreed to an investment policy statement in which Moss's portfolio will be managed under CCM's Aggressive approach but will have significantly greater exposure to technology stocks than a typical CCM aggressive portfolio.

2. Richard Bateman is a successful businessman with a $5 million portfolio. Bateman wants his portfolio managed using a conservative approach, and he specifically states that no options or futures are to be used.

A current client, Stan North, has decided to retire. North would like to reduce his risk exposure from aggressive to conservative. CCM moves North's account, including its historical performance, to the conservative composite.

At the end of 2008, CCM reports the moderate portfolio composite performance but does not include the associated number of accounts.

CCM reported the 2008 returns on its conservative composite as shown in Exhibit 1:

Exhibit 1: CCM Conservative Composite Returns: Year Ending December 31, 2007

	Market Value 12/31/2007	Asset Mix	Returns
Stocks	$95,875,000	30%	8.5%
Bonds	$182,000,000	70%	5.2%
Cash	$47,125,000	0%	3.4%
Total	$325,000,000		

The data shown in Exhibit 2 relates to Moss portfolio transactions from the 2nd quarter of 2008.

Exhibit 2: CCM Equity Returns for the Second Quarter of 2008

	Moss Portfolio
Market value 3/31/2008	$2,500,000
Cash inflows (outflows)	
4/30/2008	$300,000
5/31/2008	0
Market value 6/30/2008	$3,100,000

18.1. Campbell wants CCM's composites to be compliant with the Global Investment Performance Standards (GIPS)®. Should the Moss and the Bateman accounts be added to CCM's aggressive and conservative composites, respectively, to remain compliant with GIPS?
   A. Moss's and Bateman's accounts should be added to the "aggressive" and "conservative" composites, respectively.
   B. Moss's and Bateman's accounts should NOT be added to the "aggressive" and "conservative" composites, respectively.
   C. Moss's account should not be added to the aggressive composite, but it would be acceptable to add Bateman's account to the conservative composite.

18.2. CCM established three types of composites: aggressive, moderate, and conservative. State whether CCM's composites are *correctly* defined according to GIPS.
   A. No, CCM must define an equity and fixed-income benchmark.
   B. No, CCM must quantify risk parameters.
   C. Yes, if CCM establishes a tight allowable range.

18.3. Was CCM's movement of North's account from the aggressive composite to the conservative composite consistent with GIPS standards?
   A. Yes.
   B. No, the historical performance must remain with the aggressive composite.
   C. No, the historical performance must be excluded from both the aggressive and conservative composites.

18.4. Which of the following statements concerning CCM's performance presentation is *most* accurate? According to GIPS standards:

  A. external verification of CCM's performance measurement policies is not required.

  B. CCM must report the number of accounts in the moderate portfolio composite for 2008.

  C. the cash balance in the CCM conservative composite must be excluded from any return calculations.

18.5. Based on Exhibit 1 and using the strategic asset allocation method, the annual return of the bond category for the conservative composite is closest to:

  A. 4.5%.

  B. 4.7%.

  C. 4.8%.

18.6. Based on Exhibit 2 and using the modified Dietz method, calculate the equity performance of the Moss portfolio for the second quarter of 2008.

  A. 10.5%.

  B. 10.7%.

  C. 11.1%.

Questions 19.1–19.6 relate to portfolio manager James Hatfield and clients.

James Hatfield, CFA, manages money for several clients. The clients reside in various countries. Some of them reside in countries that do not currently have tax-advantaged accounts. Hatfield watches for changes in the tax laws of the countries to see when accounts such as tax-exempt accounts and tax-deferred accounts become available. Hatfield wants to react quickly in such cases so that his clients respond as soon as they can to changes in the availability of these accounts.

Hatfield is also doing general counseling with his clients about how they should manage their accounts for tax purposes. One of his newest clients, Chrissie Hynde, lives in a country with a flat and heavy tax regime. She already has a small portfolio of investment assets and asks for Hatfield's advice about the current allocations. Currently, her portfolio is in a taxable account and is equally allocated among interest-paying assets, dividend-paying assets and non-dividend-paying growth stocks. Hynde is young and her income is relatively low, but she is in a job that has a high degree of job security and where she expects her income to increase dramatically in about ten years and then for the rest of her career. She expects her retirement income to be equal to the wage income she will be earning when she retires. She asks Hatfield about tax-advantaged accounts. If they become available, she wants to know which tax-advantaged account, if any, would benefit her the most.

Hynde also asks Hatfield about tax drag. She has a long investment horizon, but she is considering extending it and delaying retirement. However, she plans to reduce risk over time and shift from higher return assets to lower return assets. She asks Hatfield if this strategy would increase or decrease her tax drag.

Hatfield has another client, Rick Mars, who lives in a country with a heavy capital gains tax regime. The tax regime is not expected to change. Mars asks Hatfield about harvesting losses. Mars has a position in Chromoly stock, which he accumulated over several years at successfully higher prices. Mars now plans to liquidate some of his position in Chromoly. He asks Hatfield his advice concerning the best way he should go about this.

Mars wants to make sure his portfolio of investment assets is a mean-variance optimal portfolio. In a preliminary analysis, Hatfield concludes Mars's current portfolio is optimal. As of now, however, Mars's country does not have any tax-advantaged accounts. The news has just come out that tax-exempt accounts may soon become available. Categorizing Mars's investments into the three basic categories of interest-paying investments, dividend-paying investments, and non-dividend paying growth investments, Mars asks how the availability of tax-advantaged accounts would influence the determination of the optimal weights.

19.1. What adjustment would Hatfield *most likely* make to Hynde's portfolio?
    A. Increase the allocation to interest-paying assets.
    B. Increase the allocation to dividend-paying assets.
    C. Increase the allocation to non-dividend-paying growth stocks.

19.2. Given Hynde's expectations concerning her future income and post-retirement income, would the tax-exempt account or the tax-deferred account be more beneficial?
    A. The tax-exempt account.
    B. The tax-deferred account.
    C. Neither has an advantage over the other.

19.3. Based on what we know about Hynde's plan to increase her investment horizon and choose assets with lower returns, the net effect would be:
    A. decreased tax drag.
    B. increased tax drag.
    C. an uncertain effect on tax drag.

19.4. With respect to dividend and interest income, it is likely that Mars faces favorable tax treatment for:
    A. both dividend and interest income.
    B. interest income but not dividend income.
    C. dividend income but not interest income.

19.5. Based on how Mars accumulated the position in Chromoly, Hatfield should advise Mars to:
    A. first sell the shares that were acquired first.
    B. sell the most recently acquired shares first.
    C. sell shares from each purchase and in proportions equal to the positions.

19.6. If tax-advantaged accounts become available to Mars, the optimization process would become:
    A. less complicated because the new tax regime would create a level playing field.
    B. ineffective because there is no way to create an optimal portfolio given the multiple tax effects.
    C. more complicated because the number of weights to compute would increase from three to six.

END OF AFTERNOON SESSION

PRACTICE EXAM 1
MORNING SESSION ANSWERS

The following answers are not the detailed guideline answers found in the CFA study guide, but rather the guideline answers a grader would refer to in grading a candidate's exam.

QUESTION 1

Source: Study Session 3, LOS 11.b

A. **For the exam:**
    1/n diversification: Defined contribution plan participants tend to divide their assets equally among all available alternatives.

    Discussion:
    Joe chose to divide his retirement assets equally among the offered asset classes. This reflects the behavioral trait known as 1/n diversification. Knowing generally that they should diversify their portfolios but unsure of exactly how to go about doing that, plan participants invest equal amounts in each fund in the list of funds provided by the plan sponsor. They tend to assume that all the funds provided by the employer/sponsor are appropriate for their individual portfolios. Recognizing the potential for 1/n diversification, the sponsor should provide a list of funds that if held together would provide a well-diversified portfolio.

    For the exam:
    Status quo bias: Participants tend to maintain their portfolio allocations or leave their portfolios untouched.

    Discussion:
    Status quo bias can have two effects: (1) investors will tend to stick with an original decision and maintain their original allocations without a specific reason for doing so, or (2) they will make an original allocation and then do nothing. In this case, we are not told specifically why Finnegan divided his assets equally among the five alternatives (i.e., used 1/n diversification) but he has even gone so far as to readjust the portfolio back to the original allocation without a specific goal-related reason for doing so.

> Sample scoring key: (maximum 4 points)
> 1 point for each identified weakness.
> 1 point for each supporting discussion.

Source: Study Session 4, LOS 14.f

Answer for Question 1-B

Personality Type (circle one)	Comments
Cautious Investor	**For the exam:** Averse to potential losses. Does not like to make investment decisions. **Discussion:** Cautious investors are the most risk averse of the investor types: cautious, methodical, individualistic, and spontaneous. Cautious investors are very careful, focusing on investments with low potential for loss. They tend to be overly careful in analyzing investments (or suggested investments) and making investment decisions.

Sample scoring key: (maximum 3 points)
1 point for identifying the personality type.
1 point each for the two supporting reasons.

QUESTION 2

Source: Study Session 4, LOS 14.j,l

Answer for Question 2-A

	One item that would affect Sara's risk tolerance
Ability to tolerate risk	**For the exam:** 1. Portfolio must fund all living expenses: high liquidity needs translate into reduced ability to tolerate risk. 2. Portfolio must meet expenses for father: portfolio losses would put level of father's care in jeopardy. **Discussion:** The need to fund the substantial nursing home expenses of Joe's father will require the portfolio to maintain sufficient liquidity and the need to pay all living expenses generally means the risk level of the portfolio should be moderate at best.
Willingness to tolerate risk	**For the exam:** 1. Makes own investment decisions: not afraid to do own research and make own decisions 2. Holds individual stocks: small number of individual stocks increases risk. **Discussion:** Sara makes all the investment decisions for the portfolio, so the 35% invested in the five stocks indicates her willingness to accept the risk associated with her decisions.

Sample scoring key: (maximum 6 points)
1 point for each reason.
2 points for each discussion.

Source: Study Session 4, LOS 14.k,l

Answer for Question 2-B

Constraints	Comments
i. Liquidity Requirements	**For the exam:** • $130,000 annually for father's care. • $115,000 annually for living expenses. **Discussion:** Remember to include only spending requirements that must be met by the portfolio. In this case, all expenses are met by the portfolio.
ii. Taxes	**For the exam:** • Finnegans are taxable so all investments should be made with tax effects in mind. • Any charitable contribution should be made tax efficiently. **Discussion:** This is a fairly "canned" constraint for an individual. Always look for anything unusual, such as trusts, foundations, or charitable gifts.
iii. Time Horizon	**For the exam:** Long term with 2 stages: (1) until father's care ends; (2) remaining years until death. **Discussion:** When the individual isn't retired, the typical time horizon is long term with two stages: pre-retirement and retirement. In this situation, we see a time horizon being determined by expenditures for a dependent, which is fairly common on the Level III exam. One of the more common liquidity needs for a dependent is college expenses for children. If the portfolio is large relative to the expenditure, however, the cessation of the expense in and of itself might not be sufficient to delineate a separate time horizon (i.e., reallocated portfolio).
iv. Unique Circumstances	**For the exam:** • Socially conscious investing. • Future charitable contributions. **Discussion:** Look for anything out of the ordinary, such as the desire to avoid certain stocks through socially responsible investing. A large holding of an illiquid or liquid low basis stock is another common unique circumstance.

Sample scoring key: (maximum 12 points)
3 points each.

Source: Study Session 4, LOS 16.f

C.   **For the exam:**
    i.   Valued at market value. (1 point)
    ii. Tax deduction. (1 point)

Discussion:
Had this been a large holding of Conglomerate stock instead of only 7% of the portfolio, this would be a good way to eliminate the concentrated position and, at the same time, maximize the tax deduction for the charitable gift. Had this been the transfer of the stock to a surviving spouse, the spouse would receive the stock at a stepped up tax basis equal to the current market value.

Sample scoring key: maximum 2 points.

QUESTION 3

Source: Study Session 4, LOS 14.m

Asset Class	Recommendation	Justification
Cash	higher	**For the exam:** Need more than $15,000 cash. **Discussion:** Individuals should always maintain an emergency reserve to avoid liquidating portfolio assets with every unexpected funding need that arises. For a working individual, we suggest something like 5-6 months' living expenses. For these retired individuals, a more modest amount would probably be appropriate, but more than $15,000 (1% of $1.5 million) would be advised.
Municipal Bonds	lower	**For the exam:** Low after-tax return. **Discussion:** Municipal bond returns are usually low because they are priced for high marginal tax rate investors. Since the Finnegans have a very low tax rate (15%), they should minimize the amount held. They would probably be able to increase portfolio return without an increase in risk by investing in high grade corporates or even long term Treasuries.
Domestic Equity Income Fund	higher	**For the exam:** Replace individual stocks. **Discussion:** The higher allocation will increase the potential for desired future capital gains relative to the municipal bonds. The selection of the equity income stocks will provide a better risk/reward trade-off compared to the individual stocks currently held (Sharpe ratio = (0.04 + 0.12 − 0.01) / 0.13 = 1.15. Of the individual stocks currently held, only Conglomerate has a Sharpe ratio greater than 1. The social investing mandate must be met.
Individual Domestic Stocks	lower	**For the exam:** Poor reward to risk. **Discussion:** The Finnegans current individual stock portfolio is not diversified. The risk-adjusted returns are inferior to the domestic equity income fund based on the Sharpe ratios.

Sample scoring key: (maximum 16 points)
1 point for each correct asset class weighting.
3 points for each justification as shown.

QUESTION 4

Source: Study Session 5, LOS 20. b,c,i

Statement	Determine whether you agree or disagree with *each* of the four statements made by Edwards (circle one)	If you disagree, support your opinion with *one* reason related to portfolio management
"The objectives and constraints for defined benefit pension plans and foundations are very similar. Since, unless specifically directed otherwise, the lives of both are infinite, for example, their primary return objectives are to cover the effects of inflation and thereby preserve the purchasing power of the investment portfolio."	Disagree	**For the exam:** Both also have to fund operations and benefits. **Discussion:** You'll notice that everything up to the part about the primary return objective is correct. Be careful to read the entire statement, even if it starts out correctly like this. They both want to earn the rate of inflation to maintain the purchasing power of the investment portfolio, but that is not their *primary* objective. Both require returns in excess of inflation to meet spending needs. Also, pension plans do not need to earn an inflation premium if they have nominally stated liabilities.
"Huron Foundation does not need to be concerned about the correlation between the plan sponsor financial performance and performance of the portfolio. For defined benefit plans, however, this is a significant concern."	Agree	*Note: CFA Institute does not usually require that you provide an explanation when you agree with the statement.* Since there are no contractually defined liability requirements for foundations, they usually have a greater tolerance for risk than pension plans. The main determinants for risk tolerance for foundations are time horizon and spending levels. The higher the correlation between a firm's operations and pension asset returns, the lower the risk tolerance.
"Payouts are typically based on the quality of the funding applications and proposals received each year, so Huron's liquidity needs tend to fluctuate over time. Since they are based on reasonably easily determined pension obligations, however, the liquidity needs of defined benefit pension plans do not fluctuate."	Disagree	**For the exam:** DB plans often have special liquidity needs, such as early retirement options. **Discussion:** The statement about foundation spending is correct. However, defined benefit pension plan annual expenditures can also vary dramatically. Since employee ages are not typically uniformly distributed, unequal numbers retire from year to year. Also, the firm can implement a new early retirement option or alter other plan terms that can change the amount of annual spending.

Sample scoring key: (maximum 9 points)
1 point for each correctly agreeing or disagreeing.
2 points for each discussion.

QUESTION 5

Source: Study Session 8, LOS 27.a,e,h,i

Answer for Question 5-A

Comment	Is the statement correct or incorrect? (circle one)	Explanation, if incorrect
"Although withholding taxes are frequently assessed by foreign governments on dividends and interest, the presence of domestic tax credits means that they are no longer a significant obstacle to international investing."	Incorrect	**For the exam:** Delay in receiving tax refund. **Discussion:** The withholding taxes assessed by foreign governments can be a significant obstacle to international investing. Although the taxes are often paid back to the investor after a period of time, the delay creates an opportunity cost. In some countries, the taxes are not paid back but are mitigated by tax credits provided by the domestic government. However, the credits do not benefit investors who are tax-exempt in the domestic country (e.g., foundations).
"I would recommend that the return on a stock be compared to global sector benchmarks because industry factors have increased in importance for explaining stock returns. In fact, I believe that diversifying across borders is no longer necessary as long as the investor has adequate industry representation."	Incorrect	**For the exam:** Can diversify with industries without achieving global (country) diversification. **Discussion:** It is true that industry factors have increased in importance for explaining stock returns and that as a result, global sector benchmarks are often recommended for performance evaluation. However, an investor should still diversify across borders. Consider, for example, an Italian investor. If he or she were to diversify across industries but invest only in Italian companies, they would still be exposed to the Italian country factor risk. Further, not all industries will be present in Italy and those that are may not be the best investments. The contemporary investor would be wise to diversify across both countries and industries (global investing) instead of just diversifying across countries (international investing).

Comment	Is the statement correct or incorrect? (circle one)	Explanation, if incorrect
"Differing governmental monetary and fiscal policies cause bond market correlations to be low, often lower than that between global equity markets. As a result, adding global bonds to global equity portfolios can improve the performance of a global efficient frontier, especially for lower risk portfolios."	**Correct**	*Note: CFA Institute does not usually require that you provide an explanation when the statement is correct.* The factors that cause bond market correlations to be low are differing governmental fiscal and monetary policies. If a government has unusually high budget deficits or extremely high interest rates, the country's bond market and currency will tend to move independently of other countries. The correlation between domestic and foreign bonds will tend to be low, especially when foreign bond returns are measured in U.S. dollar terms. The correlations between international bond markets can be quite low, often lower than that between international stock markets. Therefore, adding international bonds to a global portfolio offers opportunities for lower risk and higher return, especially for lower risk portfolios.

Sample scoring key: (maximum 9 points)
1 point each for correctly identifying whether the statement is correct or incorrect.
2 points for each explanation.
0 points possible if the correct/incorrect decision is wrong.

Source: Study Session 8, LOS 27.b,c

B.   2 points: to obtain the return in domestic currency (DC = the euro) terms, we use the following formula that considers the stock return (r) in yen as well as the exchange rate change(s):

$$R_{DC} = r + s + (r \times s) = 12\% + 5\% + (12\% \times 5\%) = 17.60\%$$

4 points: to calculate the contribution of currency risk, we must first calculate the risk of the stock in euros. The risk of the Japanese stock in euros must consider the risk of the Japanese stock in yen, the risk of the yen (i.e., changes in relative value), and the correlation between the relative value of the yen and the Japanese stock.

The variance (2 points) and standard deviation (1 point) of the Japanese stock in domestic currency (DC = the euro) is:

$$\sigma_{DC}^2 = \sigma^2 + \sigma_S^2 + 2\rho\sigma\sigma_S = 0.29^2 + 0.14^2 + 2(0.3)(0.29)(0.14) = 0.1281$$

$$\sigma_{DC} = \sqrt{0.1281} = 0.3579 = 35.79\%$$

1 point: the contribution of currency risk is the difference between the asset risk in euros and the asset risk in yen:

contribution of currency risk = 35.79% − 29.00% = 6.79%

Note that due to the low correlation between changes in the value of the yen and asset returns, this is much less than the 14% that might otherwise be expected as being the risk from the yen-euro exchange rate.

Sample scoring key: maximum 6 points.

QUESTION 6

Source: Study Session 13, LOS 36.b

Answer for Question 6-A

Due Diligence
1. **For the exam:** Determine persistence of the market opportunities. **Discussion:** Understand the markets being considered for investment. Determine whether active management can continue to generate a positive alpha in the future.
2. **For the exam:** Evaluate manager investment policies. **Discussion:** Identify managers with best practices and a competitive advantage among the managers under consideration.
3. **For the exam:** Evaluate the organization. **Discussion:** Determine whether the manager has low historical personnel turnover, adequate succession plans, and fair compensation.
4. **For the exam:** Evaluate personnel. **Discussion:** Conduct an interview with all the principals of the firm under consideration. Speak with current and past clients. Determine whether the principals and employees are trustworthy and competent.
5. **For the exam:** Evaluate the terms of the deal. **Discussion:** Determine whether terms are fair and reasonable based on the alternative investment category under consideration.
6. **For the exam:** Evaluate manager's service providers. **Discussion:** Ask about service providers such as lawyers, auditors, prime brokers, and lenders that deal with the manager.
7. **For the exam:** Check documents. **Discussion:** Read and understand all contract documents.

> 8. **For the exam:**
>   Maintain written records.
>
>   **Discussion:**
>   Make a written record of all the issues described above.

Sample scoring key: (maximum 6 points)
1 point each for any six of the due diligence discussions listed.

Source: Study Session 13, LOS 36.d,f

B. **For the exam:**
    Disagree (2 points)

    Hedge funds are highly correlated with endowment equities (2 points)
    -or-
    Managed futures offer better diversification potential (2 points)

    Discussion:
    Hedge funds, as mentioned by Rudd, have provided better historical Sharpe ratios than managed futures. It is also true that most alternative investments offer good diversification benefits when added to a traditional portfolio of stocks and bonds. In this situation, however, the hedge funds have also been highly correlated with the equities held by Tokay. The following calculations show the Sharpe ratios of the equity portfolio with the addition of the two different alternatives. *Note: The question does not specifically mention showing your calculations, so you would not have had to use calculations as support of your decision. If the question had told you to show your calculations, you would have performed them and referred to the resulting Sharpe ratios as support.*

    By comparing Sharpe ratios of the equity segment with managed futures versus hedge funds, we implicitly assume that the expected return and standard deviation of the remaining bond portfolio as well as its correlation with the rest of the portfolio remains unchanged. (From the exhibit we see that the correlation of Tokay bonds with both alternative classes is 0.10.) With this assumption we can simply compare the Sharpe ratios of the equity plus alternative investments segment of the portfolio using managed futures and using hedge funds to determine which will produce the better risk-adjusted expected return.

    The current value of equities held is $45 million. The amount of alternatives that will be added is $7.5 million (10% of total assets). Total equity plus alternative investments segment is therefore $52.5 million. The results show that adding managed futures to the portfolio produces a better expected Sharpe ratio than adding hedge funds:

    $$\sigma_{S,a}^2 = (w_e)^2 \sigma_e^2 + (w_a)^2 \sigma_a^2 + 2w_e w_a \sigma_e \sigma_a \rho_{a,e}$$

    where:
    $\sigma_{S,a}^2$ = variance of portfolio segment containing equities and alternatives
    w_e = weight of equities in the segment
    $\quad$ = $45 million / $52.5 million $\quad$ = 0.857
    w_a = weight of alternatives (either managed futures or hedge funds)
    $\quad$ = $7.5 million / $52.5 million $\quad$ = 0.143

Adding \$7.5 million in managed futures:

$$\sigma^2_{S,M} = w_e^2\sigma_e^2 + w_M^2\sigma_M^2 + 2w_ew_M\sigma_e\sigma_M\rho_{M,e}$$
$$= (0.857)^2(0.149)^2 + (0.143)^2(0.119)^2 + 2(0.857)(0.143)(0.149)(0.119)(-0.12)$$
$$= 0.0163 + 0.0003 - 0.0005 = 0.0161$$
$$\sigma_{S,M} = \sqrt{0.0161} = 0.1269 \;\text{(equities plus managed futures)}$$

$$\hat{R}_{S,M} = w_e\hat{R}_e + w_M\hat{R}_M = 0.857(0.098) + 0.143(0.125)$$
$$= 0.0840 + 0.0179 = 0.1019$$

$$\text{Sharpe}_{S,M} = \frac{0.1019 - 0.03}{0.1269} = 0.5666$$

Adding \$7.5 million in hedge funds:

$$\sigma^2_{S,H} = w_e^2\sigma_e^2 + w_H^2\sigma_H^2 + 2w_ew_H\sigma_e\sigma_H\rho_{H,e}$$
$$= (0.857)^2(0.149)^2 + (0.143)^2(0.101)^2 + 2(0.857)(0.143)(0.149)(0.101)(0.85)$$
$$= 0.0163 + 0.0002 + 0.0031 = 0.0196$$
$$\sigma_{S,H} = \sqrt{0.0196} = 0.1400 \;\text{(equities plus hedge funds)}$$

$$\hat{R}_{S,H} = w_e\hat{R}_e + w_H\hat{R}_H = 0.857(0.098) + 0.143(0.146)$$
$$= 0.0840 + 0.0209 = 0.1049$$

$$\text{Sharpe}_{S,H} = \frac{0.1049 - 0.03}{0.1400} = 0.5350$$

Sample scoring key: maximum 4 points.

Source: Study Session 13, LOS 36.f

C.   3 points for each:

1. **For the exam:**
    Low positive correlation with bond returns (1 point) and low negative correlation with stock returns (2 points).

    Discussion:
    Managed futures may perform best when Tokay's stock and bond investments are performing relatively poorly. Academic research suggests that historically when stocks have negative returns, the returns of managed futures are positive. In addition, managed futures have a positive correlation with bonds, thus adding managed futures to a portfolio of stocks and bonds will result in higher returns in both up and down markets.

2. **For the exam:**
    Very liquid (2 points) and provide leverage (1 point).

    Discussion:
    Managed futures provide Tokay Endowment the opportunity to swiftly respond to major price movements either upward or downward in the financial and commodity markets. The transaction does not require liquidation of other investment holdings or adding to overall portfolio risk, but the investment is highly leveraged.

Sample scoring key: maximum 6 points.

Source: Study Session 13, LOS 36.d,f,i

Answer for Question 6-D

1. Benchmarks (3 points)	**For the exam:** Custom or existing benchmarks. May not reflect true risk. **Discussion:** Tokay Endowment can either develop custom benchmarks or use benchmarks provided by Cambridge Associates and Thomson Venture Economics. Tokay must carefully evaluate the historical performance of buyout funds. Benchmark pricing data may not accurately reflect the true volatility of buyout funds. Private equity markets evaluate investments using internal rate of return based cash flow analysis.	
2. Investment characteristics (3 points)	**For the exam:** Ability to withdraw initial investment through recapitalization. High return potential. **Discussion:** Middle-market buyouts represent companies in their mature stage. The companies have a long track record and substantial revenues. Normally, the company has only a few funds or perhaps only one fund providing investment capital. (Compare this with venture capital companies where several funds may take a position in the company.) The buyout fund is heavily involved in the management of the company and normally uses debt financing for the buyout. Recapitalization is when the buyout fund issues debt through the acquired company. The debt replaces the equity of the acquired company, allowing investors to recoup their original investment. The failure rate of companies that are targeted by buyout funds is low. (Comparably, venture capital funds have a high failure rate with the companies they invest in.)	
3. Impact on the overall portfolio's risk/return profile (3 points)	**For the exam:** Small potential for return enhancement but good diversification potential. **Discussion:** Capital is normally committed for a long period of time with the potential for future cash calls. The indirect investment approach provides greater liquidity compared to using a direct investment approach. Tokay is relying on the manager's skill in choosing and managing the portfolio of companies in the buyout fund to generate strong investment returns to a greater degree than other investment vehicles. Returns/cash flows to buyout funds come more quickly than those to VC funds, but returns are usually somewhat lower.	

Sample scoring key: maximum 9 points.

QUESTION 7

Source: Study Session 13, LOS 38.a,b

Answer for Question 7-A

Comment	Is the statement correct or incorrect? (Circle One)	If incorrect, explain why.
"To derive the futures contract price using the cost of carry model, an investor would add the periodic financing and storage costs to the spot rate. From this, the convenience yield would be subtracted to obtain the no arbitrage price for a futures contract."	**Incorrect**	**For the exam:** Range of no arbitrage prices if there is a convenience yield. **Discussion:** The convenience yield is the benefit from physically holding the asset. If there is a convenience yield for an asset, one cannot calculate an exact no arbitrage price for a futures contract, but can only specify upper and lower boundaries for the futures price. The convenience yield cannot necessarily be earned by an individual investor. It can be earned by a firm that has a commercial use for the commodity, but it will vary by firm. To calculate the upper boundary futures price, the financing and storage costs would be added to the spot rate. To calculate the lower boundary futures price, the financing and storage costs would be added to the spot rate, net of the benefit from the convenience yield.
"The financing and storage costs for corn are substantial and are greater than the convenience yield. Futures contracts save the investor the costs of holding the spot. Therefore, using short-term contracts of a few months to long-term contracts of two to three years, the futures price curve will be upward sloping."	**Incorrect**	**For the exam:** Futures price falls with fall harvest. **Discussion:** It is true that, if the financing and storage costs for corn are greater than the convenience yield, the futures price curve for corn will be upward sloping. However, even in that case the futures price curve for corn will exhibit variation within the year and not always be upward sloping. At harvest, storage of corn is no longer necessary and the futures price will decline sharply. Using contracts of two to three years, the futures price curve will not be uniformly upward sloping.

Sample scoring key: (maximum 6 points)
1 point each for correctly identifying whether the statement is correct or incorrect.
2 points for each explanation.
0 points possible if the correct/incorrect decision is wrong.

Source: Study Session 13, LOS 38.b

B.   In the 5-3-2 crack spread, five gallons of crude oil will be bought to produce three gallons of gasoline and two gallons of heating oil. These outputs will be sold.

There are 42 gallons of oil in a barrel so the price *per gallon* of the crude oil is:

$70.29 / 42 = $1.6736

Using the 5-3-2 denominations for the input and outputs, the crack spread is:

(−5 × $1.6736) + (3 × $1.7500) + (2 × $1.8200) = −8.368 + 5.250 + 3.640 = $0.522/5 gallons or $0.104/gallon

Note that there is no adjustment for the interest costs from the different maturities of the contracts. Also, the crack spread here will not create a perfect hedge, because crude oil can be used for other outputs such as jet fuel and there are other inputs into the production of gasoline and heating oil.

Sample scoring key: (maximum 2 points)
2 points for calculating the crack spread.

QUESTION 8

Source: Study Session 4, LOS 16.c

A.   For the exam:

Combined Probability[1]	Real Annual Spending[2]	Expected Real Spending[3]	Present Value[4]
0.9907 = (0.8882 + 0.9171) − (0.8882 × 0.9171)	€128,750.00 = 125,000 × (1.03)	€127,552.63 = €128,750.00 × 0.9907	€122,646.75 = €127,552.63 / (1.04)
0.9586 = (0.7644 + 0.8244) − (0.7644 × 0.8244)	€132,612.50 = 125,000 × $(1.03)^2$	€127,122.34 = €132,612.50 × 0.9586	€117,531.75 = €127,122.34 / $(1.04)^2$
0.8961 = (0.6277 + 0.7208) − (0.6277 × 0.7208)	€136,590.88 = 125,000 × $(1.03)^3$	€122,399.09 = €136,590.88 × 0.8961	€108,812.35 = €122,399.09 / $(1.04)^3$
Core Capital[5]			€348,990.85 = €122,646.75 + €117,531.75 + €108,812.35
Excess Capital[6]			€851,009.15 = €600,000 + €300,000 + €300,000 − €348,990.85

For the Exam: If you see an essay question with many calculations, and, as with this question, space is provided outside the answer template for you to perform the calculations, be sure to identify each calculation and circle the answer. This will allow the grader to compare any incorrect answers to their respective calculations and award partial credit, if you set up the calculations correctly but make mathematical errors.

Discussion:

1. Combined probability is the (joint) probability that at least one of the individuals will survive to the indicated age. It is calculated as the sum of the individual probabilities minus the product of the individual probabilities.

2. Real annual spending will have to be provided in the question. In this situation you are given the current level of real spending and its expected rate of growth of 3%. The growth in real spending does not have to equal the annual rate of inflation.

3. Expected real spending is the product of the combined probability and the expected real spending. It indicates the expected amount needed to provide the annual spending needs for both individuals, given their joint probability of survival.

4. The present value of the real spending is calculated using the risk-free rate of interest. Note that we account for risk when we incorporate combined probability and real spending. Had we been given nominal spending amounts, as in other areas of the curriculum, we would have to discount at a nominal rate of interest including a premium for inflation.

5. Core capital is the amount the two individuals should have in their portfolio today to provide for the expected real spending for the next three years. It is simply the sum of the three present values of the expected real annual spending needs.

6. Excess capital is the (theoretical) amount that could be given away immediately. It is the amount currently in the Krauses' portfolio in excess of their core capital requirement. Unfortunately, both core and excess capital are calculated using mortality tables, and mortality tables are based on the *average* individual who has attained a given age.

Core capital is calculated with the assumption that neither will live longer than planned (i.e. a zero probability of living longer than planned). If spending continues as expected, however, the value of the portfolio will be zero at the end of the planning period and one or both of the individuals could be alive. As insurance against this possibility (longevity risk), individuals are encouraged to incorporate a *safety reserve* into their estate planning.

Sample scoring key: (maximum 19 points)
2 points for each correctly calculated combined probability. (6 points max)
1 point for each correctly calculated real spending amount. (3 points max)
1 point for each correctly calculated expected real spending amount. (3 points max)
1 point for each correctly calculated present value. (3 points max)
2 points for correct core capital.
2 points for correct excess capital.

Source: Study Session 4, LOS 16.i

Answer for Question 8-B

Country	Tax Jurisdiction: For the exam	Discussion
United States	**Source Jurisdiction**	Since the Krauses are German citizens, Germany will claim residence jurisdiction to tax their global income. The United States will claim source jurisdiction over income earned (generated) within its borders. This creates a *residence-source* conflict.
Germany	**Residence Jurisdiction**	

Sample scoring key: (maximum 4 points)
2 points for each correctly identified tax jurisdiction.

Source: Study Session 4, LOS 16.k

Answer for Question 8-C

Credit Method[1]	$T_{credit} = Max(T_{residence}, T_{source}) = Max(45\%, 40\%) = 45\%$ **Total tax liability = \$60,000 × 45% = \$27,000**
Exemption Method[2]	**Total tax liability = \$60,000 × 40% = \$24,000** *Foreign source income is exempt from domestic taxes.* *Only the foreign taxes are paid.*
Deduction Method[3]	$T_{deduction} = T_{residence} + T_{source}(1 - T_{residence}) = 45\% + 40\%(1 - 45\%) = 67\%$ **Total tax liability = \$60,000 × 67% = \$40,200**

Discussion:

1. Under the **credit method**, an individual is allowed to take a tax credit for foreign income taxes paid on foreign source income. The credit is applied directly to the domestic tax bill, and the individual ends up paying the higher of the two tax rates on the foreign source income. For example, in this case, the Krauses are expected to receive \$60,000, the U.S. tax rate is 40% and the tax rate in Germany is 45%.

   Assuming USD for simplicity:

   The tax bill in Germany would be \$60,000 × 0.45 = \$27,000
   The tax bill in the United States would be \$60,000 × 0.40 = \$24,000

   Under the credit method, the Krauses would be able to credit the U.S. taxes paid against their domestic tax bill. They would pay \$24,000 to the United States and \$3,000 (= \$27,000 – \$24,000) to the German government. The total tax bill is \$27,000, which coincides with the higher of the two tax rates (45%).

   Now let's reverse the tax rates. We'll assume they are 45% in the United States and 40% in Germany. The Krauses would have to pay \$27,000 (= \$60,000 × 0.45) to the U.S. tax authorities. The German government would ask for \$24,000 (= \$60,000 × 0.40), but they will allow the Krauses a credit of \$27,000 for the foreign (U.S.) taxes paid. Since the U.S. taxes will more than cover any domestic taxes due, the Krauses will have no domestic taxes due on the U.S. income. In either case, therefore, under the credit method, the Krauses would end up paying a total of \$27,000 in total taxes on the U.S. income, and this amount coincides with the higher of the two tax rates.

2. Under the **exemption method**, foreign source income is totally exempt from domestic (residential) taxation. Taxes are paid only to the foreign government at the foreign tax rate.

3. Under the **deduction method**, foreign taxes paid are deductible from total taxable income. The foreign income is taxed by the country of residence, but the domestic government will allow taxes paid to the foreign government to be applied as a tax deduction against foreign income. To determine domestic taxes on the U.S. income, first calculate the amount of taxes paid to the U.S. government:

   \$60,000 × 0.40 = \$24,000 taxes to U.S. government

Deduct the amount of taxes paid to the U.S. government from U.S. income to determine the amount of U.S. income that is subject to German taxes:

$60,000 – $24,000 = $36,000 taxable in Germany

Applying the tax rate in Germany we arrive at the amount of domestic taxes on the U.S. income:

$36,000 × 0.45 = $16,200.

Total taxes on the U.S. income would be $24,000 + $16,200 = $40,200, which is equivalent to a combined tax rate of $40,200/$60,000 = 67%.

Professor's Note: As long as you know the difference between exemption, deduction, and credit, you can figure out any tax bill without memorizing formulas. For example, if you forget the equation for the combined tax rate you can always use this "long" method to calculate taxes due and the combined tax rate under the deduction method.

Sample scoring key: (maximum 9 points)
3 points for each correctly computed total tax liability.

QUESTION 9

Source: Study Session 13, LOS 36.u,v

A.   **For the exam:**

    i.   Buy the bonds; short the stock. (3 points)

    ii.   Bonds increase in value more than stocks. Distressed firms don't pay dividends. Even if they have to pay dividends, interest received on bonds will be greater. (1 point each)

Discussion:
If the company's prospects improve, both the market price of distressed bonds and the market price of the stock will appreciate. Therefore, Baker would profit on the bonds, but have some offsetting loss on the short stock position. As the company's situation improves, the debt should appreciate more than the stock due to debt's senior credit position. Since the arbitrage is long bonds and short the stock, it will earn the difference between the accrued interest on the bonds and any dividends paid on the stock. In a distressed situation, however, dividends will have probably been suspended. Typically, to conserve cash, any company in a distressed situation will not quickly resume paying dividends, allowing the distressed debt investor to earn the accrued interest without having to pay dividends on the short stock position.

Sample scoring key: maximum 6 points.

Source: Study Session 13, LOS 36.u,v

B.   2 points each:

    i.   Event risk

       For the exam:
       Associated with the individual firm. Important.

       Discussion:
       Event risk can be significant, but because the event is usually related to the specific company situation, this risk is not highly correlated with overall stock or bond market returns.

    ii.   Market liquidity risk

       For the exam:
       Distressed debt usually illiquid. Important.

       Discussion:
       Lack of liquidity is a significant risk of distressed debt. There are few participants in the distressed debt markets. To motivate a transaction, the seller would be forced to lower her price significantly. In addition, implementing a successful business plan can take years. Investors must be willing to accept the long-term nature of distressed debt investing. Otherwise, full return potential of the investment will not be realized.

iii. Market risk

For the exam:
Systematic risk. Least important.

Discussion:
Least important of the three, since the returns to most distressed debt investing are associated with either the improved situation of the individual firm or from a pre-packaged bankruptcy and subsequent IPO or sale (whole or in pieces) to another firm. Distressed debt returns are not highly correlated with market trends.

Sample scoring key: maximum 6 points.

Source: Study Session 13, LOS 36.v

C.   **For the exam:**
Judge might rule against distressed debt holders.

Discussion:
J factor risk refers to the effect of the judge on the results of any bankruptcy proceeding, especially prepackaged bankruptcies, which can be important in distressed debt strategies. The judge may rule more in favor of debt or equity security holders, and thus have a dramatic impact on their respective returns.

Sample scoring key: maximum 2 points.

QUESTION 10

Source: Study Session 8, LOS 26. i,n

A.   **For the exam:**
CPs 3 and 4

Discussion:
We are told that the investor cannot utilize short selling or other borrowing to finance the investment. In that case, even if you are not specifically told to use the two adjacent corner portfolios, you will find the two corner portfolios whose expected returns *most closely* bracket the required return. The required return is 8.5% and the expected returns from CPs 3 and 4 are the closest to (and surrounding) that required return.

Sample scoring key: (maximum 2 points)
1 point for each correctly identified corner portfolio.

Source: Study Session 8, LOS 26. i,n

B.   **For the exam:**
$8.5 = 9.3w_3 + 8.2(1 - w_3)$
$8.5 = 9.3w_3 + 8.2 - 8.2w_3$
$0.3 = 1.1\ w_3$
$w_3 = 0.27 \rightarrow w_4 = 0.73$

For the exam:
Notice that a mathematical error in this calculation will carry through to part C (i.e., double jeopardy). In a situation like this you should always show as much of the first calculation as possible. In that way, the graders will recognize that the incorrect answers for Part C are caused by the mathematical error in the first calculation, not by your lack of knowledge, and they will award partial or even full credit for Part C. Of course, even though you use incorrect weights, you must show your calculations for Part C to demonstrate that you understand that calculation.

Discussion:
To determine the appropriate weights of corner portfolios 3 and 4 we set the weighted average of their expected returns equal to the required return. Defining the weight of one in terms of the other (here we defined the weight of CP 4 in terms of CP 3), we solve for their weights. Thus, 27% invested in corner portfolio 3 and 73% in corner portfolio 4 is the most appropriate allocation.

By using the corner portfolio theorem, the weights of the two corner portfolios, and their expected standard deviations, we can solve for the resulting *maximum* standard deviation to ensure that the combination does not violate the risk constraint:

$\sigma_p = 0.27(12.1\%) + 0.73(9.0\%) = 3.267\% + 6.570\% = 9.837\%$

You'll notice that the standard deviation of the combination is less than but very close to the maximum standard deviation specified in the vignette. 9.837% is the *maximum* standard deviation, however, as it does not consider diversification. Since the correlation of the two corner portfolios is certainly less than 1.0, the actual standard deviation of the combination will be somewhat less.

For the exam:
When a question on the exam asks you to determine the best two corner portfolios to combine without using leverage but says nothing about supporting your answer or showing calculations, you can be assured that the resulting portfolio will not violate the risk constraint (in this question the maximum standard deviation = 10.0%). If the question asks you to support your selection of corner portfolios with two reasons, calculate the standard deviation as we have done. Then, your two reasons are: (1) expected returns bracket the required return, and (2) standard deviation does not violate the risk constraint.

Sample scoring key: (maximum 3 points)
3 points; 0 if weights are incorrect.

Source: Study Session 8, LOS 26. i,n

C.   **For the exam:**
(0.27) (25.4%) + (0.73) (12.9%) = 16.275%

Discussion:
To calculate the proportion of U.S. equities in the resulting combination of corner portfolios, multiply the weight of U.S. equities in each of the selected corner portfolios by the weight of the respective corner portfolio and then sum. In this case, we use corner portfolios 3 and 4 with foreign equity weights of 25.4% and 12.9%, respectively:

U.S. equities weight = (weight of CP_3) × (weight of foreign equities in CP_3) +
(weight of CP_4) × (weight of foreign equities in CP_4)

= (0.27) (25.4%) + (0.73) (12.9%)

= 6.858 + 9.417 = 16.275%

Sample scoring key: (maximum 3 points)
2 points if set up correctly but weights were calculated incorrectly in part A.

Source: Study Session 8, LOS 26. i,n

D.   **For the exam:**
(1) CP 4; highest Sharpe ratio (1 point each; no points if Sharpe ratio not mentioned)
(2) $w_{Rf} < 0$; $w_{CP4} > 1.0$ (2 points, but only if the answer for part 1 is correct)

Discussion:
When the manager is able to combine the risk free asset with the most appropriate corner portfolio and short selling is permitted, you will always use the corner portfolio with the highest Sharpe ratio. The portfolio with the highest Sharpe is the tangency portfolio on the **capital allocation line** (CAL). Any portfolio that falls on the CAL will provide the highest available return per unit of risk as measured by the Sharpe ratio, which is also the slope of the CAL. Since, in this case, the required return is greater than the return provided by the tangency portfolio (CP 4), we must borrow at the risk free rate (by short-selling the risk free asset) and invest the proceeds in CP 4. This makes the final weight of CP 4 in the portfolio greater than 1.0 and the weight of the risk free asset negative. The final portfolio, the combination of the risk free asset and CP 4, will fall to the *right* of the tangency portfolio on the CAL, meaning it will have a higher expected return and standard deviation than the tangency portfolio. It will have exactly the same Sharpe ratio, however.

The required return is 8.5%, CP 4 provides an expected return of 8.2%, and the risk free return is 3%, so:

$$8.5 = 8.2w_4 + 3.0(1 - w_4)$$
$$8.5 = 8.2w_4 + 3.0 - 3.0w_4$$
$$8.5 - 3.0 = 8.2w_4 - 3.0w_4$$
$$5.5 = 5.2w_4$$
$$w_4 = 1.05769 \rightarrow w_{Rf} = -0.0579$$

(Notice the negative weight of the risk-free asset, indicating a short position)

Checking the math: always a good idea if you have time
$$1.05769(8.2) - 0.05769(3.0) = 8.6731 - 0.1731 = 8.5\%$$

The standard deviation of the combination is a weighted average of the standard deviations of the tangency portfolio and the risk free asset. Since the standard deviation of the risk free asset is zero, the standard deviation of the final portfolio is the weight of the tangency portfolio multiplied by its standard deviation:

$$w_4 = 1.05769$$
$$\sigma_P = 1.05769(9.0) = 9.519\%$$

The portfolio meets the risk constraint: standard deviation $\leq 10.0\%$.

For the exam:

For more on answering corner portfolio questions on the Level III exam, check out the online Level III library volume on corner portfolios.

Sample scoring key: maximum 4 points.

QUESTION 11

Source: Study Session 17, LOS 46.p

Answer for Question 11

$$S_P = \frac{\overline{R}_P - \overline{R}_F}{\sigma_P}; \; T_P = \frac{\overline{R}_P - \overline{R}_F}{\beta_P}$$

$$\text{Jensen's alpha} = R_P - \left[R_F + \beta_P\left(R_M - R_F\right)\right]$$

$$M_P^2 = \overline{R}_F + \left[\frac{\overline{R}_P - \overline{R}_F}{\sigma_P}\right]\sigma_m = \overline{R}_F + \left(\overline{R}_P - \overline{R}_F\right)\frac{\sigma_m}{\sigma_P}$$

Measure	Portfolio	Calculation	Value
Sharpe, S	1	(0.42 – 0.06) / 1.2	0.300
	2	(0.25 – 0.06) / 0.4	0.475
	3	(0.16 – 0.06) / 0.2	0.500
Treynor, T	1	(0.42 – 0.06) / 1.8	0.200
	2	(0.25 – 0.06) / 1.2	0.158
	3	(0.16 – 0.06) / 0.5	0.200
M^2	1	0.06 + (0.42 – 0.06)(0.50 / 1.2)	0.210
	2	0.06 + (0.25 – 0.06)(0.50 / 0.4)	0.298
	3	0.06 + (0.16 – 0.06)(0.50 / 0.2)	0.310
Jensen	1	0.42 – [0.06 + 1.8(0.20 – 0.06)]	0.108
	2	0.25 – [0.06 + 1.2(0.20 – 0.06)]	0.022
	3	0.16 – [0.06 + 0.5(0.20 – 0.06)]	0.030

Sample scoring key: (maximum 12 points)
1 point for each correct calculation for 12 points.

QUESTION 12

Source: Study Session 8, LOS 26.g,h,n

A.   **For the exam:**
Portfolio E
- Sufficient cash for early retirement payments.
- Meets shortfall risk: $[9.04 - (-8.0)] / 8.19 = 2.08$.
- No exposure to lumber stocks.

Discussion:
Early retirement payments are 10% of portfolio assets, so the selected allocation must have at least 10% in cash equivalents. In addition, due to the desire for a more conservative asset allocation, the portfolio should avoid stocks that are highly correlated with the sponsor, such as lumber industry equities.

> Sample scoring key: (maximum 6 points)
> 2 points for selecting Portfolio E.
> 2 points each for two correct justifications for Portfolio E.

Source: Study Session 8, LOS 26.g,h,n

B.   Portfolio *A* is not most appropriate because it:
- has insufficient cash.
- does not meet the shortfall risk: $[8.65 - (-8.0)] / 8.53 = 1.95$

Portfolio *B* is not most appropriate because it has:
- insufficient cash.
- exposure to lumber industry equities.

Portfolio *C* is not most appropriate because it:
- does not meet the shortfall risk: $[9.06 - (-8.0)] / 8.83 = 1.93$
- has exposure to lumber industry equities.

Portfolio *D* is not most appropriate because it:
- has insufficient cash.
- does not meet the shortfall risk: $[8.29 - (-8.0)] / 8.35 = 1.95$

> Sample scoring key: (maximum 4 points)
> 1 point each for identifying one reason why the other four portfolios are not appropriate.

PRACTICE EXAM 1
AFTERNOON SESSION ANSWERS

To get detailed answer explanations with references to specific LOS and SchweserNotes[TM] content, and to get valuable feedback on how your score compares to those of other Level III candidates, use your Username and Password to gain Online Access at schweser.com and choose the left-hand menu item "Practice Exams Vol. 1."

13.1.	B	16.3.	A	19.5.	C
13.2.	B	16.4.	C	19.6.	A
13.3.	A	16.5.	A	20.1.	A
13.4.	B	16.6.	A	20.2.	C
13.5.	A	17.1.	B	20.3.	B
13.6.	C	17.2.	B	20.4.	A
14.1.	C	17.3.	A	20.5.	A
14.2.	A	17.4.	B	20.6.	A
14.3.	A	17.5.	B	21.1.	C
14.4.	B	17.6.	B	21.2.	B
14.5.	C	18.1.	C	21.3.	C
14.6.	B	18.2.	B	21.4.	A
15.1.	B	18.3.	B	21.5.	C
15.2.	C	18.4.	C	21.6.	B
15.3.	B	18.5.	C	22.1.	B
15.4.	B	18.6.	B	22.2.	A
15.5.	B	19.1.	C	22.3.	B
15.6.	A	19.2.	A	22.4.	C
16.1.	A	19.3.	B	22.5.	C
16.2.	C	19.4.	A	22.6.	B

PRACTICE EXAM 1
AFTERNOON SESSION ANSWERS

QUESTION 13

Source: Study Session 1

13.1. **B** At the time Ulster accepted Phillips (and the Jones Family Trust) as a client, she was unaware of the referral arrangement between Fried and the tax consultant. In addition, Ulster informed the client of the referral agreement terms after being fully briefed on the matter. No other information in the case indicates that her acceptance of Phillips as a client violated the Standards. Given the full disclosure, it is understood that Phillips approves of Fried's need to periodically advise the tax consultant of potential tax issues relating to the client's portfolio. After discovering, however, that Fried has been violating Standard VI(C) Referral Fees by not disclosing the arrangement with the tax consultant, she should not have accepted additional clients from Fried. Standard I(A) Knowledge of the Law requires that members and candidates not knowingly participate or assist in any activity that violates applicable law, rules, and regulations, including the Code and Standards. If a member or candidate knows of a violation, they must dissociate from the activity. Members and candidates may find it necessary to report the violation to their supervisor or compliance officer as part of their attempt to dissociate from the violating activity. By accepting West as a client, Ulster has violated Standard I(A). (Study Session 1, LOS 2.a)

13.2. **B** As part of the referral arrangement, Fried is obligated to inform the tax consultant of potential tax issues that arise as a result of managing the portfolios of the referred clients. This is a violation of Standard III(E) Preservation of Confidentiality. Members and candidates are required to keep client information (such as tax status) confidential unless the information involves illegal activities, in which case the member or candidate may have a legal obligation to disclose the information. This is an especially relevant issue in this case since the referral arrangement has not been disclosed and the client has had no opportunity to allow or refuse the communication of her portfolio tax status to the consultant. (Study Session 1, LOS 2.a)

13.3. **A** During the meeting, Ulster describes the services the firm can provide. However, she neglected to mention that her firm has no experience managing private equity investments and even assures West that DIS will have no problem managing this portion of the portfolio. Thus, Ulster has misrepresented the services that her firm can provide to the client in violation of Standard I(C) Misrepresentation. (Study Session 1, LOS 2.a)

13.4. **B** According to Standard III(B) Fair Dealing, members and candidates must deal fairly with all clients. This applies to recommendations made by the member or candidate and investment action taken by the member or candidate on behalf of the client. Different service levels are acceptable as long as they are offered to all clients. In this scenario, it is not the existence of different service levels that violates Standard III(B) but the fact that trade allocation policies between the service levels are unfair. Clients who enroll for the least expensive services are put at a great disadvantage to other clients. Disclosure of the unfair policy does not absolve the member or candidate from their responsibility to treat clients fairly. (Study Session 1, LOS 2.a)

13.5. **A** Ulster has failed to recognize that while the derivative strategy successfully lowered the volatilities of her clients' portfolios and raised the returns, the strategy may not have been suitable for all portfolios. In particular, the Jones Family Trust investment policy statement strictly forbids the use of derivative instruments, and therefore the derivatives strategy is unsuitable for the account. Ulster should not have used the strategy for the Jones Family Trust account or for any other account that would deem the strategy unsuitable and has thus violated Standard III(C) Suitability. (Study Session 1, LOS 2.a)

13.6. **C** Fried has violated Standard VI(B) Priority of Transactions by placing his own sell order ahead of his clients' sell orders. Even though Fried has used a limit order with a 5% premium to the current stock price (and his order never gets executed), he has still acted in his own interest before acting in his clients' interest. Fried should have placed his clients' trades before placing his own. (Study Session 1, LOS 2.a)

QUESTION 14

Source: Study Session 2

14.1. **C** The IPS review policy is inadequate. It is good that IPS are reviewed at any time upon client request, but it is also likely that clients may be unaware of when such a review might be appropriate. It is incumbent upon the manager to initiate a review of the client's IPS. The Asset Manager Code recommends such reviews on an annual basis, or more frequently if changes in client circumstances justify them. The process for making changes in style/strategy is adequate. (Study Session 2, LOS 6.b)

14.2. **A** The IPO program creates a substantial conflict of interest between managers and clients. Managers wanting to boost their participation in an IPO would be motivated to place orders in accounts where such an investment might not be appropriate. The employee participation in and of itself might be acceptable, so long as clients' interests were placed ahead of employees'. In this case, there is no evidence of such a priority of transactions, and further, the fact that CA has no exact numbers on the program indicates that the firm is not tracking employee trading activity, which is poor policy. (Study Session 2, LOS 6.b)

14.3. **A** It is perfectly reasonable for CA to offer certain services or products only to clients meeting specified criteria, such as assets under management. (Study Session 2, LOS 6.b)

14.4. **B** Riley was incorrect. The pricing methodology should be disclosed to clients, whether one or multiple sources are used. Simpson was correct. Multiple sources are acceptable, so long as full disclosure is made. (Study Session 2, LOS 6.b)

14.5. **C** This type of trading is clearly market manipulation. Even though the 100 shares may be insignificant, the trade sets the price for the entire position. Such trades, especially entered as buy orders, are an unethical attempt to manipulate prices higher and justify a higher return for the period. However, even a sell transaction made under similar circumstances would be market manipulation. (Study Session 2, LOS 6.b)

14.6. **B** BTN obviously assists in the investment decision-making process at CA. Using soft dollars to purchase BTN is acceptable. BTR might assist in the investment decision-making process, but managers have not performed any due diligence to verify the quality of the service. With no proven track record or other apparent means of verifying BTR's value, buying the service violates the managers' duty to have a reasonable basis for making investment decisions. Also, the very small capitalization firms may not be suitable for all clients. Unless CA has specific policies and monitoring in place to ensure only soft dollars from appropriate accounts are used to purchase research from BTR, they could also be in violation of Standard III: C, Suitability, as well as AMC Standard B:5.a. (Study Session 2, LOS 6.b)

QUESTION 15

Source: Study Session 7

15.1. **B** Constant returns to scale assumes that the percentage change in total factor productivity is zero, so that if labor and capital increase by a given percentage, economic output will increase by the same amount. (Study Session 7, LOS 24.a)

15.2. **C** The percentage change in capital and labor can be obtained from the national accounts. The Solow residual is equal to the percentage change in total factor productivity and is estimated as follows:

$$\text{Solow residual} = \%\Delta A = \%\Delta Y - \alpha(\%\Delta K) - (1-\alpha)\%\Delta L$$

(Study Session 7, LOS 24.a)

15.3. **B** To determine the country with the highest expected real GDP growth rate, use the following formula to solve for the expected real GDP growth rate for each country.

$$\%\Delta Y \cong \%\Delta A + \alpha(\%\Delta K) + (1-\alpha)(\%\Delta L)$$

Country 1: $\%\Delta Y \cong 2.0\% + 0.7(4.0\%) + (1-0.7)(9.0\%) = 7.5\%$
Country 2: $\%\Delta Y \cong 4.0\% + 0.4(4.5\%) + (1-0.4)(7.5\%) = 10.3\%$
Country 3: $\%\Delta Y \cong 3.0\% + 0.3(8.5\%) + (1-0.3)(5.5\%) = 9.4\%$

(Study Session 7, LOS 24.b)

15.4. **B** The H-model should be employed to evaluate the intrinsic value of the equity market for Country 4, because the H-model assumes that the current "super-normal" growth rate will decline linearly to a long-term sustainable growth rate:

$$\text{H-Model: } P_0 = \frac{D_0}{r - g_L}\left[(1 + g_L) + \frac{N}{2}(g_S - g_L)\right]$$

The (current) rate of supernormal growth is estimated using the data for year 1. This growth rate will decline linearly over the next 20 years to the long-term, sustainable growth rate, which is estimated using the data for year 21:

$$g_S \cong 5.2\% + 0.4(6.9\%) + (1-0.4)(8.9\%)$$
$$\cong 5.2\% + 2.76\% + 5.34\% = 13.30\%$$
$$g_L \cong 0.5\% + 0.7(1.7\%) + (1-0.7)(2.0\%)$$
$$\cong 0.5\% + 1.19\% + 0.6\% = 2.29\%$$

The estimated intrinsic value of the equity market for Country 4 is:

$$P_0 = \frac{15}{0.12 - 0.0229}\left[(1 + 0.0229) + \frac{20}{2}(0.133 - 0.0229)\right]$$

$$= 154.48[1.0229 + 1.101] = 328.10$$

(Study Session 7, LOS 24.c)

15.5. **B** The Yardeni model calculates the fair earnings ratio (i.e., the ratio of earnings to price) as the yield on long term bonds less a growth factor.

$$\frac{E_1}{P_0} = Y_B - d(LTEG) = 0.075 - 0.15 \times 0.05 = 0.0675$$

The intrinsic forward P/E ratio is the inverse of the ratio of earnings to price computed using the Yardeni model.

$$\frac{E_1}{P_0} = 0.0675 \Rightarrow \frac{P_0}{E_1} = \frac{1}{0.0675} = 14.81$$

The actual forward P/E ratio can be calculated from the actual current P/E ratio by using the long-term earnings growth rate:

$$\frac{P_0}{E_1} = \frac{P_0}{E_0 \times (1 + LTGR)} = 15 \times \frac{1}{1.05} = 14.28$$

The actual forward P/E is less than the intrinsic forward P/E indicating that Country 5's equity market is slightly undervalued. (Study Session 7, LOS 24.g)

15.6. **A** In this case, the top-down approach is most appropriate as the fund is only concerned with the direction of currencies and markets and not the relative returns between securities. (Study Session 7, LOS 24.e)

QUESTION 16

Source: Study Sessions 14 and 15

16.1. **A** To hedge the interest payments on the U.K. bonds, Point University needs to enter into a currency swap in which it pays GBP (at a rate of 5.3% per GBP of notional principal) and receives USD (at a rate of 4.9% per USD of notional principal). Such an arrangement will effectively lock in an exchange rate for the term of the swap. First, we must determine the face value of the U.K. bonds. Since the U.K. bonds are trading at face value, the USD allocation in the portfolio can be converted at the current exchange rate to determine the GBP face value:

U.K. Bond face value = Portfolio value × U.K. Bond allocation × GBP/USD exchange rate

U.K. Bond face value = USD 800,000,000 × 0.05 × 0.45 GBP/USD = GBP 18,000,000

Next calculate the interest due every six months from the bonds:

GBP 18,000,000 × (0.047 / 2) = GBP 423,000

In order to pay GBP 423,000 in the swap (so that a USD amount can be received), the notional principal of the swap based on a U.K. swap rate of 5.3% is calculated as follows:

$$\text{Notional Principal} \left(\frac{\text{Annual Swap Rate}}{\text{Number of Periods per year}} \right) = \text{Swap Payment}$$

Rearranging the equation to isolate the Notional Principal yields the following:

$$\text{Notional Principal} = \text{Swap Payment} \left(\frac{\text{Number of Periods per year}}{\text{Annual Swap Rate}} \right)$$

$$\text{Notional Principal} = \text{GBP}423,000 \left(\frac{2}{0.053} \right) = \text{GBP}15,962,264 \approx 16,000,000$$

We could also convert the notional principal into a USD amount:

$$\text{GBP } 15,962,264 \left(\frac{1}{0.45 \text{ GBP/USD}} \right) = \text{GBP } 15,962,264 \left(2.22 \text{ USD/GBP} \right) = \text{USD}35,436,226$$

(Study Session 15, LOS 43.f)

16.2. **C** In order to adjust the allocation of an existing equity portfolio, two futures contracts are needed. The first contract should have an underlying equal (or highly similar) to the existing equity exposure to be reduced. This contract is sold to reduce a portion of the existing portfolio to a zero beta, effectively canceling the exposure to that equity sector. The second futures contract should have an underlying equal to the desired equity exposure. This contract is purchased to provide the desired equity exposure. The number of contracts to use is calculated using the following formula:

$$\text{number of contracts} = \left(\frac{\beta_{\text{target}} - \beta_{\text{position}}}{\beta_{\text{futures contract}}} \right) \left(\frac{\text{Value of position}}{\text{Futures price} \times \text{multiplier}} \right)$$

For Point University, should sell 416 mid-cap contracts:

$$\text{number of contracts} = \left(\frac{0 - 1.3}{1.1} \right) \left(\frac{80,000,000}{908 \times 250} \right) = -416.5 \approx -416 \text{ contracts}$$

Note that the negative sign indicates that the contracts should be sold.

(Study Session 15, LOS 41.e)

16.3. **A** The number of European index contracts to purchase is 778:

$$\text{number of contracts} = \left(\frac{1.2 - 0}{1.05} \right) \left(\frac{80,000,000}{2,351 \times 50} \right) = 777.78 \approx 778 \text{ contracts}$$

(Study Session 15, LOS 41.e)

16.4. **C** There are three types of exposure to exchange rate risk. Economic exposure is the loss of sales that a domestic exporter might experience if the domestic currency appreciates relative to a foreign currency. Translation exposure refers to the fact that multinational corporations might see a decline in the value of their assets that are denominated in foreign currencies when those foreign currencies depreciate. Transaction exposure is the risk that exchange rate fluctuations will make contracted future cash flows from foreign trade partners decrease in domestic currency value or make planned purchases of foreign goods more expensive. Haikuza has hedged transaction exposure. (Study Session 15, LOS 41.f)

16.5. **A** Basis is the difference between the spot and futures exchange rates at a point in time. The magnitude of the basis depends upon the spot exchange rate and the interest rate differential between the two economies. The basis converges to zero as the futures contract nears maturity and the spot rate and futures rate become equal. When the maturity of the futures used to hedge a position does not equal the maturity of the position itself, the hedge is exposed to basis risk. Haikuza has decided to use a 12 month futures contract even though the next gold purchase will occur in 9 months. The difference in the term of the futures and the term of the actual purchase exposes Haikuza to basis risk. If Haikuza had perfectly matched the term of the futures contract and the term of the gold purchase, there would have been no basis risk. Haikuza could have also used a short-term contract strategy, using futures contracts with maturities of less than 9 months, rolling the position forward as the contracts expire. This strategy would also expose the firm to basis risk and would likely incur higher transaction costs to reestablish the hedge multiple times. (Study Session 14, LOS 40.d)

16.6. **A** The minimum variance hedge ratio is calculated as follows:

$$h = h_T + h_E = 1 + \frac{Cov(R_L, R_C)}{\sigma^2_{R_C}}$$

where :
h   = the minimum variance hedge ratio
$h_T = 1$ = the portion of the ratio compensating for translation risk
$h_E = \dfrac{Cov(R_L, R_C)}{\sigma^2_{R_C}}$ = the portion of the ratio compensating for economic risk

The equation above demonstrates that to compensate for translation risk, 100% of the principal must be hedged (h_T). However, to compensate for economic risk, the relationship between local asset returns and returns on the currency is accounted for using the covariance between these variables and the variance of the currency returns (h_E). For Haikuza, the minimum variance hedge ratio is:

$$h = 1 + \frac{-0.184}{0.92} = 1 - 0.2 = 0.8$$

Thus, for every futures contract sold to hedge translation risk, 0.2 contracts must be purchased to hedge economic risk for a total of 0.8 contracts per dollar to be sold in the hedge. (Study Session 14, LOS 40.b)

QUESTION 17

Source: Study Session 9

17.1. **B** The fund compares emerging market bond issues to U.S. bond issues of similar credit risk, interest rate risk, and liquidity risk. The analyst is starting at the bottom (i.e., at the individual issue level), not at the economy-wide level as in the top-down approach. (Study Session 9, LOS 29.a)

17.2. **B** Statement 1: In the primary bond market in the United States, there are a declining number of callable and putable bonds being sold. The option adjusted spread accounts for options imbedded in bonds and is therefore becoming less useful for analyzing the attractiveness of bond investments. Thus, Watson is incorrect.

Statement 2: Watson is correct. Swap spread analysis allows a fixed rate bond to be transformed into a floating rate bond, and vice versa. It is therefore useful in comparing the relative attractiveness of fixed-rate and floating-rate bond markets. (Study Session 9, LOS 29.b, e)

17.3. **A** She makes her trade based on which issues she believes could be downgraded, in light of her forecasts for a U.S. economic slowdown. She reallocates away from credit risky bonds towards investment grade bonds. This describes a credit-defense trade. (Study Session 9, LOS 29.d)

17.4. **B** Smith is swapping bonds in order to obtain a higher yield. The Quincy Corporation bond has a yield that is 50 basis points higher. This describes a yield/spread pickup trade.

However, notice also that the Quincy Corporation bond has a lower credit rating, which probably accounts for its higher yield. Given its higher credit risk, its yield is more likely to rise in the future than the yield on the Mahan Corporation bond. If the yield on the Quincy bond does rise, its price will fall.

Smith has failed to evaluate the Quincy bond on a total return basis (i.e., he has not examined the return from both the yield and the potential change in price). If the yield on the Quincy bond rises high enough, its price could fall such that its total return is lower.

Note that it is probably true that the liquidity of the Mahan bond is lower because the Quincy bond is newly issued and newly issued bonds typically have higher liquidity. However, he has already sold the Mahan bond, so this is not a consideration. (Study Session 9, LOS 29.d)

17.5. **B** Corporate bullets and MBS can react differently to an increase in interest rate volatility. Increased volatility is due to increased uncertainty in yields, which typically produces increased risk premiums (increased yield spreads over Treasuries). The increase in risk premiums will probably vary directly with the risk of the bonds, but most if not all outstanding corporate bonds could see a net increase in yield with an accompanying drop in price (the increase in the spread is greater than the drop in Treasury rates). MBS, on the other hand, include call options which increase in value with increased interest rate volatility. As long as rates do not fall enough to stimulate refinancing, a small drop in Treasury rates combined with increased volatility will provide positive outcomes for holders of MBS. Swapping out of corporate bullets into MBS is considered a structural trade, because it is based on the assumption that different bond structures react differently to changing circumstances. (Study Session 9, LOS 29.d, e)

17.6. **B** Bond B is likely to have the greatest liquidity. Its characteristics are common to those bonds with the greatest liquidity. It is large (greater than a billion dollars in issue), sold publicly, and is a medium term note (maturity of five to twelve years). Privately placed bonds are less liquid than publicly sold bonds.

Note that bond liquidity is cyclical with the economy and declines as defaults increase. The longer term trend however is for increasing liquidity in the global bond market. (Study Session 9, LOS 29.c)

QUESTION 18

Source: Study Sessions 9 and 10

18.1. **C** Historical variance measures for individual bonds are not good predictors of future risk because the bonds are constantly moving towards maturity. Therefore, the variance in the past was for a bond with higher interest rate sensitivity than the bond will have in the future. The historical standard deviation would include price changes due to interest rates. Duration does directly address volatility due to changes in interest rates, and a portfolio duration measure is much simpler to calculate than the historical variance and covariance numbers needed to measure bond portfolio standard deviation. (Study Session 10, LOS 30.c)

18.2. **B** Portfolio duration is simply a weighted average, taken as follows:

Sector	% of portfolio	Duration	Duration Contribution
U.S. Treasury	14.6%	7.54	1.101
U.S. agencies	23.7%	9.02	2.138
U.S. corporates	31.8%	4.52	1.437
U.S. mortgages (MBS)	11.4%	1.33	0.152
Non-U.S. governments	18.5%	3.22	0.596
	100.0%		5.424

Since 5.42 > 5.25, the portfolio has slightly more interest rate risk than the benchmark. (Study Session 8, LOS 28.d)

18.3. **B** The spread for Treasury securities is zero, so adding Treasuries reduces the weighted average portfolio spread duration. The spread duration of 6.25 is greater than the effective duration of 5.42, indicating more sensitivity to spreads than to interest rate levels. A 50 basis point change in the zero volatility spread (another name for static spread) should lead to a 6.25 / 2 = 3.125% change in portfolio value. (Study Session 9, LOS 28.h)

18.4. **C** Both suggestions are correct. The interest rate risk of the MBS could be hedged by using a combination of 2-year and 10-year Treasury securities or futures. An investor would take long or short positions in the futures such that the average price change of the MBS and the futures position offset each other for a set of assumed level and twist changes in the yield curve. The spread risk should not be hedged. Since Hickock believes the OAS is high, any hedge would take away the potential upside from any narrowing of the spread (remember a narrowing spread means increasing bond values). (Study Session 10, LOS 31.d)

18.5. **C** Because MBS are amortizing securities with a prepayment option, the cash flows will be significantly affected by the shape of the yield curve. The duration of MBS securities will have more sensitivity to changes in interest rates, and will decrease rapidly as rates fall. MBS securities can exhibit negative convexity in a declining interest rate environment. (Study Session 10, LOS 31.b)

18.6. **B** The underlying logic of this hedge is to provide protection against both changes in the level of interest rates and changes in the shape of the yield curve. The single security hedge would not protect against twists in the yield curve. The T-bill/30-year portfolio would hedge the extremes, but, especially considering that interest rate volatility is usually the highest for short and intermediate maturities, it provides little protection against changes in the shape of the curve between those extremes. (Study Session 10, LOS 31.d)

QUESTION 19

Source: Study Session 16

19.1. **C** effective spread (buy order) = 2 × (actual execution price – midpoint of the market at the time an order is entered)

effective spread for the order of 700 shares = 2 × (79.25 – [(79.25 + 79.00) / 2)]) = 0.25

effective spread for the order of 1,300 shares = 2 × (80.00 – [(80.10 + 79.75) / 2)]) = 0.15

Average effective spread (arithmetic) equals the mean effective spread over all transactions for Technology Company. In this case: average effective spread = (0.25 + 0.15) / 2 = 0.20. The weighted-average effective spread is:

$$\frac{700}{2,000}(0.25) + \frac{1,300}{2,000}(0.15) = 0.0875 + 0.0975$$
$$= 0.185$$

For the exam:
You will note that the letter answer to this question does not change if you use the arithmetic or weighted-average method. If asked as part of an essay question on the exam, be sure to use the method requested.

(Study Session 16, LOS 44.b)

19.2. **A** The Technology Company trade was based on information-motivated trading. Simpson's analyst must have obtained some piece of information that motivated her to have Simpson acquire more shares of Technology Company. Simpson quickly executed the order through a market order.

Since the trade was completed in a single day using market orders, it is not likely motivated by value considerations. Value-motivated investors are usually patient and utilize limit orders to ensure getting the desired prices. Also, a liquidity-motivated trade is used to either (1) reinvest temporary cash or (2) generate cash for necessary liquidity concerns, such as meeting client withdrawals. Since the Technology Company trade was a leveraged purchase, it was not performed to generate or to reinvest cash. (Study Session 16, LOS 44.j)

19.3. **B** The factors listed by Simpson that make a market liquid are not all correct. The major factors that contribute to making a market liquid are the presence of many buyers and sellers, diversity of opinion and information, convenience and market integrity. A liquid market will have narrow bid-ask spreads, not wide bid-ask spreads. Simpson's discussion of the factors evaluated when assessing market quality is correct. To evaluate market quality, the following factors must be assessed: market liquidity, market transparency, and the certainty with which investor orders will be completed. (Study Session 16, LOS 44.e)

19.4. **A** Implementation shortfall can be decomposed into explicit costs, realized profit/loss, delay costs, and missed trade opportunity cost (MTOC).

Paper portfolio investment $= (35 \times 100,000) = 3,500,000$

$$\text{Explicit costs} = \frac{\text{commission}}{\text{paper portfolio investment}} = \frac{(2,500 + 2,500)}{3,500,000} = 0.00143 = 0.143\%$$

©2010 Kaplan, Inc.

The additional components of total implementation shortfall can be calculated as follows:

$$\text{Nano's execution price} = \left[\left(36.75 \times \left(\frac{50,000}{100,000}\right)\right) + \left(40.00 \times \left(\frac{50,000}{100,000}\right)\right)\right] = 38.375$$

$$\text{realized loss} = \left(\frac{\text{Nano's execution price} - \text{day one closing price}}{\text{benchmark price}}\right) \times \left(\frac{\text{shares purchased}}{\text{shares ordered}}\right)$$

$$\text{realized loss} = \left(\frac{38.375 - 36.50}{35.00}\right) \times \left(\frac{100,000}{100,000}\right) = 0.05357$$

$$\text{delay costs} = \left(\frac{\text{day one closing} - \text{benchmark price}}{\text{benchmark price}}\right) \times \left(\frac{\text{shares purchased}}{\text{shares ordered}}\right)$$

$$\text{delay costs} = \left(\frac{36.50 - 35.00}{35.00}\right) \times \left(\frac{100,000}{100,000}\right) = 0.04286$$

$$\text{MTOC} = \left(\frac{\text{cancellation price} - \text{benchmark price}}{\text{benchmark price}}\right) \times \left(\frac{\text{shares not purchased}}{\text{shares ordered}}\right)$$

$$\text{MTOC} = \left[\left(\frac{0 - 35.00}{35.00}\right) \times \left(\frac{0}{100,000}\right)\right] = 0$$

Total implementation shortfall = 0.00143 + 0.05357 + 0.04286 + 0 = 0.09786 (sum of components method)

(Study Session 16, LOS 44.f)

19.5. **C** $\quad \text{total implementation shortfall} = \dfrac{\text{paper portfolio gain} - \text{real portfolio gain}}{\text{paper portfolio investment}}$ (direct method)

$$\text{paper portfolio gain} = (40 - 35) \times 100,000 = 500,000$$

$$\text{real portfolio gain} = \text{terminal value} - \text{investment}$$

$$\text{terminal value} = (40 \times 100,000) = 4,000,000$$

$$\text{investment} = \left[(36.75 \times 50,000) + 2,500\right] + \left[(40 \times 50,000) + 2,500\right] = 3,842,500$$

$$\text{real portfolio gain} = 4,000,000 - 3,842,500 = 157,500$$

$$\text{total implementation shortfall} = \frac{500,000 - 157,500}{3,500,000} = 0.09786$$

(Study Session 16, LOS 44.g)

19.6. **A** The Institute report specifies four characteristics of best execution:

1. Best execution cannot be judged independently of the investment decision. Some strategies might have high trading costs, but that alone does not mean the strategy should not be pursued as long as it generates the intended value.

2. Best execution cannot be known with certainty ex ante; it depends on the particular circumstances of the trade. Each party to a trade determines what best execution is.

3. Although best execution can be measured ex post over time, it cannot be measured for a single trade, because a particular trade may have been subject to extreme market conditions. Over time, however, a trader's effectiveness can be ascertained.

4. Relationships and practices are integral to best execution. Best execution is ongoing and requires diligence and dedication to the process.

Business relationships are indeed integral to the concept of best execution. Also, high portfolio turnover, in and of itself, does not necessarily imply the manager is not pursuing a best execution strategy. Best execution, concerned with the implementation of portfolio decisions, implies that trades should generate the intended value, and this says nothing about the frequency of trading. In the vignette, we are not told whether the considerable portfolio turnover (once per year) is excessive or whether it is an intentional strategy designed to achieve the intended increase in wealth. If over many trades the strategy produces the intended wealth gain, we could potentially classify it as best execution. In this case, with no information other than "as long as the portfolio value is greater after trading costs," we would most likely conclude this does not meet CFA Institute guidelines for best execution.

(Study Session 16, LOS 44.n)

QUESTION 20

Source: Study Session 15

20.1. **A** In a long straddle, the investor purchases a call option and a put option with the same strike price. The strategy is suitable in an environment in which volatility is expected to be high, but the direction of the volatility is uncertain. The straddle benefits if the price of the underlying moves by a large amount, either up or down. The strategy does poorly if the stock price remains constant. Fund A's objective is to profit from changes in market volatility using option strategies. Fund A's market expectations are that volatility in the near future will be higher, but the direction is uncertain. Thus, Fund A would be well suited to undertake a long straddle option strategy. A short butterfly strategy and a long bull call strategy would both benefit from higher volatility with uncertain direction. However, both provide limited profit potential for both increases and decreases in the price of the underlying. A long straddle on the other hand has unlimited profit potential for increases in the price of the underlying and profit potential for decreases in the price of the underlying limited only by the price falling to zero. (Study Session 15, LOS 42.b)

20.2. **C** In a long butterfly call strategy, the investor purchases a call with a low strike price (X_1), purchases a call with a high strike price (X_3), and sells two calls with a strike price between the high and low strike prices (X_2). The long butterfly strategy is actually a combination of a bull call spread and a bear call spread. The strategy is designed to have the highest payoff and profit when volatility is low and the price of the underlying at expiration is equal to X_2.

The maximum profit of the strategy is calculated as follows:

$$X_2 - X_1 - c_1 + 2c_2 - c_3$$

where:
X_2 = Strike price of the option with the middle strike price
X_1 = Strike price of the option with the low strike price
c_1 = Premium of option with the low strike price
c_2 = Premium of the option with the middle strike price
c_3 = Premium of the option with the high strike price

Using the data in Figure 2, the maximum profit on the butterfly spread strategy is equal to:

$$1,500 - 1,475 - 35.40 + 2(18.10) - 7.90 = 17.90$$

(Study Session 15, LOS 42.b)

20.3. **B** First, calculate the payoff of the option at expiration:

notional principal × max(0, underlying rate at expiration − exercise rate)(days in underlying rate / 360)

$50,000,000 × \max(0, 0.073 − 0.06)(180 / 360) = 325,000$

Next, calculate the compounded value of the option premium:

option premium[1 + (current LIBOR + spread)(days until option expiration / 360)]

$120,000[1 + (0.065 + 0.015)(110 / 360)] = 122,933$

Next, calculate the effective loan proceeds:

loan proceeds − compounded value of option premium

$50,000,000 − 122,933 = 49,877,067$

Next, calculate the interest on the loan taken in 110 days:

loan proceeds(underlying rate at option expiration + spread)(days in underlying rate / 360)

$50,000,000(0.073 + 0.015)(180 / 360) = 2,200,000$

Finally, calculate the effective annual interest rate on the loan:

$$\left(\frac{\text{Loan proceeds} + \text{Interest on loan} - \text{Option payoff}}{\text{Effective loan proceeds}} \right)^{(365/\text{days in underlying rate})}$$

$$\left(\frac{50,000,000 + 2,200,000 - 325,000}{49,877,067} \right)^{(365/180)} - 1 = 8.29\%$$

If the manager had not utilized the interest rate option, the rate on the loan would have been 8.8% = 7.3% + 1.5%. (Study Session 15, LOS 42.c)

20.4. **A** The manager of Fund is correct regarding the potential arbitrage opportunities associated with the strategy. The box-spread strategy is a combination of a bull call spread (purchase a call with low exercise price X_1 and sell a call with higher exercise price X_2) and a bear put spread (sell a put with exercise price X_1 and purchase a put with exercise price X_2). The strategy is executed solely within the options market and does not require a position in the underlying, an assumption about an option pricing model, or an assumption regarding the volatility of the underlying security. The combination of options results in a payoff equal to $X_2 − X_1$ no matter what the price of the underlying security is at option expiration. Because the strategy has a known payoff, the return should be equal to the risk-free rate. Thus, the price of entering a box-spread today should equal $(X_2 − X_1) / (1 + R_f)^T$ where R_f is the risk-free rate. If the price of entering a box-spread is less than this amount, an arbitrage opportunity exists. (Study Session 15, LOS 42.b)

20.5. **A** The manager of Fund C is correct regarding the method of determining the delta hedge position (Comment 1), but is not correct regarding adjustments to the delta hedge position (Comment 2). In a delta hedge, a short position in call options is offset with a long position in the underlying security (or vice versa). The delta of the option is used as the hedge ratio and is approximately equal to the change in option price divided by the change in the price of the underlying security. The number of shares of stock to purchase to establish the delta hedged position is calculated as:

#Short Call Options × Option Delta = #Shares to Purchase

Rearranging the equation, we see that the option delta can be thought of as the number of shares to purchase per call option sold short.

Option Delta = #Shares to Purchase / #Short Call Options

Since Fund C already holds positions in the shares of the underlying securities, the manager will need to write the call options. We can rearrange the equation above one more time to determine that the number of call options to short per share of the underlying held is equal to the inverse of the option delta.

#Short Call Options / #Shares to Purchase = 1 / Option Delta

The delta of a call option will change in response to a change in any of the variables affecting the option value (i.e., volatility, time, price of the underlying, etc.). Any time the delta of the option changes, the delta hedge must be adjusted. In addition, the hedge is an approximation and is only effective for small changes in the price of the underlying security. (Study Session 15, LOS 42.e)

20.6. **A** Gamma is a measure of the change in delta resulting from a change in the price of the underlying security. Gamma is largest for options that are at-the-money and/or near expiration. This implies that at-the-money options nearing expiration have unstable deltas which will move rapidly with any change in the price of the underlying security. Delta hedging in such an environment is difficult. (Study Session 15, LOS 42.f)

QUESTION 21

Source: Study Session 14

21.1. **C** The first part of Nicholson's comment is correct. Thomasville's contract with Boston Advisors is asymmetric because managers are paid for profits but not penalized for losses. As a result, Thomasville will pay for Amato's positive performance, even though Boston Advisors only earned a *net* of $5 million ($20 – $15) for Thomasville. The loss incurred by Garvin is not penalized in the contract. Thomasville would have been better off investing in two managers with, say profits of $2.5 million each. The small positive profits would result in lower performance fees and higher net profits for Thomasville.

The second part of Nicholson's comment is incorrect. Thomasville's compensation contract with Boston Advisors more closely resembles a call option (from Boston Advisors' perspective) as it pays off as returns increase but expires worthless if they decrease. That is, managers at Boston are paid if there are profits but do not suffer if there are losses. This increases the manager's incentive to take risk, which is apparently what Garvin did in the last quarter. Entering the fourth quarter, he may have had no profits and realized that he had to earn a return quickly in order to earn the 20% compensation fee. This may have been why he sustained his largest losses in the fourth quarter. (Study Session 14, LOS 39.d)

21.2. **B** To calculate the monthly VAR, we must first calculate a monthly expected return and monthly standard deviation. Note that to obtain a monthly standard deviation from an annual standard deviation, we must divide the annual standard deviation by the square root of 12. We then calculate a monthly percent VAR by subtracting 1.65 times the monthly standard deviation from the monthly expected return. The monthly dollar VAR is calculated last using the fund's asset base:

Monthly expected return = 14.4% / 12 = 1.20%

Monthly standard deviation = $\left(21.5\% \middle/ \sqrt{12} \right) = 6.2065\%$

Monthly percent VAR = 1.20% – (1.65 × 6.2065%) = –9.0407%

Monthly dollar VAR = $80 × 9.0407% = $7.2 million. (Study Session 14, LOS 39.e)

21.3. **C** Fluellen is incorrect regarding the Moffett option. There is no *current* credit risk of this option because it is a European option and cannot be exercised until maturity. It only has potential credit risk (i.e., the risk of non-payment at maturity, at which time the value of the option will likely be different than its current value). However, it would be correct to say that the *value of the potential credit risk* is its current market value, which is the $2.86.

Fluellen is incorrect regarding the McNeill option. There is no credit risk in an option to the seller (Thomasville). Once the option is sold, it is the buyer of the option who faces the risk that the seller will not honor the contract. That is, the only possible inflow to the writer (seller) of the option is the premium received. (Study Session 14, LOS 39.i)

21.4. **A** The VAR measure calculated for the Special Strategies Portfolio is accurate. At a 5% VAR, losses exceeding the threshold of $13.9 million should occur about 5% of the time. With 250 trading days and a 5% VAR, losses exceeding the threshold should occur in 12.5 (5% × 250) days out of a year. This is very close to the 13 observed.

However, the fact that the losses usually exceed $13.9 million by a significant amount suggests that the fund has the potential to suffer very large losses. Because of this, scenario analysis should be performed as a supplement to VAR so management can be aware of the potential for large losses and better protect the firm against such a scenario.

Note also that although the calculated VAR has been accurate, the presence of options and their non-normal return distributions indicates that the variance-covariance VAR should probably not be used as a final risk measurement. The variance-covariance or analytical VAR assumes a normal distribution of returns. Delta normal VAR is a version of the variance-covariance VAR in which the deltas for options are used as part of the VAR methodology in determining potential losses. Note: since the delta normal method is not explained in the Level III curriculum, you will not have to explain it on the exam. (Study Session 14, LOS 39.f)

21.5. **C** The swap with the highest credit risk is swap C. At the beginning of a swap's life, the parties would not enter into the contract if credit risk was too high and any existing credit risk would be priced into the contract. So swaps A and B probably have low credit risk because they have been recently initiated.

Credit risk is highest for interest rate swaps near the middle of their life because as the swap ages, the counterparties' credit worthiness may have changed. As the swap nears its maturity and the number of remaining settlement payments decreases, credit risk decreases.

In a currency swap, the credit risk is highest between the middle of its life and its maturity due to the exchange of principal on the maturity date. Thus, swap C, which is three-quarters into its life, likely has the highest credit risk. (Study Session 14, LOS 39.i)

21.6. **B** Fluellen was incorrect when she said that cross-default provisions prevent debtors from defaulting on one obligation when they default on others. Cross-default-provisions can be to the detriment of the debtor because the provisions state that if a debtor is in default on one contract, they are in default on all of them. So, if a debtor defaults on a contract to a third party, the contract with the first creditor is declared in default. These provisions are common in derivative-based credit contracts so that creditors can limit their losses.

Fluellen is incorrect regarding the calculation of credit risk and credit VAR. Credit risk and credit VAR are difficult to estimate due to the lack of historical default data, the inability to determine the correlations between different credit events, and the inability to forecast recovery rates. (Study Session 14, LOS 39.i)

QUESTION 22

Source: Study Sessions 17 and 18

22.1. **B** Under GIPS, all fee-paying, discretionary portfolios must be included in at least one composite. There is no minimum number of portfolios or minimum asset level for composite formation, so the Contrarian composite can be formed. However, the number of portfolios and dispersion does not have to be reported because there are less than six portfolios in the composite. (Study Session 18, LOS 48.b, l)

22.2. **A** The Cypress University portfolio is still a discretionary portfolio (i.e., the ethical investing restriction does not limit the ability of the manager to implement the investment strategy because Nigel does not hold any stocks in the countries of concern). Therefore, the historical and future record of performance for the Cypress University portfolio should be kept in the Global Equity Growth composite.

If, at some point, the ethical investing concern *does* limit the ability of the manager to implement the investment strategy, it would be deemed nondiscretionary and its *future* record of performance would not be included in the Global Equity Growth composite. Its historical record of performance would not be removed. (Study Session 18, LOS 48.g)

22.3. **B** Statement 1: The GIPS requirements that Gano states here are correct. Additionally, beginning January 1, 2010, portfolios must be valued at calendar month end and on the dates that any large external cash flows are received.

Statement 2: Gano is incorrect. It is true that composites are groups of portfolios that represent a specific investment strategy or objective and that a definition of them must be made available upon request. However, for periods prior to January 1, 2010, the requirement for composite return calculation is *quarterly*. Beginning in January 1, 2010, *monthly* return calculations for composites are required. (Study Session 18, LOS 48.d,f)

22.4. **C** The Global Equity Growth benchmark is fully hedged against currency risk but the manager is not, thus the manager is using active currency management.

The manager of the Emerging Markets Equity composite does not weight the country markets differently from the benchmark so her country and currency weights are the same as the benchmark. In addition, she does not hedge foreign currency exposures, so she is using passive currency management.

In both cases, the manager's active or passive currency position is determined by first examining the benchmark position and then examining the manager's position relative to that of the benchmark. (Study Session 17, LOS 47.d)

22.5. **C** From their description, it is apparent that frontier markets have fundamentally different investment characteristics than emerging markets. Thus, the investment strategy has fundamentally changed. Under GIPS, composites are defined by their investment strategy. Therefore, a new composite should be created to reflect the change in the investment strategy. The benchmark for the new composite should reflect the new investment strategy. (Study Session 18, LOS 48.h)

22.6. **B** To perform a multi-year excess return calculation, one cannot simply add or compound the excess returns over all years. Instead, the excess return in the first period must be compounded at the benchmark return for the second period. The excess return in the second period must be compounded at the portfolio return for the first period. These are then added together. The same is true for multi-year attribution analysis and the calculation of each attribute's contribution over all years. (Study Session 17, LOS 47.e)

©2010 Kaplan, Inc.

Practice Exam 2
Morning Session Answers

QUESTION 1

Source: Study Session 16, LOS 44.1

A.   **For the exam:** (2 points each for any two of the following)
  1. Automated trading according to set rules.
  2. Minimizes trading costs and risk.
  3. Breaks large orders into several smaller orders.
  4. Minimizes market impact.

Discussion:
In algorithmic trading, a computer uses quantitative rules to determine the optimal sizes of trades to minimize costs and risk. Larger trades are often broken into several smaller trades so as to blend into the typical market flow of orders. Algorithmic trading strategies can be classified as logical participation strategies, opportunistic strategies, and specialized strategies.

Sample scoring key: maximum 4 points

Source: Study Session 14, LOS 44.m

Answer for Question 1-B

Stock	Appropriate trading strategy	Justification
1. Star	Implementation shortfall strategy	**For the exam:** High urgency level **Discussion:** Although the Star trade is a small percentage of daily volume and has a narrow spread as a percentage of the last price, the urgency level is high thus the implementation shortfall algorithmic trading strategy is appropriate. $\text{narrow spread} = \dfrac{39.76 - 39.74}{39.75} = 0.0005$ $\text{small \% of daily volume} = \dfrac{700,000}{11,500,000} = 6.1\%$

Stock	Appropriate trading strategy	Justification
2. Moon	Use a broker or crossing system	**For the exam:** Large relative average daily volume and large spreads. **Discussion:** The Moon trade's wide spread and large percentage of daily volume suggests a broker or crossing system should be used. In addition, the trade has a low urgency level. $$\text{wide spread} = \frac{150.37 - 149.62}{150.00} = 0.005$$ $$\text{large \% of daily volume} = \frac{500,000}{2,200,000} = 22.7\%$$ *Note: this is NOT an algorithmic trading strategy.*
3. Sun	Simple participation strategy based on VWAP, TWAP, or another benchmark	**For the exam:** Narrow spread, low urgency, and small relative average daily volume **Discussion:** The Sun trade has a narrow spread as percentage of last price, low urgency level, and trades at a small percentage of daily volume which makes the simple participation *algorithmic* trading strategy best suited for this trade. $$\text{narrow spread} = \frac{80.02 - 79.98}{80.00} = 0.0005$$ $$\text{small \% of daily volume} = \frac{500,000}{6,000,000} = 8.3\%$$

Sample scoring key: (maximum 6 points)
1 point for each algorithmic trading strategy.
1 point for each justification.

Source: Study Session 16, LOS 44.l

Answer for Question 1-C

Circle one	Defend Your Selection
Incorrect (1 point)	**For the exam:** (2 points) • Traders needed to monitor automatic trading process and manage more complicated trades. • Role of trader has changed with greater emphasis on thinking strategically and tactically rather than managing broker relationships. **Discussion:** Rather than eliminating traders, algorithmic trading strategies will make them more productive by increasing the amount that can be traded at a lower cost with less error. The role of a trader has changed under algorithmic trading as greater emphasis is placed on strategic and tactical decision making rather than managing broker relationships. The automated trading process needs to be monitored thus the role of a trader would not be eliminated.

Sample scoring key: (maximum 3 points)
1 point for incorrect.
2 points for one correct statement.

QUESTION 2

Source: Study Session 18, LOS 48.i,l

Answer for Question 2-A

Comment	Is the comment consistent with the requirements of GIPS? (circle one)	If not, recommend the change that will bring the firm into GIPS compliance
"We have not reported the performance for our real estate composite because we only have eight portfolios in it, which is less than the minimum number of portfolios required to form a composite. Once we have the required ten portfolios necessary for composite creation, we will begin reporting performance for the real estate composite."	No	**For the exam:** Firm required to report performance of composite regardless of how many portfolios are in it. **Discussion:** There is no minimum required number of portfolios necessary for composite creation. Richardson may have been thinking of the requirement for reporting the number of portfolios in a composite. To be GIPS compliant firms must report the number of portfolios in a composite and a measure of internal dispersion unless there are five or less portfolios in the composite.
"We have different policies for when portfolios are added to a composite. The time period for inclusion of new portfolios is longer for the private equity composite than it is for the small cap equity composite."	Yes	*Note: It is usually the case that CFAI does not require you to provide an explanation when the statement is correct. The discussion below is to help you better understand the material.* This policy is consistent with the GIPS standards. Depending on the type of asset, it can take several months to find a suitable investment for an investor's funds. Finding an investment in the private equity world can often take longer than in the case of publicly traded equity. It may also be the case that clients deposit their funds over an extended period. GIPS allows different portfolio inclusion policies for each of a firm's composites, as long as the policies are applied consistently within composites.

Sample scoring key: (maximum 6 points)
1 point each for correctly identifying whether the comment is consistent with the GIPS standards.
4 points for recommending the change necessary to bring the firm into compliance with the GIPS standards.
0 points possible if the yes/no decision is wrong.

Source: Study Session 18, LOS 49.p

B.   For the calculation, your objective would be to provide the calculations as shown below. You should show your work on the exam in case you make a mathematical mistake. This provides you with the potential for receiving partial credit if your process for calculating the answer is correct.

Discussion:

To obtain the capital and income return, we must first calculate the capital employed (C_E), which utilizes the capital at the beginning of the period (C_0), the capital contribution, and the capital disbursement. If the capital contribution came at 0.43 into the quarter, then the manager had use of those funds for 0.57 of the quarter. We weight the capital contribution of $800,000 by this portion.

If the capital disbursement came at 0.87 into the quarter, then the manager lost use of these funds for 0.13 of the quarter. We weight the capital disbursement of $620,000 by 0.13 and subtract it as follows.

$$C_E = C_0 + \sum_{i=1}^{n} (CF_i \times w_i)$$

$$C_E = \$15,000,000 + \$800,000(0.57) - \$620,000(0.13) = \$15,375,400$$

To determine the capital return (R_C), we examine the capital gain or loss, capital expenditures, and sale of properties. Capital expenditures (E_C) are those used for improving a property and are subtracted because they will be reflected in the property's ending value and the manager should not receive credit for this additional value.

The proceeds from the sale of properties (S) are added in because the drop in ending property value from a sale should not be counted against a manager.

Using the figures from the example:

$$R_C = \frac{MV_1 - MV_0 - E_C + S}{C_E}$$

$$R_C = \frac{\$17,100,000 - \$16,300,000 - \$510,000 + \$930,000}{\$15,375,400} = 7.9\%$$

To determine the income return (R_i), we use the investment income (INC) minus the non-recoverable expenses (E_{NR}) minus debt interest (INT_D) minus property taxes (T_P). Essentially, we subtract the cost of doing business on a periodic basis from investment income as below.

$$R_i = \frac{INC - E_{NR} - INT_D - T_P}{C_E}$$

$$= \frac{\$546,000 - \$125,000 - \$78,000 - \$148,000}{\$15,375,400} = 1.3\%$$

The total return for the quarter is the sum of the capital return and the income return:

$$R_T = R_C + R_i = 7.9\% + 1.3\% = 9.2\%$$

Sample scoring key: (maximum 6 points)
3 points for calculating the capital return.
3 points for calculating the income return.

QUESTION 3

Source: Study Session 5, LOS 20.i,j

Answer for Question 3-A

Objectives	Comments

1. Return (3 points)	**For the exam:**
	• $(1.045)(1.04)(1.0035) - 1 = 9.06\%$
	  (3 points)
	
	Discussion:
	The point breakdown for the return calculation is as follows:
	      Inflation adjustment (4%) and fee adjustment (0.35%)—1 point
	      Multiplying, not adding terms—1 point
	      Return (9.06%)—1 point
	
	Note that adding rather than multiplying would earn only 1 of 3 possible points. A total return approach should be used with consideration of current income requirements, but not to the exclusion of long-term capital gains. The long-term return requirement is 9.06% with 4.5% of that being paid out with the remaining 4.56% protecting the purchasing power and covering expenses.

2. Risk tolerance (2 points)	**For the exam:** Above average. **Discussion:** The fund needs to meet the 4.5% spending rate, so it can tolerate more risk in the form of a higher weighting to equity securities. Spending rates above 5% would be considered high and usually lead to an erosion of principal which should be avoided.

Constraints	Comments
1. Time horizon (2 points)	**For the exam:** Long term. **Discussion:** Most endowments are established to permanently fund a specific activity thus they have an infinite time horizon as in the case of the Shailor College endowment fund.
2. Liquidity (2 points)	**For the exam:** Annual spending needs of 4.5% plus 0.35% for management fees. **Discussion:** Under "normal" circumstances, endowments have only an ongoing requirement to provide a portion of the sponsor's annual operating budget. Be on the lookout, however, for such things as funding a new building, providing new scholarships or endowed professorship, et cetera. If you should see things like that on the exam, they should be included in the liquidity constraint and under unique circumstances.
3. Legal (1 point)	**For the exam:** Prudent investor rules apply. **Discussion:** There are few federal regulations governing the administration of endowments. Most states have adopted the Uniform Management Institutional Fund Act (UMIFA) as the governing regulation for endowments. If no specific legal considerations are mentioned then the best answer would be "Prudent Investor rules apply."

Objectives	Comments
4. Taxes (1 point)	**For the exam:** Tax exempt. (1 point) **Discussion:** Investment income is tax-exempt. However, watch for income generated by donated businesses. Even though the endowment legally owns the business, the business's income is subject to taxation.
5. Unique (1 point)	**For the exam:** None. **Discussion:** Endowments can have many unique circumstances due to the diverse nature of different causes to be funded. Socially responsible investing is frequently taken into consideration when deciding upon the individual investments.

Sample scoring key: maximum 12 points.

Source: Study Session 5, LOS 20.i.j; Study Session 8, LOS 26.o

Answer for Question 3-B

Recommended Change	Explanation (For the exam)
1. Too much cash	Cash drag; reduced portfolio return
2. Increase corporate bonds	Long term, steady income; less risk than equity.
3. Increase large caps	Long-term capital growth with less risk than small caps.
4. Reduce small caps	Too high especially considering 60% allocation to higher risk assets (small caps, hedge funds, venture capital)
5. Reduce venture capital	Too high considering 60% allocation to higher risk assets (small caps, hedge funds, venture capital)
6. Reduce overall allocation to higher risk assets	60% total allocation to higher risk assets (small caps, hedge funds, venture capital)
7. Add global securities	Increased diversification (less risk) and increased expected return.

Discussion:
You probably noticed that the proposed allocation is somewhat bi-polar. It contains 60% high risk (standard deviation) assets and 30–40% low(er) risk assets (depending on how you classify REITs and large cap stocks). Although the allocation might provide the necessary return and liquidity, there is considerable room for improvement from both a return and a risk perspective.

In general, the risk tolerance of an endowment is based on the proportion of the sponsor's annual operating budget it must provide, but most endowments (obviously) would be classified as having average ability to tolerate risk. We are not told how much of Shailor's annual budget must be met by the endowment, but we can assume the endowment has an average ability to tolerate risk.

An allocation of 60% to high risk assets (small caps, VC, and hedge funds) is probably too high for any endowment, even with the diversification benefits these assets provide. There is almost no fixed income (corporate bonds) other than Treasuries, which provide low risk and high liquidity but very low return. Cash drag (pulling down the portfolio return) is the result of holding too much cash and cash equivalents. Given an average ability to tolerate risk and typical annual liquidity needs, a 20% allocation to Treasuries is simply too high. The endowment should be able to increase return without significantly increasing its exposure to risk. Cash and equivalents should be reduced to 10% or less, especially when corporate bonds are increased.

With their typically low liquidity needs, endowments are able to hold riskier assets that provide high expected returns, high stand-alone risk, but low correlations with the plan's other assets (stocks and bonds). These will increase the plan's overall expected return without a considerable impact on risk, as long as their allocations are moderate. Given Shailor's 60% total allocation to small caps, venture capital, and hedge funds, something has to be reduced. Given the size of the fund, they should be able to hold approximately 5% ($25 million) each in venture capital and hedge funds while diversifying their exposure in those areas. If those asset classes are properly reduced, a 20% or so allocation to small caps would probably be okay.

The allocation would also benefit from exposure to global securities, which would provide increased expected return and diversification benefits (remember, the domestic SML shifts up when global securities are allowed).

> Sample scoring key: (maximum 12 points)
> 1 point for each correct recommended change (maximum 4 points)
> 2 points for each correct explanation (maximum 8 points)

QUESTION 4

Source: Study Session 11, LOS 32.b,d,i

Comment	Circle one	Supporting statement
"Active management is appropriate for large-cap stocks, where managers can take big enough positions to capitalize on pockets of inefficiency."	Incorrect	**For the exam:** More public information available on large caps; hard to generate excess returns. **Discussion:** Large cap stocks tend to be more efficiently priced due to the amount of publicly held information and the amount of analyst and portfolio manager attention paid to them. Excess returns (i.e., alphas) are very difficult to generate with large caps. More likely to generate alphas in small and micro cap markets or other markets where privileged information is somewhat easier to obtain.
"Because the S&P 500 Index is price-weighted, out-performing stocks tend to have more and more influence on its value."	Incorrect	**For the exam:** S&P is market-value weighted. **Discussion:** Stocks of larger firms are weighted more heavily in market value-weighted indexes, such as the S&P 500, thus there is a large firm bias. For the same return on a large and small firm in the index, the larger firm will have a greater affect on the value of the index. In a similar fashion, higher priced stocks have a greater impact on the value of a price weighted index, such as the DJIA.
"The Shailor College endowment should employ a passive index vehicle, such as a Russell 2000 index fund, for our small-cap stock portfolio. The market for small-cap stocks tends to be more efficient than the market for large-cap stocks and would provide more opportunities for us to benefit from active management."	Incorrect	**For the exam:** Easier to generate alpha with small caps. **Discussion:** See the discussion for answer 1. Active management tends to be more productive with small caps, due to the greater likelihood of obtaining privileged information.

Sample scoring key: (maximum 6 points)
1 point for each correct/incorrect decision that is correct.
2 points for each supporting statement as long as the correct/incorrect decision is correct.

QUESTION 5

Source: Study Session 17, LOS 46.f

Comment	Agree or Disagree (circle one)	If you disagree, support your decision with one reason related to the characteristics of valid benchmarks
"For a benchmark to be considered valid, it must be investable. To be investable, I should be able to recreate and hold the benchmark as a portfolio."	Agree	You are not typically asked to support your decision when you agree with the statement. In this case, the statement is basically the definition of investability, so it is a correct statement.
"Although I agree with you that market value-weighted benchmarks are generally considered the most valid, the benchmark you have applied in my performance appraisal is not truly market value-weighted because you have not included the total market capitalization of all the benchmark firms."	Disagree	**For the exam:** Need to adjust for float. **Discussion:** Any global equity index should be adjusted for float, and this is especially true with emerging market indexes.
"Perhaps as an alternative we could use a multi-factor model-based benchmark. Factor model-based benchmarks are considered valid benchmarks and, since they are based on sound statistical methods, their results are irrefutable."	Disagree	**For the exam:** Can be ambiguous. **Discussion:** You can construct several different benchmarks with the same factor exposures, yet they could behave differently.
"If you do not like the idea of multi-factor-based benchmarks, we can always go back to comparing my performance to the average equity manager. At least that way I know exactly who I'm up against."	Disagree	**For the exam:** Not known ahead of time. **Discussion:** Referred to as median manager, or simply manager universes, the average manager is not known ahead of time. Also, this measure is subject to survivorship as managers can stop reporting or go out of business over the period.

Sample scoring key: (maximum 12 points)
3 points for agreeing with first statement.
1 point each for disagreeing with remaining three statements.
2 points for each correct explanation *only if* agree/disagree decision is correct.

QUESTION 6

Source: Study Session 10, LOS 30.e

A. **For the exam:**

$$\# \text{ contracts} = \left(\frac{D_T - D_P}{D_f}\right)\left(\frac{V_P}{P_f\,(\text{multiplier})}\right)$$

-

$$D_f = \frac{D_{CTD}}{\text{conv. factor}}$$

$$\# \text{ contracts} = \left(\frac{5 - 6.8}{6.5 \big/ 1.3}\right)\left(\frac{250,000,000}{100,000}\right) = -900$$

(3 points for the calculation: 1 point for the numerator, 1 point for the denominator, 1 point for correct answer)

- The contracts should be sold. (1 point)

Discussion:
On the exam, always write out the equation. If you make a calculation error you may get partial credit for having the correct equation. The contracts should be sold, as indicated by the minus sign in the answer. Mulder wants to decrease portfolio duration, which is accomplished by selling futures.

Sample scoring key: maximum 4 points.

Source: Study Session 10, LOS 30.d

B. **For the exam:**
- Futures offer greater liquidity. (1 point for any one of the following advantages: greater liquidity, lower transaction costs, or efficiency.)
- Basis risk is the risk that the difference between the cash securities price and the futures price will change unexpectedly. Any difference between the CTD security underlying the derivative and the security being hedged can give rise to basis risk. (2 points)

Discussion:
Compared to cash market instruments, futures are: more liquid, less expensive because transaction costs are less, and easier to short futures than the actual bond because there is greater depth in the futures market.

Since this is a cross-hedge (i.e., using Treasury futures to modify or fully hedge the risk of a corporate bond portfolio), the strategy is subject to basis risk. If the basis should unexpectedly widen or narrow significantly, the hedge will be valued incorrectly. Think in terms of the values used to determine the number of contracts. A significant change in the basis represents a change in the relative values of the portfolio and the futures position, and the resulting duration of the strategy could be more or less than desired.

Sample scoring key: maximum 3 points.

Source: Study Session 10, LOS 30.g

Answer for Question 6-C

	Credit forward at a contract spread of 250bp
i. The maximum potential loss to Mulder.	**For the exam:** • The maximum loss would occur if the spread declined to zero which is an unlikely event. • $\text{payoff} = (\text{spread at maturity} - \text{contract spread}) \times \text{notional principal} \times \text{risk factor}$ $\quad = (0.0 - 0.025) \times \$10,000,000 \times 3 = -\$750,000$ (2 points) **Discussion:** Mulder is worried about the quality of the bonds decreasing and is purchasing a credit spread forward which will pay off if the spread on the bond increases above the contract spread due to the price of the bond decreasing. The credit forward is a zero sum game because if the spread at maturity is less than the contract spread, the forward buyer will have to pay the forward seller.
ii. The payoff if the spread narrows to 200bp at the maturity of the derivative.	**For the exam:** • $\text{payoff} = (\text{spread at maturity} - \text{contract spread}) \times \text{notional principal} \times \text{risk factor}$ $\quad = (0.020 - 0.025) \times \$10,000,000 \times 3 = -\$150,000$ (1 point) • Mulder would have to pay \$150,000 (1 point) **Discussion:** A spread of 200 bp means the price of the bond went up from the original 250 bp spread. The 200 bp spread is below the contract spread and knowing that credit spread forwards are zero sum games this means Mulder will owe the payoff amount to the seller of the credit spread option.

Sample scoring key: maximum 4 points.

QUESTION 7

Source: Study Session 12, LOS 33.a,b

Answer for Question 7-A

Comment	Moral Hazard	Description
"Because he has obtained the approval of several investment initiatives related to traditional wired network technologies, Baltus has managed to shift a significant amount of FRI investments away from wireless communications technology to increase his importance in the firm."	Entrenchment strategy	**For the exam:** Manager invests in marginal product he knows well to make him look good. **Discussion:** Baktus has managed to invest in technology with which he is familiar, even though it is outdated. This allows him to perform well but adds little or no value to the firm. It produces job security for Baltus at the expense of the firm's shareholders.
"Korkov … has convinced FRI's investment committee to invest in several media production ventures. The media companies FRI has invested in generally require long investment periods and have high levels of risk, making them relatively expensive capital projects that divert attention away from FRI's core operations."	Extravagant projects	**For the exam:** Manager invests in pet projects to increase size of firm and increase compensation. **Discussion:** When managers have excess cash they often "waste" it on extravagant projects to increase the size of their firms. In this case, Korkov is probably additionally motivated by his compensation package which includes stock options. Taking on risky projects presents the opportunity for Korkov's options to increase significantly in value.

Sample scoring key: (maximum 6 points)
1 point for each correctly identified moral hazard.
2 points for correct description, only if moral hazard is correctly identified.

Source: Study Session 12, LOS 33.e

B.   **For the exam:**
Incentives:
1. Interest and principal payments reduce amount of free cash.
2. Must plan ahead to meet debt payments and avoid possible bankruptcy.
3. Bondholders exert some control over management actions.
4. Makes the managers' claims residual to bondholders.

Disincentives:
1. Can diminish liquidity.
2. Makes bankruptcy more likely.
3. With increased risk, can increase cost of capital.
4. Produces bargaining inefficiencies.
5. Managers become more risk averse with increased debt.

Discussion:
Incentives:
*   Managers must pay closer attention to free cash flows generated by the firm when leverage is increased in order to meet debt service payments and make profitable investments. If close attention is not paid, the firm will become internally illiquid. This can result in risk failure and subsequent termination of those managers who contributed to the failure.
*   Managers are prevented from consuming perks or investing in unnecessary investment projects since excess free cash flow is removed from the firm.
*   If managers are significant shareholders in the firm, increasing the number of debtholders increases the degree to which managers are residual claimants on the cash flows of the firm. Since the cash flows will be determined by management's actions, they will have greater incentive to act in the best interest of the shareholders (which is their own best interest).
*   If managers do not manage the firm well and the debt goes into default, the firm's creditors effectively take control of the firm. Most managers desire to avoid working under the likely conservative and restrictive policies that would be instituted by controlling creditors.

Limitations:
*   *Cost of Illiquidity*—Increasing the level of debt too much can restrict the cash flows of the firm to the point that management cannot fund ongoing operations or invest in new profitable projects. Even if managers do act in the best interest of shareholders as a result of the increased debt level, unforeseen events that may be beyond management's control may negatively impact the already cash strapped firm. Capital markets may be unwilling to extend the needed funds to the poorly performing firm.
*   *Bankruptcy Costs*—The costs of bankruptcy are high. Whether the firm enters into a Chapter 7 liquidation or a Chapter 11 reorganization, the stakeholders of the firm are likely to lose at least a portion of the value of their investment in the firm. Increasing the level of debt increases the risk of bankruptcy. If debt levels are pushed too high, the motivating effect is outweighed by the probability of default and eventual bankruptcy.

Sample scoring key: (maximum 8 points)
2 points each for any two incentives and for any two disincentives.

QUESTION 8

Source: Study Session 4, LOS 17.b,c

Answer for Question 8-A

Stage	Nature of the position in Tides stock and type of risk faced (circle one)	State and explain Wilson's probable desire for diversification
Entrepreneur	Portfolio concentrated in one privately held stock. **Both types of risk**	**For the exam:** Little desire for diversification; feels in control; strong emotional tie to the stock. **Discussion:** Entrepreneurs have little or no fear of unsystematic risk and hence almost no desire for diversification because they feel they control their own destinies.
Executive	Portfolio concentrated in one publicly held stock. **Both types of risk**	**For the exam:** Little desire for diversification; feels in control; strong emotional tie to the stock. **Discussion:** The higher in the firm, the more the executive acts like an entrepreneur. Since Wilson is in total control, his role is very similar to when he was an entrepreneur.
Investor	Stock is one of many publicly traded stocks in a well-diversified portfolio. **Market risk**	**For the exam:** Desire for diversification; no emotional tie with any stock. **Discussion:** As an investor, Wilson would have little if any emotional tie with the firm. His primary goal now, as an investor only, is diversification. Diversification removes specific (unsystematic) risk.

Sample scoring key: (maximum 12 points)
1 point each for identifying correct risk exposure.
1 point each for correctly identifying nature of the stock position.
1 point each for correctly identifying desire for diversification.
1 point each for correct explanation of desire for diversification.

Source: Study Session 4, LOS 17.d

Answer for Question 8-B

Strategy	Description of strategy
Public exchange fund	**For the exam:** Fully diversify by combining large position with many other investors with large positions in other stocks. Partnership—illiquid; locked up for 7–10 years. **Discussion:** Private exchange funds are professionally managed. The manager collects different large positions from several different investors and combines them into a large, diversified portfolio. Since the risk of the holding is reduced significantly, it provides collateral for borrowing. At the dissolution of the partnership each investor receives his proportional share of the total portfolio.
Completion portfolio	**For the exam:** Diversification is achieved slowly over time by adding other securities or use as collateral to borrow and buy other securities immediately. Liquidity determined by individual's desire to hold the stock and whether a market for the stock. **Discussion:** This strategy is generally most useful to an individual with a large portfolio consisting of many assets including a large position in a low basis security. The individual can combine the other assets with the low basis position or sell them and use the proceeds to combine other assets with the low basis asset to achieve diversification. In addition, the individual will typically utilize loss harvesting and dividend reinvesting to gradually reduce the low basis position over time.
Equity collar	**For the exam:** Sell a call; buy a put. Reduces risk without diversifying. Liquidity determined by individual's desire to hold the stock, whether is a market for the stock, and the degree of hedge. (Could be several naked option positions.) **Discussion:** By selling the call, the individual using the equity collar gives up a lot of upside potential, but by purchasing the put, the individual is hedged against the downside. The "tightness" of the collar depends on the relative strike process of the put and call. A concern with equity collars is the *constructive sale rule*. If tax authorities rule that the collar removes too much risk, effectively locking in a sale price, they rule the investor has sold the shares and must pay income taxes on any gains. *Note: Relate this strategy to that utilized by lending institutions with fixed rate liabilities and floating rate assets. By using interest rate collars they give up some upside potential to protect their assets on the downside.*

Sample scoring key: (maximum 6 points)
1 point for explaining each strategy, the degree of diversification achieved, and the liquidity of each position.

QUESTION 9

Source: Study Session 4, LOS 14.j,l

A.   **For the exam:**
   Generate return sufficient to provide law school tuition, pay his living expenses, pay his brother's care, and maintain purchasing power of portfolio.

   Portfolio value = 87,500 × 2 × $45 = $7,875,000

   Required after-tax real return = [($45,000 + $175,000)(1.03)] / $7,875,000 = 2.88%

   Required after-tax nominal return = 2.88% + 3.00% = 5.88% (arithmetic)

   or

   Required after-tax nominal return = (1.0288)(1.03) = 5.97% (geometric)

Discussion:

When asked to formulate the return requirement, you are effectively being asked to list the spending requirements. This has become a common tactic of CFA Institute in these questions. It is actually a good thing for you to do, even if not asked, because it makes you think about the spending requirements and you are less likely to forget something. Although you were not specifically told that Wilson wants to maintain the purchasing power of his portfolio, I strongly recommend that you always think that way and add (or compound) the appropriate expected rate of inflation. In this case, the return only has to compensate for general inflation, but in some cases there is a specific rate of inflation that will apply to a given expense. For example, medical expenses frequently rise at a rate of inflation that is higher than the general rate. Be sure that you adjust the spending requirements by the appropriate rate of inflation.

The typical methodology to calculate required return is determining the value of the portfolio at the beginning of the year and the expenses that must be met over the year. The ratio of the two is the real return the portfolio must earn. You then either add or compound by the rate of inflation to determine the inflation-adjusted return the portfolio must earn. Note that even though you have already increased the spending requirements by the rate of inflation you must add inflation again to maintain the purchasing power of the portfolio itself.

Sample scoring key: (maximum 10 points)
2 points for correct portfolio value.
4 points for formulation of return requirement; 1 point for each component listed.
1 point for adjusting spending requirements for inflation.
2 points for correct real return.
1 point for adding inflation to the real return.

Source: Study Session 4, LOS 14.k,l

Answer for Question 9-B

Wilson's ability to tolerate risk would be considered: (circle one)	Support with two reasons
Above average	**For the exam:** 1. Significant flexibility. 2. Large portfolio relative to spending needs. **Discussion:** The two reasons given are fairly common. Always look for *flexibility* in the client. Flexibility refers to the client's ability to alter lifestyle and spending needs, which usually leads to an above average ability to tolerate risk. It is typically the result of age and personal circumstances. Wilson is quite young with a substantial portfolio, and that provides a plethora of alternatives. For example, he could choose not to work, he could start another business, he could finish law school and practice law, and so on. If you listed some of these alternatives without specifically writing *flexibility*, that would suffice as an answer.

Sample scoring key: (5 points maximum)
1 point for correctly identifying above average ability to tolerate risk.
2 points each for any two of the reasons mentioned.

QUESTION 10

Source: Study Session 4, LOS 19.a

Answer for Question 10-A

(1) Change in the discount rate on human capital (your choice)	(2) Effect on the value of human capital (circle one)	(3) Effect on the amount of life insurance (circle one)	(4) Support with one reason
Increase	Decrease	Decrease	**For the exam:** Life insurance replaces lost HC; higher discount reduces PV of human capital.

(1) Change in the discount rate on human capital (your choice)	(2) Effect on the value of human capital (circle one)	(3) Effect on the amount of life insurance (circle one)	(4) Support with one reason
Decrease	Increase	Increase	**For the exam:** Life insurance replaces lost HC; lower discount increases PV of human capital.

Discussion:

You will notice that your choice in the first column of the template determines the correct answers in the other three columns.

Human capital, the present value of future labor-related income, is calculated using a discount rate corresponding to the nature of the human capital (HC). As HC becomes more equity-like (variable and/or correlated with financial markets) the appropriate discount rate increases. Someone with equity-like HC, for example, will generally have a smaller HC due to the high discount rate and a corresponding reduced amount of life insurance needed to replace it in the case of premature death. Another way to consider this is that an individual with a highly variable income stream would likely have a high tolerance for risk, and this high tolerance for risk (i.e. uncertainty) would lead to a tolerance for loss of HC. The opposite is also true. The more steady and certain (bond-like) the HC, the higher its PV and the greater the optimal amount of life insurance.

> Sample scoring key: (maximum 4 points)
> 1 point each for selections in columns 2 and 3 that are correct given the selection in column 1.
> 2 points for correct justification in column 4.

Source: Study Session 4, LOS 14.m and LOS 19.c,d

Answer for Question 10-B

Asset Class	Recommended allocation (circle one)	Support with one reason
Cash	0% to 5%	**For the exam:** Low liquidity needs; cash drag. **Discussion:** Always minimize the amount of cash. Wilson has minimal need for cash in his portfolio. The low return on cash pulls the portfolio return down (cash drag).
Bonds	36% to 45%	**For the exam:** HC bond-like; low correlation with stocks. **Discussion:** In Exhibit 3 we see that Wilson's HC has a very low correlation with stocks and is in fact more highly correlated with cash and bonds. Treating the HC as part of the portfolio, we can allocate the portfolio more heavily to stocks.
Stocks	51% to 60%	**For the exam:** HC bond-like; low correlation with stocks. **Discussion:** In Exhibit 3 we see that Wilson's HC is more correlated with cash and bonds. Treating the HC as part of the portfolio, we can allocate the portfolio more heavily to stocks.

Sample scoring key: (maximum 9 points)
1 point for each correct allocation.
2 points for each correct justification.

QUESTION 11

Source: Study Session 5, LOS 20.b

A.   **For the exam:**
5% + 1.75% = 6.75%

Discussion:
The committee wants to build a plan surplus by setting the return objective 175 basis points above the 5% minimum required rate of return set by the plan's actuary. The discount rate used by the actuary is a very common way for the question to provide you with the minimum required return. Based on assumptions employed by the actuary, if the portfolio produces that return, it will be able to meet pension obligations.

The minimum 10% return PHL's President Mauer mentioned is irrelevant. Since the plan should be run for the sole benefit of the beneficiaries, the president's comments should not affect the return objective set by the fund. This is a common distracter used by CFA Institute in this type of question and is aimed at making you think in terms of willingness to tolerate risk, which is typically of no consequence with institutional investors.

Sample scoring key: 2 points for calculating the correct return objective.

Source: Study Session 5, LOS 20.c

Answer for Question 11-B

Risk factor	Indicate whether PHLP has below-average, average, or above average ability to tolerate risk compared with the average for the corporate helicopter leasing industry (circle one)	Justify each response with *one* reason
i. Sponsor financial status and profitability	**Above average**	**For the exam:** Financially sound; lower D/E and higher ROE than industry. **Discussion:** PHL is currently in a good position to make contributions to PHLP if needed. This gives PHLP an above average ability to take risk compared with the industry average.
ii. Workforce age	**Above average**	**For the exam:** Workforce younger than industry; longer time horizon. **Discussion:** Although 12% of the workforce is more than 50 years old, this is less than the 16% industry average. PHLP has an above-average ability to take risk compared to the average for PHL's industry because the younger age of its employees increases the duration of PHLP's liabilities.
iii. Retired employees	**Below average**	**For the exam:** Lower ratio of active to retired. **Discussion:** A lower ratio of active to retired employees usually indicates a shorter time horizon and an aging active employee group. This reduces the relative duration of the PHLP's liabilities and increases the likelihood of PHL having to make special contributions to the fund. These give PHLP a below average ability to take risk compared to the average for PHL's industry.

Sample scoring key: (maximum 9 points)
1 point each for correctly indicating the risk tolerance level.
2 points for each correct justification.

Source: Study Session 5, LOS 20.c

Answer for Question 11-C

Factor	Indicate whether the factor increases, does not affect, or decreases PHLP's ability to tolerate risk (circle one)	Justify *each* response with *one* reason
i. Sponsor (PHL) and pension fund (PHLP) common risk exposures	Decreases	**For the exam:** Reduces PHL's ability to provide funds if drop in pension fund earnings. **Discussion:** Unless McCormick can persuade the Investment Committee to reduce PHLP's 15% exposure to these securities, this factor decreases PHLP's ability to take risk. The desire to increase exposure should not be considered.
ii. Retirement plan features	Decreases	**For the exam:** Early retirement options shorten plan liability duration. **Discussion:** 12% of PHL's workforce qualify for early retirement. We are not given any indication of how many will elect to retire, but since the option is newly implemented, PKLP must be ready to meet increased liquidity needs. Liquidity requirements associated with this potential increase in payouts reduce PHLP's ability to take risk.

Sample scoring key: (maximum 6 points)
1 point each for correctly identifying how the factor will affect risk tolerance.
2 points for each correct justification.

Source: Study Session 5, LOS 20.b

Answer for Question 11-D

	Constraint	Formulate *each* of the constraints in PHLP's investment policy statement and justify *each* response with *one* reason.
i.	Liquidity requirement	**For the exam:** Low liquidity needs: • Long time horizon relative to the industry. **Discussion:** PHL has a relatively young and stable workforce compared to the industry averages. The plan is unlikely to need to make large payouts in the near future given the average duration of 17 years for PHLP's liabilities. PHLP may want to set aside a reserve, however, to deal with the possibility of employees taking advantage of PHLP's early retirement option at some time in the future.
ii.	Time horizon	**For the exam:** Long, single-stage time horizon. • Average employee younger than industry. **Discussion:** With a stable workforce with an average age less than the industry average, PHLP's time horizon is longer than average. When dealing with pension plans, always look at workforce characteristics for indications of the plan's time horizon, liquidity needs, risk tolerance, and unique circumstances. Taxes are not typically a concern since pension plans are tax exempt.

Sample scoring key: (maximum 4 points)
1 point for each correctly formulated constraint.
1 point for each correct justification.

QUESTION 12

Source: Study Session 13 LOS 36.s

Answer for Question 12-A

Hedge Fund Style	Description
Convertible arbitrage	**For the exam:** Capitalize on mispriced convertibles. Buy or sell the bond; hedge equity risk with opposite position in underlying stock. Gain from short rebate and coupons on bond. If firm volatility or value increases, option portion of bond increases in value. **Discussion:** This is effectively a delta hedge strategy. The manager eliminates (reduces) the equity risk with the hedge, receives interest and coupons, and hopes the volatility of the firm increases. As with any relative value strategy, the manager also gains from the prices of the assets moving back into equilibrium. Used also with warrants and convertible preferred stock.
Equity market neutral	**For the exam:** Achieve a zero beta with long and short positions; gain by holding undervalued, shorting overvalued securities. **Discussion:** Managers pair together stocks with equal betas, one long and one short, to eliminate systematic risk. They gain from the ability to identify over- and under-valued securities while facing no systematic risk.
Hedged equity	**For the exam:** Gain from holding short and long positions in over-valued and under-valued securities. Does not have to be market neutral. **Discussion:** Hedged equity managers gain from long and short positions without the specific goal of attaining zero systematic risk. Net portfolio position can be anywhere from net long to short, depending on the manager's forecasts.
Global macro	**For the exam:** Take very large positions in financial and non-financial assets to take advantage of systematic (market) swings rather than changes in individual security prices. **Discussion:** Managed futures are sometimes classified as a global macro strategy. GM managers sometimes use derivatives to increase their exposures.

Sample scoring key: (maximum 12 points)
3 points for each correctly described strategy. Description must include the basic strategy as well as how profits are generated.

Source: Study Session 13 LOS 36.c

Answer for Question 12-B

	Alternative investments special issues
1	**For the exam:** Tax issues; frequently must deal with partnerships and other ownership forms with unique tax structures.
2	**For the exam:** Suitability; holding periods might not be suitable to client.
3	**For the exam:** Decision risk; extreme returns can make client want to change strategy quickly at disadvantageous point.

Discussion:
In addition to the due diligence necessary for any investment, alternative investments present several unique special issues. These include tax issues, suitability, communication with the client, decision risk, and the size of the position needed. Many private wealth clients have large positions in closely held equities. When this is the case, the alternative will probably not have the necessary liquidity. Also, the amount that must be invested in most alternatives is considerable. If it will take up too large a portion of the portfolio, the alternative is again unsuited for the client. Many times investing in alternatives involves buying into a partnership or other private investing relationship. These investment vehicles often have peculiar tax issues that might not be suitable for the client. Communication with the client is required, meaning the manager must thoroughly describe the return and risk of the alternative. Often times, clients are unable to comprehend the true nature of the investment, and this can lead to their wanting to liquidate the position at an inopportune time after a large positive or negative return.

Sample scoring key: (maximum 6 points)
2 points each for any three correctly described alternative investment special issues.

Practice Exam 2
Afternoon Session Answers

To get detailed answer explanations with references to specific LOS and SchweserNotes[TM] content, and to get valuable feedback on how your score compares to those of other Level III candidates, use your Username and Password to gain Online Access at schweser.com and choose the left-hand menu item "Practice Exams Vol. 1."

13.1.	C	16.3.	A	19.5.	C
13.2.	A	16.4.	B	19.6.	B
13.3.	B	16.5.	B	20.1.	B
13.4.	B	16.6.	A	20.2.	B
13.5.	C	17.1.	B	20.3.	B
13.6.	B	17.2.	B	20.4.	C
14.1.	B	17.3.	C	20.5.	B
14.2.	B	17.4.	B	20.6.	A
14.3.	C	17.5.	A	21.1.	A
14.4.	C	17.6.	C	21.2.	B
14.5.	A	18.1.	A	21.3.	B
14.6.	B	18.2.	A	21.4.	C
15.1.	B	18.3.	B	21.5.	B
15.2.	B	18.4.	C	21.6.	A
15.3.	C	18.5.	A	22.1.	B
15.4.	C	18.6.	B	22.2.	B
15.5.	B	19.1.	C	22.3.	C
15.6.	B	19.2.	C	22.4.	C
16.1.	C	19.3.	A	22.5.	C
16.2.	C	19.4.	C	22.6.	C

PRACTICE EXAM 2
AFTERNOON SESSION ANSWERS

QUESTION 13

Source: Study Session 1

13.1. **C** There is no evidence to suggest that the contact was inappropriate. Green is trying to gauge investor sentiment relative to technology stocks. While a fire wall within the firm would be advisable, since no company-specific information was exchanged, the contact was relatively harmless. Also, there is no violation of Standard II(A) Material Nonpublic Information because there was no inside information discussed. (Study Session 1, LOS 2.a)

13.2. **A** Green has taken a small number of oversubscribed IPOs to represent the entire market for technology IPOs. This is clearly a misrepresentation of the true market situation. Thus, Green has violated Standard I(C) Misrepresentations which prohibits such misstatements of fact. Also, IPOs may not be suitable for all accounts, but Green has recommended that all of Federal Securities' portfolio managers add the IPO shares to their portfolios. Green did not violate the confidentiality of the investment banking clients since he was unaware of, and did not disclose, any details of the upcoming IPOs. Also, Green was not in possession of any material nonpublic information. (Study Session 1, LOS 2.a)

13.3. **B** By telling the institutional client that the IPO shares will double the performance that he experienced last year, Green has essentially guaranteed the performance of the IPO shares in violation of Standard I(C) Misrepresentation. Green has also given the client a recommendation in advance of all other institutional and, presumably, many individual clients. This is a violation of Standard III(B) Fair Dealing. (Study Session 1, LOS 2.a)

13.4. **B** While disclosures such as the one detailed in Characteristic 2 are required by CFA Institute Standards of Professional Conduct, this disclosure has nothing to do with restricting information flow between different departments and is not one of the minimum requirements of a firewall as laid out by Standard II(A) Material Nonpublic Information. The minimum elements include control of interdepartmental communication through a clearance area such as the compliance or legal department; use of restricted, watch, and rumor lists to review employee trades; documentation of procedures that restrict information sharing between departments and of enforcement of such procedures; and heightened review of proprietary trading during periods in which the firm has knowledge of material nonpublic information. (Study Session 1, LOS 2.a)

13.5. **C** Standard IV(A) Loyalty governs Ybarra's and Cliff's actions in this case. Neither Ybarra nor Cliff have non-compete agreements and are therefore not precluded from preparing to go into competition with Federal Securities while still employed by the firm. In making such preparations, however, members and candidates must not breach their duty of loyalty to their current employer. Ybarra has breached his duty by contacting Federal Securities' existing clients to solicit their business. Thus, he is in violation of Standard IV(A). Cliff has not violated the Standard. She is allowed to make preparations to compete before leaving Federal Securities and has not done anything to interfere with Federal's operations. She is allowed to market her services to Federal clients as long as she does not do so before leaving the company and does not use Federal's client lists or other resources to do so. Cliff has purchased the client list on her own and is not planning to market to Federal clients until after she resigns from the firm. (Study Session 1, LOS 2.a)

13.6. **B** According to Standard VI(A) Disclosure of Conflicts, members and candidates must make full and fair disclosure of any and all matters that interfere with their independence and objectivity. Green's board membership has the potential to influence his research recommendations. Even though he currently does not sit on the board, he expects to return to board membership in the near future. Clients, prospects, and his employer would all need to be notified of such information to assess the level of objectivity in Green's reports on the company in question. Green's inheritance of the put options on a company he covers also presents a situation in which his objectivity may be compromised. Even though it may be remote, the incentive to be pessimistic about the subject company exists since Green would like to benefit from the increase in the value of the put options. He must disclose this conflict to clients, prospects, and his employer as well. Generally, any conflict that may impair a member's or candidate's independence and objectivity will need to be disclosed to clients, prospects, and the employer. (Study Session 1, LOS 2.a)

QUESTION 14

Source: Study Session 2

14.1. **B** CFA Institute distinguishes gifts/entertainment received from those who can influence managers' behavior, from gifts/entertainment/additional compensation from clients. It is up to firm's discretion what constitutes "minimal value"—this is a judgment call. $100 U.S. is a good guideline, but CFA Institute does not specify a dollar amount. According to CFA Institute's Asset Manager Code of Professional Conduct, Appendix 6A—Loyalty to Clients, managers must refuse to engage in any business relationship, or accept any gift, which would potentially impair loyalty, independence, and objectivity. Additional compensation from clients is allowed, under Standard IV(B) Duties to Employers—Additional Compensation Arrangements, as long as there is written permission obtained from all parties involved. Employers must first provide consent. There is no restriction on the value of additional compensation which may be received from a client, as long as proper permission is received. (Study Session 2, LOS 6.b)

14.2. **B** General statements regarding fees and costs are not enough. Disclosures of all fees and costs must be made. Also, in accordance with the "Disclosures" section of the Asset Manager Code of Professional Conduct, managers must provide returns gross- and net-of-fees. In addition, managers must show an itemization of charges if requested by the client. (Study Session 2, LOS 6.b)

14.3. **C** In the case of "directed brokerage," the client is in charge. In Statement 1, since the client is directing the manager to purchase the goods or services, the practice does not violate any loyalty duty. Thus, Statement 1 is incorrect. In the case of Statement 2, there may be situations in which clients may recommend brokers who do not provide the best service or execution. There is not much the manager can do in these cases, but the manager is obligated to at least inform the client that they may not be receiving the best execution. Statement 2 is correct. (Study Session 2, LOS 6.b)

14.4. **C** Proxies do have economic value to the client, which must be safeguarded. Managers must not just vote proxies blindly with management. Non-routine proxy issues do necessitate more review and analysis. The proxy voting policies and process must be disclosed to the client, however, if a cost-benefit analysis shows that there are cases where voting of all proxies may not benefit the client, then all proxies do not have to be voted. (Study Session 2, LOS 6.b)

14.5. **A** Both provisions are correct. Off-site back-up would be a minimum provision. Also, the periodic testing is needed in order to identify gaps in the plan, and to educate employees. This is in accordance with the CFA Institute Asset Manager Code of Professional Conduct, under Section D—Appendix 6A—Recommendations and Guidance—Compliance and Support. (Study Session 2, LOS 6.b)

14.6. **B** CFA Institute clearly encourages firms to adopt not only the Code and Standards, but additionally the Asset Manager Code of Conduct. The Standards do not require adoption of the Asset Manager Code, but it provides a proper ethical framework for a firm to work within. However, these are insufficient on a stand alone basis; they must be supplemented by detailed processes and procedures specific that the individual firm. (Study Session 2, LOS 6.b)

QUESTION 15

Source: Study Session 7

15.1. **B** For an equity long-short hedge fund, the bottom-up approach is the most appropriate forecasting approach. Individual security investments are determined by identifying over- or under-valued securities. Thus, managers will start at the "bottom" by analyzing individual securities and probably not move upward (broader) in the analysis. The net market exposure of the fund is not determined through an economy-wide analysis, as in top-down analysis. Rather it will vary based on the amount of long and short exposures. (Study Session 7, LOS 24.e)

15.2. **B** An increase in retirement age increases the labor force growth rate and leads to increased GDP growth. A decrease in the savings rate means less capital is available meaning higher interest rates, decreased investment in capital stock, and a decrease in economic growth. An increase in pollution controls increases costs of production and decreases economic growth. The reduction in economic output due to increased pollution controls could be only short term (Study Session 7, LOS 24.b)

15.3. **C** Real GDP growth can be estimated as follows:

$$\%\Delta Y \cong \%\Delta A + \alpha(\%\Delta K) + (1-\alpha)(\%\Delta L)$$

where:
$\%\Delta A$ = percentage change in total factor productivity
$\%\Delta K$ = percentage change in capital
$\%\Delta L$ = percentage change in labor

$$\%\Delta Y \cong 1.25\% + 0.6(-0.50\%) + (1-0.6)(2.50\%)$$
$$\%\Delta Y \cong 1.25\% + -0.30\% + 1.00\% = 1.95\%$$

For the period 1991–2000, growth in total factor productivity contributed more to real GDP growth than the growth in labor or the growth in capital. (Study Session 7, LOS 24.b)

15.4. **C** The first step is to estimate real GDP growth.

$$\%\Delta Y \cong \%\Delta A + \alpha(\%\Delta K) + (1-\alpha)(\%\Delta L)$$
$$\cong 2.35\% + 0.6(1.25\%) + (1-0.6)(0.42\%) = 3.27\%$$

Next, the intrinsic value of the market index can be estimated using the Gordon growth model.

$$P_0 = \frac{D_0(1+g)}{r-g} = \frac{75 \times (1+0.0327)}{0.08 - 0.0327} = \frac{77.45}{0.047} = 1637.42$$

(Study Session 7, LOS 24.c)

15.5. **B** Comment 2 is correct. Comment 1 is incorrect. When the earnings yield for the S&P 500 is greater than the yield on Treasuries, the level of the index is low relative to expected earnings, making the earnings yield too high. Thus, equities would be considered under-valued. Comment 3 is incorrect because earnings and prices are restating according to CPI in the 10-year average price/earnings ratio model, so the model does account for inflation. (Study Session 7, LOS 24.f)

15.6. **B** The equity q ratio is computed as:

$$\text{equity } q = \frac{\text{market value of equity}}{\text{mv of assets} - \text{mv of liabilities}} = \frac{20}{50 - 26} = 0.8333$$

The ratio is less than one, so the equity index is considered to be undervalued. (Study Session 7, LOS 24.g)

QUESTION 16

Source: Study Session 11

16.1. **C** The way a long-only portfolio earns a positive alpha is through the selection of undervalued securities. Stock selection is how Kiley generates his performance. Kiley's portfolio is potentially exposed to both systematic and unsystematic risk. (Study Session 11, LOS 32.m)

16.2. **C** The change in allocations in Exhibits 1 and 2 indicate large changes in investment style. Allocations moved from a growth-oriented style in the first 5-year period to a value-oriented style in the second 5-year period. The returns based analysis confirms these findings—the slopes changed markedly for LCV (large increase in the second 5-year period) and LCG (large decrease in the second 5-year period). (Study Session 11, LOS 32.i,k)

16.3. **A** The most extreme negative decision that a long-only manager can make is to drop the allocation to the sector to zero. The active weight is the difference between the manager's allocation and the benchmark allocation: $0 - 3\% = -3\%$. (Study Session 11, LOS 32.m)

16.4. **B** In an alpha and beta separation approach, the investor gains systematic risk exposure by allocating funds to (low-cost) passive index managers, while separately adding alpha via allocation of funds to market-neutral long-short managers. (Study Session 11, LOS 32.t)

16.5. **B** The information coefficient (IC) measures manager skill. The information coefficient will be high, because the correlation between alpha forecasts and alpha realizations is expected to remain high. The investor breadth (IB) measures the number of independent investment decisions made within the investor's portfolio. The investor breadth will be low, because GenM employs a small number of active managers (the satellites managers), who, in turn, are mandated to consider only a small number of securities. The Information ratio = IC $\times$ (IB)$^{1/2}$. The information ratio could be higher or lower, depending on the level reached for each of the variables. (Study Session 11, LOS 32.p)

16.6. **A** Advantage 1 is correct. A Completeness Fund compliments or "completes" the actively managed portfolio so that the investor's portfolio has risk exposure similar to that of the benchmark. The advantage of the Completeness Fund approach is capturing the stock selecting ability of active managers, while making the overall portfolio risk profile similar to its benchmark.

Advantage 2 is incorrect. Misfit risk is defined as the standard deviation of the differences between the returns on the managers' normal portfolio and the investor's benchmark. Although the completeness fund approach in its purest form would eliminate misfit risk, the elimination of misfit risk would prevent the fund from receiving the benefit of active management. If the Completeness Fund eliminates misfit risk, it will also eliminate the additional returns associated with the stock selecting ability of active managers. (Study Session 11, LOS 32.r)

QUESTION 17

Source: Study Session 3

17.1. **B** Common characteristics of overconfidence are frequent trading (high turnover), high risk levels (high beta), and the illusion of knowledge (extensive data and research reports, which do not necessarily indicate superior performance going forward). Relying on staff input may or may not be good portfolio management, but it is not a sign of overconfidence. (Study Session 3, LOS 12.a)

17.2. **B** Regret minimization is the desire to avoid feeling the pain of making a poor financial decision. Regret minimization can impact new investment decisions because the investor wishes to avoid repeating the pain of a previous financial loss. The portfolio manager's under-weighting in technology is this kind of regret minimization. Note that this could also be a symptom of myopic loss aversion. (Study Session 3, LOS 8.b, 9.a)

17.3. **C** Gambler's fallacy is a belief in extreme mean reversion. You could think of it as the "it's due" syndrome as in, "He hasn't had a hit in 15 at-bats…he's due." Another example is flipping a coin and having it come up heads several times in a row. Someone who is subject to gambler's fallacy would start to think tails is "due" and to overestimate the probability of tails on the sixth flip.

The fallacy also arises when investors inappropriately predict a reverse in a trend, such as the portfolio manager's erroneous assumption about oil prices. The manager starts to see the probability of a reversal as increasing in value as the sector increases in value. Anchoring incorporates recent events into future projections. (Study Session 3, LOS 7.a)

17.4. **B** Assuming that good companies make good investments is representativeness. Think of representativeness as "if-then." (If this, then that.) In this case, the committee member applies if-then by assuming that *if* a company is good (however defined) *then* it is a good investment. Representativeness can also be exhibited as an overreaction to the historical investment success of a company. The investor uses the past performance as the "if" and good future performance as the "then." The basic idea of mental accounting is that decision makers tend to debit costs associated with transactions to different "mental accounts." A precondition is that these mental accounts are regarded independently of each other. Thus, mental accounting becomes important in the context of relative evaluation. Hindsight bias is the tendency on the part of investors to overestimate what they knew or should have known. (Study Session 3, LOS 9.a)

17.5. **A** By selling a stock that has declined in value, the manager would be accepting a loss. By hanging on to these poor performing stocks, the manager is avoiding any admission of an error on her part, and is demonstrating loss aversion. Money illusion refers to underestimating the effects of inflation by focusing on nominal returns rather than real (inflation-adjusted) returns. (Study Session 3, LOS 8.a)

17.6. **C** Statement 1 is incorrect. The behavioral trait is regret minimization, not overreaction. The concept of regret minimization leads to herding behavior. Window dressing is a herding mentality in which portfolio managers show investors that they only invest in stocks that outperform (winners) and avoid poor performing stocks (losers). The overreaction concept asserts that random events can greatly influence an investor's decision making.

Statement 2 is incorrect. The trading described is similar to dollar cost averaging, which is a framing dependence issue that mitigates loss aversion. Anchoring leads to an under-reaction to new information, which does not apply to the portfolio manager's trading strategy. (Study Session 3, LOS 8.a, b)

QUESTION 18

Source: Study Session 10

18.1. **A** Higgins describes a cross hedge strategy. The investor sells the first foreign currency forward for a second foreign currency that is expected to appreciate to a greater degree than the currency of the bond. When the bond is sold or matures, the investor sells the second foreign currency for the domestic currency at the spot rate.

Tyler is describing a proxy hedge strategy. The investor uses a second foreign currency to hedge the first foreign currency. Here the investor would use a forward contract where dollars would be bought and euros would be sold (remember the Bergen Petroleum bond is denominated in Norwegian NKr). If the NKr and euro are positively correlated, the movement of the NKr and euro will offset one another. The short euro position in the forward contract and the long NKr position from the liquidation of the bonds would offset so that the net return from the two positions would be zero. The dollar-euro forward contract provides the currency hedge. (Study Session 10, LOS 30.j)

18.2. **A** The returns for the unhedged and hedged positions are calculated as follows. Assume the U.S. dollar is currency d and the Norwegian NKr is currency f. The forward rate is denoted as F, and risk-free rates in each currency are denoted as i.

The unhedged return is the return on the bond plus the expected change in the NKr:

$= 7.00 - 0.40 = 6.60$

To obtain the hedged return, we first calculate the approximate forward discount for the Norwegian NKr relative to the domestic currency:

$F_{d,f} = i_d - i_f = 2.50 - 4.80 = -2.30$

The hedged return is the return on the bond plus the forward discount for the NKr:

$= 7.00 - 2.30 = 4.70$

The highest return is from the unhedged position. Assuming the investor is risk-neutral (i.e., is only concerned with return), the unhedged position should be taken. (Study Session 10, LOS 30.j)

18.3. **B** Higgins is incorrect because although interest rate parity does utilize both spot rates and forward rates, the relationship does *not* posit that forward rates have predictive power for future spot rates. Interest rate parity states that when interest rates are higher in the foreign country, there will be a forward discount for that country's currency, (i.e., the foreign currency will have a lower value in the forward rate relative to the spot rate). Likewise, if interest rates are lower in the foreign country, there will be a forward premium for that country's currency (i.e., the foreign currency will have a higher value in the forward rate relative to the spot rate).

Although interest rate parity depends on covered interest arbitrage, Tyler is incorrect because if the U.K. rate is 5.5%, the Japanese rate is 2.3%, and the Japanese yen is at a forward premium of 4.1%, then the investor should borrow pounds at 5.5%, invest in Japan, and convert back to pounds in one year earning the yen forward premium. The return in Japan would be 2.3% + 4.1% = 6.4%, inclusive of the forward premium. The risk-free, covered interest arbitrage profit would be 6.4% − 5.5% = 0.9%, before transactions costs. (Study Session 10, LOS 30.j)

18.4. **C** Higgins is incorrect. He is correct that emerging country debt is usually denominated in a hard currency and that emerging country currency crises sometimes spread from one country to another (i.e., contagion does occur). However, the quality in emerging market sovereign bonds has increased over time. In addition, emerging market governments can implement fiscal and/or monetary policies to offset potentially negative events and they have access to major wide-world lenders (e.g., World Bank, International Monetary Fund).

Tyler is correct because investing outside the emerging market bond index does provide the potential for excess returns. The major emerging market bond index, the Emerging Markets Bond Index Plus (EMBI+), is concentrated in Latin American debt (e.g., Brazil, Mexico). The portfolio manager can earn an alpha by investing in emerging country bonds outside of this region. (Study Session 10, LOS 30.l)

18.5. **A** In breakeven spread analysis, the analyst determines the yield change that makes the returns on bonds equivalent. To determine the breakeven yield change at which the investor would be indifferent between purchasing two bonds, we must first compare the bonds' yields over the holding period. Over the one-year time horizon, the Horgen bond has a yield advantage of 1% (9% – 8%). For the returns to be equivalent over the one-year time horizon (once the investor has purchased the bonds), the price for the Horgen bond must fall by 1%. For its price to fall, its yield must increase. The breakeven change in price of the Horgen bond will be:

change in price = duration × change in yield

In this case, the change in yield is the widening of spread that must occur to make the investor indifferent between the two bonds. You can solve for the widening (W) by:

1.0% = 7.25 × W   (7.25 is the duration of the Horgen bond)

0.1379% = W = 13.79 basis points

Therefore, if the Horgen bond's yield rises by more than 13.79 basis points, the value of the bond would decline by an amount that would offset the yield advantage, making the Midlothian bond more attractive. If the Horgen yield decreases, the price appreciation would add to the favorable yield differential of investing in the Horgen bond. Note that we calculated the breakeven yield change using the bond with the longer duration. (Study Session 10, LOS 30.k)

18.6. **B** Breakeven spread analysis measures the change in price, resulting from yield spread widening, that would offset the favorable yield differential of one bond over another. Breakeven spreads do not provide any explicit measure of exchange rate risk. The calculation of the breakeven spread is based on duration. (Study Session 10, LOS 30.k)

QUESTION 19

Source: Study Session 15

19.1. **C** Number of futures = $V(1 + R_F)^T / P_f$ (multiplier)

Number = $[3,000,000,000(1 + 0.03)^{5/12}] / (250)(1,058) = 11,482.71$ contracts; remember the S&P 500 futures quoted contract price is multiplied by 250 to get the contract size. (Study Session 15, LOS 41.a)

19.2. **C** payoff = # contracts$(250)(P_{f1} - P_{f0})$

payoff = $-11,482(250)(1,125 - 1,058) = -192,323,500$ (Study Session 15, LOS 41.a)

19.3. **A** Current asset allocation is 88% bonds and 12% stocks; recommended asset allocation is 75% bonds and 25% stocks. Requires selling $3,250,000,000 (13% of $25 billion) in bonds and buying an equivalent amount of stocks.

contract size = $250 \times \$1,058 = \$264,500$;

number of equity futures = $[(\beta_T - \beta_P) / \beta_f] \times [V_P / (P_f)(\text{multiplier})]$

$[(1 - 0) / 1] \times (3,250,000,000 / \$264,500) = 12,287.33 \sim 12,290$ equity futures contracts

(Study Session 15, LOS 41.d)

19.4. **C** dollar value of portfolio = 162,225,000,000 yen / 108.15 = $1,500,000,000

contract size = (multiplier)(P_f) = $5.00 \times 10,337 = \$51,685$

number futures = $[(\beta_T - \beta_P) / \beta_f] \times [V_P / (P_f)(\text{multiplier})]$

$[(0 - 0.90) / 1.0] \times (\$1,500,000,000 / \$51,685) = -26,119.76$ contracts (short)

(Study Session 15, LOS 41.f)

19.5. **C** UGG would hedge payment risk by buying a forward currency contract. UGG cannot resolve all their liquidity issues using futures contracts (e.g., forward contracts are more liquid than futures contracts for risk management of foreign currency). UGG would use yield beta in the process of adjusting their exposure to bonds, not equities. (Study Session 15, LOS 41.b)

19.6. **B** Futures contracts on corporate bonds do not exist, therefore Choice A is incorrect. Forwards are the most frequently used method of hedging exchange rate risk in practice. Futures markets are used less frequently to manage exchange rate risk since they are relatively newer than the foreign exchange forward market and provide less liquidity. Choice C is incorrect since hedging the Japanese equity portfolio and the currency risk between the dollar and the yen would lock in the U.S. risk-free rate, not the Japanese risk-free rate. Also, management would have to know the exact future value if the equity to hedge. (Study Session 15, LOS 41.g)

QUESTION 20

Source: Study Session 15

20.1. **B** The duration of a pay fixed/receive floating swap for four years with quarterly payments would be equal to the duration of a 4-year floating rate bond with quarterly payments minus the duration of a 4-year fixed rate bond with quarterly payments. The duration of the 4-year floating rate bond would be approximately one-half of the payment interval, or $0.5 \times 1/4 = 0.125$. The duration of the 4-year fixed rate bond (based on the assumption given in the vignette) would be 75% of four years, or 3.0. Therefore, the swap duration is $0.125 - 3.0 = -2.875$. (Study Session 15, LOS 43.b)

 Professor's Note: Due to conflicting convention, you would likely be provided the duration of the floating arm of the swap on the exam. If not, I recommend that you use ½ the payment interval.

20.2. **B** The duration of Swap B, a pay fixed/receive floating swap for five years with semiannual payments, would be equal to the duration of a 5-year floating rate bond with semiannual payments minus the duration of a 5-year fixed rate bond with semiannual payments. The duration of the 5-year floating rate bond would be one-half of the payment interval, or $0.5 \times 0.5 = 0.25$. The duration of the 5-year fixed rate bond would be 75% of five years, or 3.75. Therefore the swap duration will be $0.25 - 3.75 = -3.50$.

The required notional principal to achieve a portfolio duration of 4.5 using Swap B would be:

$$NP = V_P[(MD_T - MD_p) / MD_{swap}] = \$800M \times [(4.5 - 6.5) / -3.5] = \$457M$$

(Study Session 15, LOS 43.d)

20.3. **B** Creating a short position in a synthetic dual currency bond would require issuing a fixed rate bond denominated in dollars and then entering into a swap as the dollar receiver or equivalently, the Yen payer. Since the investment policy statement does not allow Skinner to leverage the portfolio, this strategy to offset the Yen exposure is inappropriate. Michaels's comment on the swap is correct, however. The synthetic dual-currency bond would require entering into the swap as a fixed-rate yen payer. It is also true that the swap would increase the credit risk of the portfolio. (Study Session 15, LOS 43.f)

20.4. **C** A receiver swaption gives the holder the right to enter into a receive fixed–pay floating swap at a future date. Therefore, the swaption has value when interest rates decline. The call feature on the callable bond will also have value when interest rates decline (positive value for the issuer, negative value for the investor). Since the holder of a callable bond (the long) has effectively sold a call option to the issuer of a callable bond, purchasing the swaption will offset the call option position. (Study Session 15, LOS 43.h)

 Professor's Note: Remember that the words "receiver" and "payer" in the name of the swaption refer to the fixed arm of the swap. A receiver swaption, for example, gives the holder the option to enter a swap as fixed rate receiver.

20.5. **B** To increase the duration of the portfolio, Skinner would want to hold a position that moved inversely with interest rates (i.e., decreases in value as interest rates increase). The swap position that accomplishes this objective is a pay floating/receive fixed. As interest rates decrease, Skinner would receive the same fixed payments but would pay out lower floating rate payments. (Study Session 15, LOS 43.b)

20.6. **A** The swap would reduce the cash flow risk, since Barter will have locked in a fixed payment by using the swap. However, the duration of the fixed rate payments will be much higher than the duration of the floating rate payments, thus increasing the market value risk. (Study Session 15, LOS 43.c)

QUESTION 21

Source: Study Sessions 8 and 13

21.1. **A** Since Hope is only concerned with the foundation's spending rate, an asset-only approach (AO) is appropriate. If Hope considers a large capital spending program, the asset-liability approach (ALM) is appropriate. (Study Session 8, LOS 26.d)

21.2. **B** International equities form a separate asset class with its own distinct risk and return profile. Return and risk metrics for domestic and international equities should not be commingled. The lost information could be critical in understanding the foundation's future performance. (Study Session 8, LOS 26.i)

21.3. **B** The appropriate comparison is the Sharpe ratio of the new asset class to the product of the Sharpe ratio of the existing portfolio and the correlation between the new asset and the existing portfolio.

$$\frac{\hat{R}_{new} - R_F}{\sigma_{new}} > \left(\frac{\hat{R}_p - R_F}{\sigma_p} \right) Corr\left(R_{new}, R_p \right)$$

If the above equation holds, an investor can achieve a superior efficient frontier by adding the new asset class to the existing portfolio. The equation does not, however, provide an indication of the optimal amount of the new asset class to add to the portfolio.

Venture capital: $\dfrac{0.114 - 0.035}{0.189} = 0.418 < 0.43 = \left(\dfrac{0.121 - 0.035}{0.1} \right) 0.50$

Adding venture capital reduces the Sharpe ratio. Do not add venture capital.

Hedge funds: $\dfrac{0.135 - 0.035}{0.103} = 0.917 > 0.645 = \left(\dfrac{0.121 - 0.035}{0.1} \right) 0.75$

Adding hedge funds increases the Sharpe ratio. Add hedge funds.

(Study Session 13, LOS 36.f)

21.4. **C** Both of the comments made in the report by Meyer are incorrect. The general partner of a private equity (venture capital) LP usually earns a management fee on committed capital, not invested capital, which may be significantly less than the amount of capital committed by the limited partners (i.e., the investors). The rest of the statement regarding the structure of a private equity investment is correct.

As for the comment on the strategy related to private equity investment, committed capital is not required all at once. The general partner makes capital calls over a period of up to five years (the commitment period). Limited partners must be ready to provide the funds when a capital call is received, so long-term liquidity is a consideration over the commitment period. The rest of the comments related to private equity investing strategy are correct. (Study Session 13, LOS 36.k, l)

21.5. **B** Equity market neutral strategies take long positions in undervalued securities and short positions in overvalued securities such that the exposure to market, industry, sector, etc., risk is zero (i.e., neutral). The trades in Fund Y combine a long and short exposure such that the beta (market risk) is 0.01, which is approximately zero or neutral to market risk. The trades are also within the same industry. Furthermore, the net investment of zero indicates that the long and short positions were of equivalent dollar value. It is most likely that Fund Y is following an equity market neutral strategy. Fund Z is following a global macro strategy since it is attempting to take advantage of directional movements in markets. Fund X is following a hedged equity strategy. Hedged equity strategies, like equity market neutral strategies, involve taking long positions in undervalued and short positions in overvalued securities, but they are not structured to be market, industry, sector, or dollar neutral. Fund X is net short and has used securities in different industries to achieve its strategy. (Study Session 13, LOS 36.p)

21.6. **A** Stale pricing is not one of the hedge fund biases that typically create difficulties in using hedge fund indexes as benchmarks. Survivorship bias is a problem, since many hedge fund indexes delete the performance of failed funds from the index's historical record, which biases the returns upward over time. Hedge fund indexes also may backfill the performance of funds recently added to the index. Since only funds that are performing well are likely to be added to the index, the backfilled returns are likely to bias the index's historical performance upward. (Study Session 13, LOS 36.s)

QUESTION 22

Source: Study Session 6

22.1. **B** Using the Grinold and Kroner model, the expected return on a stock market is its dividend yield plus the inflation rate plus the real earnings growth rate minus the change in stock outstanding plus changes in the P/E ratio:

$$\hat{R}_i = \frac{D_1}{P_0} + i + g - \Delta S + \Delta\left(\frac{P}{E}\right)$$

where :

$\hat{R}_i$ = expected return on stock market i

D_1 = dividend next period

P_0 = current stock price

i = expected inflation rate

g = real growth rate in total earnings

ΔS = change in number of shares outstanding

$\Delta\left(\dfrac{P}{E}\right)$ = change in P/E ratio

The highest expected return is for Bergamo. The expected equity market return calculations for Alzano (A), Bergamo (B), and Lombardo (L) are:

$$\hat{R}_A = 2.70\% + 2.80 + 4.80\% - (-0.20\%) + 0.70\% = 11.20\%$$
$$\hat{R}_B = 0.60\% + 5.30 + 5.70\% - 1.20\% + 1.10\% = 11.50\%$$
$$\hat{R}_L = 3.60\% + 1.90 + 2.20\% - (-0.80\%) + (-0.20\%) = 8.30\%$$

Note that when the change in stock outstanding decreases (i.e., stock is repurchased), this is to the investor's benefit (the repurchase yield is positive). Changes in the P/E ratio also affect the expected return. If investors think, for example, that stocks will be less risky in the future, the P/E ratio will increase, and the expected return on stocks increases. (Study Session 6, LOS 23.c)

22.2. **B** The data show that yields are declining as maturity increases, therefore the yield curve is inverted. The downward sloping yield curve indicates that the economy is likely to contract in the future. (Study Session 6, LOS 23.i)

22.3. **C** Given that the Linden economy is likely to contract in the future, Wieters should recommend that the Balduvi Endowment move toward government and investment grade bonds, because inflation and interest rates will decrease and economic growth will slow. Stocks, especially cyclical stocks, should be underweighted. High yield bonds should also be underweighted, because the default risk premium on them may grow as the economy slows. Therefore, Wieters should recommend Portfolio C for the Balduvi Endowment. (Study Session 6, LOS 23.f, g, n, o, q)

         ©2010 Kaplan, Inc.

22.4. **C** Mora is likely susceptible to the confirming evidence trap. The confirming evidence trap is when analysts give too much credence to evidence that supports their existing or favored beliefs. Note that Mora's prior belief from her master's degree training was that the default risk premium has predictive power for stock returns. In the analysis, it appears that lagged changes in the stock market have a strong relationship with future stock returns. Mora's conclusions seem to focus solely on the default risk premium.

It could be argued that she is also susceptible to the anchoring trap because she puts too much weight on the first set of information she received (from her master's studies). (Study Session 6, LOS 23.b)

22.5. **C** Wieters is likely susceptible to the recallability trap. The recallability trap is when analysts let past disasters or dramatic events weigh too heavily in their forecasts. Although the 80-year history indicates that Lombardo stocks returns average 13.6%, Wieters projects returns much lower. He may be letting the credit crisis of 2007-2008 overly influence his predictions.

It might be argued that he is also susceptible to the status quo trap, because his prediction is influenced by recent events, but in this trap he would probably predict closer to the recent value of −12.6% in his forecasts. (Study Session 6, LOS 23.b)

22.6. **C** Statement 1: Mora's statements on emerging market debt are correct.

Statement 2: Mora is incorrect. It is true that emerging market debt is particularly susceptible to financial crises and that an emerging government must have foreign currency reserves to defend its currency in the foreign exchange markets. However, most emerging debt is denominated in a non-domestic currency. The currency of emerging bonds is usually a hard currency (e.g., dollars, euros, etc.) and an emerging government must have a hard currency to pay back the principal and interest. The default risk for emerging market debt is thus much higher. (Study Session 6, LOS 23.k, o)

PRACTICE EXAM 3
MORNING SESSION ANSWERS

QUESTION 1

Reference: Book 1, Study Session 4, LOS 14.j,k

Cross-reference to CFA Institute assigned reading: Reading 14

Answer for Question 1

For the Exam:

		Investment Policy Statement for Middendorf
Objectives	Risk Tolerance	**Ability:** Middendorf's situation indicates an above average risk tolerance. **Willingness:** Her statements indicate below average willingness to tolerate risk. **Overall:** Middendorf's overall risk tolerance is below average.
	Return Objectives	There is no numerical return objective. The goal is to maximize her after-tax return within her risk objectives.
Constraints	Time Horizon	Long-term, 2-stage (pre-retirement and retirement)
	Liquidity	Her liquidity needs, in light of the $750,000 payment pending, are minimal.
	Legal/Regulatory	There are no special legal or regulatory issues.
	Taxes	She is taxed as an individual, and her tax situation is straightforward. Taxes related to diversifying the portfolio must be considered.
	Unique Circumstances	She is single with no dependents. Her portfolio is concentrated, and this matter should be addressed.

Discussion:

Investment Policy Statement for Middendorf		
Objectives	Risk Tolerance	**Ability:** Middendorf's ability is a function of her assets, income, and personal characteristics which form the basis for the constraints section of the IPS. *Assets:* significant net worth. Argues for an above average level of risk tolerance. *Income:* substantial. Above average level of risk tolerance. *Personal characteristics:* long time horizon, manageable liquidity needs, no special legal/regulatory issues, straightforward tax situation, single with no dependents. All argue for above average risk tolerance. **Willingness:** Middendorf's willingness is a function of her personality traits, which we must infer from her statements. She states that she is concerned about the recent volatility exhibited by her portfolio, though we do not have statistical information from which we can assess whether or not this was excessive. She also indicates a desire for a lower volatility portfolio going forward. Both of these statements indicate an average to below average willingness to bear risk. **Overall:** If ability is less than willingness, the level dictated by ability should be the binding constraint. If ability is greater than willingness, the investor should be counseled with a view toward increasing the level of willingness to match ability. The resulting level of willingness becomes the binding constraint. Since we have no information that would lead us to believe that the level of willingness has been increased, her overall risk tolerance is average to below average.
	Return Objectives	Since there is no portfolio income requirement for the foreseeable future, there is no numerical return target. Her objective is simply to maximize total after-tax return, subject to the portfolio meeting her risk objectives.

Constraints	Time Horizon	Middendorf is 52, with no plans to retire in the foreseeable future, so her overall time horizon is at least 25–35 years. She has a 2-stage time horizon: employment and retirement.
	Liquidity	She does not require income from her portfolio. She needs liquidity to fund her planned travel and for emergency situations. The $750,000 severance payment, net of taxes, will be more than sufficient to meet her liquidity needs for the foreseeable future. Her portfolio liquidity requirement is low.
	Legal/Regulatory	There are no special legal or regulatory issues.
	Taxes	Middendorf is taxed as an individual. She may have to pay taxes on portfolio income and capital gains, depending upon the extent to which her assets are held in tax-sheltered accounts. Any investment actions must take tax status into consideration, including those relating to the diversification of the concentrated stock position.
	Unique Circumstances	She is single with no dependents. Her portfolio is concentrated, and this matter should be addressed (i.e., diversified) as soon as possible.

Sample Scoring Key:
1 point for each of the three risk components (ability, willingness, overall).
2 points for each of the return components (no numerical target, maximize subject to risk objectives).
2 points for each constraint.

QUESTION 2

Reference: Book 1, Study Session 4, LOS 16.c, d

Cross-reference to CFA Institute assigned reading: Reading 16

Answer for Question 2-A

Combined Probability	Real Annual Spending	Expected Real Spending	Present Value
0.9980 = (0.9248 + 0.9736) − 0.9248 × 0.9736	$150,000	**$149,700** = $150,000 × 0.9980	**$146,765** = $149,700 / (1.02)
0.9912 = (0.8418 + 0.9446) − 0.8418 × 0.9446	$150,000	**$148,680** = $150,000 × 0.9912	**$142,907** = $148,680 / $(1.02)^2$
0.9781 = (0.7501 + 0.9125) − 0.7501 × 0.9125	$150,000	**$146,715** = $150,000 × 0.9781	**$138,253** = $146,715 / $(1.02)^3$
0.9569 = (0.6489 + 0.8771) − 0.6489 × 0.8771	$150,000	**$143,535** = $150,000 × 0.9569	**$132,604** = $143,535 / $(1.02)^4$
0.9251 = (0.5371 + 0.8381) − 0.5371 × 0.8381	$150,000	**$138,765** = $150,000 × 0.9251	**$125,684** = $138,765 / $(1.02)^5$
Core Capital			**$686,213** = $146,765 + $142,907 + $138,253 + $132,604 + $125,684
Excess Capital			**$313,787** = $200,000 + $500,000 + $300,000 − $686,213

Sample Scoring Key: (Maximum 24 points)
2 points for each correctly calculated combined probability. (10 points max)
1 point for each correctly calculated expected real spending amount. (5 points max)
1 point for each correctly calculated present value. (5 points max)
2 points for correct core capital.
2 points for correct excess capital.

 Professor's Note: If you see an essay question with this many calculations and extra space to perform them, be sure to identify each calculation and circle the answer, so that the grader can compare the calculation to the answer you entered in the template.

Answer for Question 2-B

More beneficial to gift or bequest the fund?	Gift	Bequest
Value as Tax-Free Gift	PV = \$300,000; N = 5; Tax rate: 35%; Expected return: 7% FV(tax-free gift) = **\$374,750** $\qquad\qquad\quad = \$300{,}000[1 + 0.07(1 - 0.35)]^5$ $\qquad\qquad\quad = \$300{,}000(1.0455)^5$	
Value as Bequest	PV = \$300,000; N = 5; Tax rate: 25%; Expected return: 7% Inheritance tax-rate = 20% FV(bequest) = **\$309,972** $\qquad\qquad\quad = \$300{,}000[1 + 0.07(1 - 0.25)]^5(1 - 0.2)$ $\qquad\qquad\quad = \$300{,}000[(1.0525)^5](0.8)$	
Relative Value	**1.2090** = \$374,750 / \$309,972	

Sample Scoring Key: (Maximum 8 points)
3 points for FV gift.
3 points for FV bequest.
1 point each for correct relative value and correctly identifying gift as best alternative.

QUESTION 3

Reference: Book 3, Study Session 11, LOS 32.e,i,s
Book 3, Study Session 11, LOS 33.b,d,e

Cross-reference to CFA Institute assigned reading: Readings 32 and 33

A. **For the Exam:**
(Note: From the information provided we know we will have to use the Fundamental Law of Active Management to assess the performance of the two managers.)

true active return = manager's total return − manager's normal portfolio return

Sycamore: 12 − 15 = −3%
Malta: 16 − 14 = +2%

$$\text{total active risk} = \sqrt{\left(\text{true active risk}\right)^2 + \left(\text{misfit active risk}\right)^2}$$

Sycamore: 2.86%
Malta: 2.14%

$$\text{true information ratio} = \frac{\text{true active return}}{\text{true active risk}}$$

Sycamore: −1.05
Malta: 0.94

Performance evaluation:

Sycamore:

Compared to the fund manager's benchmark, the Sycamore manager outperformed the benchmark and generated a positive alpha. However, based on the normal benchmark portfolio, the Sycamore manager underperformed the Malta fund manager (i.e., negative active return).

Malta:

Compared to the fund manager's benchmark, the Malta manager underperformed the benchmark and generated a negative alpha. However, based on the normal benchmark portfolio, the Malta manager outperformed the Sycamore fund manager (i.e., positive active return).

Discussion:

The manager's total active return can be decomposed into "true" and "misfit" components. The true return is the manager's total return minus the appropriate benchmark, the manager's normal portfolio. The normal portfolio has a level of systematic risk exposure that is typical of the manager's portfolio. Thus, the true active return is "true" in the sense that it measures what the manager earned relative to the level of risk normally assumed.

true active return = manager's total return − manager's normal portfolio return

Sycamore: 12 − 15 = −3%
Malta: 16 − 14 = +2%

The misfit return is the manager's normal portfolio return minus the investor's benchmark. The misfit active return is "misfit" to the extent that the benchmark is not consistent with the manager's style.

misfit active return = manager's normal portfolio return – investor's benchmark return

Sycamore: 15 – 11 = +4%
Malta: 14 – 18 = –4%

To derive the true active risk, we need to know the total active risk and misfit risk:

$$\text{total active risk} = \sqrt{(\text{true active risk})^2 + (\text{misfit active risk})^2}$$

Sycamore: $4.0\% = \sqrt{(\text{true active risk})^2 + (2.8\%)^2} = 2.86\%$

Malta: $4.1\% = \sqrt{(\text{true active risk})^2 + (3.5\%)^2} = 2.14\%$

The true information ratio is simply a reward to risk measure:

$$\text{true information ratio} = \frac{\text{true active return}}{\text{true active risk}}$$

Sycamore: $\dfrac{-3.0}{2.86} = -1.05$

Malta: $\dfrac{2.0}{2.14} = 0.94$

If the information ratio is positive, the manager has generated positive risk-adjusted returns, and the larger the ratio, the better the portfolio manager's performance.

Performance evaluation:

Sycamore's performance relative to its benchmark suggests that the portfolio has generated positive alpha. Conversely, Malta's performance suggests that it has generated negative alpha.

However, the benchmarks are misspecified. Judged against the appropriate benchmark—one that has the same level of systematic risk typically assumed by the portfolio—we can see that the Sycamore has actually underperformed, while Malta has outperformed.

Here's a **key point** to make on the exam: The true information ratio provides a more accurate measure of the manager's performance, and by this measure, Malta has outperformed.

Sample Scoring Key:
2 points for the calculations of each firm's true information ratio.
2 points for the discussion of each firm's performance.

B. i. **For the Exam:**

Kishwaukee appears to be a large-cap value fund, while Rockford appears to be a small-cap growth fund. Value stocks tend to have higher earnings volatility than growth stocks.

Discussion:

It appears that Kishwaukee is a large-cap value fund. Relative to the broad market, its holdings have a high dividend yield, low earnings growth, high median market cap, low P/B ratio, and low P/E ratio, which are all characteristics of a large-cap value fund. Additionally, it also has greater representation in the financial and utility industries. It appears that Rockford is a small-cap growth fund. Relative to the broad market, its holdings have a low dividend yield, high earnings growth, low median market cap, high P/B ratio, and high P/E ratio, which are all characteristics of a small-cap growth fund. Additionally, it also has greater representation in the technology and healthcare industries. Relative to growth stocks, value stocks tend to have higher earnings volatility. Thus, we would expect Kishwaukee's holdings to have higher earnings volatility.

ii. **For the Exam:**

Jensen is using holdings-based style analysis, and Miller is using returns-based style analysis. Holdings-based analysis will detect changes in style more quickly than returns-based style analysis.

Discussion:

Jensen is using holdings-based style analysis because she characterizes the holdings of the manager's portfolio by examining its contents. Miller is using returns-based style analysis because she uses a regression approach where the manager's returns are regressed against various security indices. Holdings-based analysis will detect changes in style (style drift) more quickly than returns-based style analysis. The reason is that returns-based analysis typically uses monthly returns over the past several years. Thus, a portion of the analysis is based on data that may no longer reflect the manager's emphasis. Holdings-based style analysis uses the portfolio's current contents to characterize the portfolio and provides a more up-to-date picture of the portfolio's contents.

iii. **For the Exam:**

Kishwaukee is a mutual fund and mutual funds are generally less tax efficient than an ETF such as Rockford.

Discussion:

Kishwaukee is a mutual fund and mutual funds are generally less tax efficient than an ETF such as Rockford. When an investor wants to liquidate their ETF shares, they sell to another investor, which is not a taxable event for the ETF. Additionally, when an ETF redeems a large number of ETF shares for an institutional investor, the ETF may exchange the ETF shares for the basket of stocks underlying the ETF. This also is not a taxable event for the ETF. In an index mutual fund, redemptions typically involve a sale of the underlying securities for cash, which is a taxable event that is passed onto shareholders. Thus, an ETF is more tax efficient for the investor than a mutual fund.

> Sample Scoring Key:
> 3 points for the discussion of each issue.

Answer for Question 3-C

Comment	Correct or incorrect? (circle one)	Explanation
"I am encouraged that PharmaScreen has institutions that hold their stock. The institutions will help monitor management and will use their influence to effect the change needed with PharmaScreen's management."	Incorrect	**For the Exam:** The amount of PharmaScreen stock held by a single institution is likely too small for there to be an incentive to monitor management. **Discussion:** Although Jensen is correct that, in general, institutions help monitor management, the amount of PharmaScreen stock held by a single institution is likely too small and liquid for there to be an incentive to monitor management. PharmaScreen's largest investor is Cape Fear, which holds a small amount of this small-cap stock. Given that Cape Fear is a large hedge fund, their small holding in PharmaScreen would be insignificant to them. The fact that Cape Fear has sold their publicly traded shares indicates that they might sell more shares rather than pushing for change. If the holdings of Cape Fear or another institution were larger or less liquid, they would be more likely to force change at the firm.
"PharmaScreen's management needs a compensation structure that more closely aligns the interests of management and shareholders. One possible solution would be to weight management's compensation more heavily toward out-of-the-money stock options so that they have a strong incentive to increase the stock price. The drawback of this form of compensation is that management would have an incentive to undertake too much risk."	Correct	**For the Exam:** Stock options align the interests of management with shareholders, but out-of-the-money options may induce management to undertake too much risk in an attempt to increase the stock price. **Discussion:** An appropriately structured grant of stock options should work to align the interests of management with those of the shareholders (i.e., that the value of the equity be increased). However, if the options are sufficiently far out of the money, it may appear to management that it is unlikely the options will be in the money prior to expiration under normal circumstances. Thus, management may have an incentive to seek projects that have large potential returns but are excessively risky, in the hope that the options come into the money. In essence, the options have given managers an incentive to gamble with shareholder capital.

> Sample Scoring Key:
> 1 point for identifying whether the statement is correct or incorrect.
> 2 points for the explanation of why each is correct or incorrect.
> 0 points possible if correct/incorrect decision is wrong.

D. i. **For the Exam:** (note the question only asks for two reasons)
- Debt eliminates excess cash which managers may waste.
- Debt requires that managers ensure firm liquidity to repay debt.
- Debt motivates managers to keep the firm's control out of the debt-holders' hands in a bankruptcy.
- Debt allows manager-owners to more clearly see the end result of their efforts.

Discussion:

1. Debt motivates management because it takes excess cash out of management hands. With the pressure to make periodic interest and principal payments, management does not have the luxury of spending cash on frivolous projects and perks.

2. To ensure that the firm has cash flow for future investments after repaying its debt, the managers must assure the firm's liquidity. The risk of insufficient liquidity provides an incentive effect for management.

3. If the firm lacks liquidity to the degree where debtholders force the firm into bankruptcy, the managers lose control of the firm and possibly their jobs.

4. If managers hold the majority of the firm's equity, then the issuance of debt, rather than equity, means they don't have to share their residual claim on profits. If equity had been issued instead, the managers-owners would be sharing residual profits with other equity holders.

ii. **For the Exam:** (note the question only asks for one limitation)
- Illiquidity can prevent the firm from investing in new projects.
- Bankruptcy is more likely with more debt and bankruptcy is costly.

Discussion:

1. The threat of illiquidity that motivates management can also deny the firm investment in new projects. The illiquidity may be due to circumstances beyond management's control.

2. If the firm is severely liquidity constrained and cannot pay the interest on its debt, it might be forced into bankruptcy. Bankruptcy costs can be substantial.

Sample Scoring Key:
2 points for the discussion of each reason why debt is an effective mechanism.
2 points for the discussion of the limitation of debt as an effective mechanism.

QUESTION 4

Reference: Book 3, Study Session 9, LOS 28.d
Book 4, Study Session 14, LOS 39.a,f,h,l
Book 4, Study Session 15, LOS 42.f

Cross-reference to CFA Institute assigned reading: Readings 28, 39, and 42

Answer for Question 4-A

Comment	Correct or incorrect? (circle one)	Explanation
"Antelope must evaluate the risk of its bond positions and equity index option positions carefully because of recent volatility in interest rates and in the stock markets. For bonds and options, standard deviation is not the preferred risk management tool. Necessary and sufficient risk measures for bonds and options are the duration of bonds and delta of options."	Incorrect	**For the Exam:** The durations and deltas are not sufficient; convexity and gamma should also be used. **Discussion:** Although it is true that standard deviation is not preferred as a measure of bond and option risk, the durations of bonds and the deltas of options are not sufficient by themselves. Second-order effects should also be used. For bonds, this would be convexity; for options it would be gamma.
"One risk management tool Antelope should consider is maximum loss optimization. This tool involves recognizing those factors with the greatest potential to damage the value of Antelope's portfolio. Antelope could then take steps to limit the damage from these factors."	Correct	**For the Exam:** Maximum loss optimization can model the non-normal events arising from Antelope's options and nontraditional assets. **Discussion:** In maximum loss optimization, the risk factors that have the greatest potential impact on the portfolio are identified. Once the factors are identified, procedures are put in place to limit their impact. This tool is especially valuable for assets with non-normal return distributions because this method does not assume normally distributed returns.

Sample Scoring Key:
1 point for identifying whether the statement is correct or incorrect.
1 point for the explanation of why each is correct or incorrect.
0 points possible if correct/incorrect decision is wrong.

B.   i.   **For the Exam:**

In Antelope's case, a centralized system should be used. The critical flaw, in a multi-manager setting, is that a decentralized risk management system will not account for interactions between manager positions.

Discussion:

Although a decentralized risk management system makes those individuals with the most knowledge (those closest to the action) responsible for risk, a centralized system allows upper management to view risk for the firm as a whole so that the interactions (i.e., correlations) between manager positions can be accounted for. This is especially true in Antelope's case, because the firm has positions in many alternative assets that are likely to have low correlations with traditional assets. A centralized system also allows senior management to monitor for "rogue" managers.

ii.   **For the Exam:**

In Antelope's case, the variance-covariance or analytical VAR should not be used because Antelope holds assets with non-normal returns. The variance-covariance VAR assumes returns are normally distributed.

Discussion:

Although the variance-covariance VAR allows for the correlations of risks across portfolios, the presence of options and nontraditional assets with non-normal return distributions suggests that Antelope should use the historical method or the Monte Carlo method. These methods do not assume a normal distribution of returns.

Sample Scoring Key:
2 points for the discussion of each issue.

C.   The three ratios to use in your answer are the Sharpe ratio (total risk), the Sortino ratio (downside risk), and the RoMAD (maximum drawdown). Note that although the M-squared measure also uses total risk (standard deviation) to evaluate risk-adjusted return, the required data (i.e., market return, market risk, risk-free rate) are not provided in Figure 1. Jensen's alpha and the Treynor measure evaluate performance based on systematic risk (not total risk) using beta, which is also not provided.

For the Exam:

$$\text{Sharpe ratio} = \frac{\overline{R_P} - \overline{R_F}}{\sigma_P}$$

$$\text{Davis} = \frac{20.6 - 4.5}{33.2} = 0.48$$

$$\text{Brooks} = \frac{21.3 - 4.5}{31.2} = 0.54$$

Sharpe: Brooks has outperformed Davis.

$$\text{Sortino ratio} = \frac{\overline{R_P} - \text{MAR}}{\text{downside deviation}}$$

$$\text{Davis} = \frac{20.6 - 5.3}{15.05} = 1.02$$

$$\text{Brooks} = \frac{21.3 - 5.3}{16.5} = 0.97$$

Sortino: Davis has outperformed Brooks.

$$\text{RoMAD} = \frac{\overline{R_P}}{\text{maximum drawdown}}$$

$$\text{Davis} = \frac{20.6}{15.2} = 1.36$$

$$\text{Brooks} = \frac{21.3}{13.7} = 1.55$$

RoMAD: Brooks has outperformed Davis.

Discussion:

The Sharpe ratio is the portfolio's excess return over the risk-free rate ($R_P - R_F$) divided by the portfolio total risk as measured by standard deviation (σ_P):

$$\text{Sharpe ratio} = \frac{\overline{R}_P - \overline{R}_F}{\sigma_P}$$

$$\text{Davis} = \frac{20.6 - 4.5}{33.2} = 0.48$$

$$\text{Brooks} = \frac{21.3 - 4.5}{31.2} = 0.54$$

The greater the Sharpe ratio, the greater the excess return received per unit of total risk assumed. Since Brook's value is larger (0.54 > 0.48), he has outperformed Davis on the basis of this measure.

The Sortino ratio is the portfolio's excess return over some minimum acceptable return (MAR) divided by the downside deviation (the standard deviation of the returns falling below the MAR):

$$\text{Sortino ratio} = \frac{\overline{R}_P - \text{MAR}}{\text{downside deviation}}$$

$$\text{Davis} = \frac{20.6 - 5.3}{15.05} = 1.02$$

$$\text{Brooks} = \frac{21.3 - 5.3}{16.5} = 0.97$$

The idea behind the Sortino ratio is that volatility is only "bad" when the deviation is below the target return, that the manager should not be penalized for the volatility of returns exceeding the MAR. Thus, only the downside deviation is used in its calculation. The greater the Sortino ratio, the greater the excess return per unit of downside risk assumed. Since Davis's value is larger (1.02 > 0.97), he has outperformed Brooks on the basis of this measure.

The return over maximum drawdown (RoMAD) is the portfolio's return divided by the maximum drawdown (i.e., the largest percentage loss, peak to trough, over some specified period of time):

$$\text{RoMAD} = \frac{\overline{R}_P}{\text{maximum drawdown}}$$

$$\text{Davis} = \frac{20.6}{15.2} = 1.36$$

$$\text{Brooks} = \frac{21.3}{13.7} = 1.55$$

The RoMAD is a reward to risk ratio, so the greater the RoMAD, the better the performance. Since the RoMAD for Brooks is greater (1.55 > 1.36), he has outperformed Davis on the basis of this measure.

> Sample Scoring Key:
> 1 point for the calculation of each measure for each manager and 1 point for each evaluation (1 point for each ratio). Total: 9 points

For the Exam:

The Sortino Ratio is most appropriate. Since Davis has beaten his benchmark every year, his volatility is on the upside; standard deviation and maximum drawdown overstate his true risk.

Discussion:

The vignette states that Davis has had tremendous success and has beaten his benchmark every year. Using standard deviation or maximum drawdown as a risk measure would penalize Davis because his volatility is derived exclusively from returns in excess of his benchmark. Therefore, the most appropriate measure is the Sortino ratio because it assumes that the relevant risk is failure to achieve the minimum acceptable return or MAR. (Note that Davis could exceed his benchmark in a given period but still fail to achieve the MAR.)

> Sample Scoring Key:
> 1 point for identification of the correct measure and 2 points for the justification. Total: 3 points

QUESTION 5

Reference: Book 2, Study Session 5, LOS 20.i
Book 3, Study Session 11, LOS 32.t

Cross-reference to CFA Institute assigned reading: Readings 20 and 32

Answer for Question 5-A

Comment	Correct or incorrect? (circle one)	Explanation
"The trust officers at the bank may want to suggest an alpha-beta separation approach. This approach is particularly useful in less efficient markets such as small cap markets."	Incorrect	**For the Exam:** Alpha-beta separation approach works best in efficient markets. -OR- It may be difficult or costly to implement in small-cap markets. **Discussion:** In an alpha and beta separation approach, the investor may gain a systematic risk exposure (beta) through a low-cost index fund or ETF while adding an alpha through a long-short strategy. This strategy may be particularly suitable for those markets that are highly efficient and difficult to generate an alpha from. A limitation of the alpha and beta separation approach is that it may be difficult or costly to implement short positions in markets such as emerging markets or small-cap markets.

"Portfolio managers should be aware, however, that some institutions may not be able to use an alpha-beta separation approach because of institutional constraints."	**Correct**	**For the Exam:** An alpha-beta separation approach requires a short position, which some investors may be restricted from using. **Discussion:** Some investors, such as institutions, may not be able to use an alpha and beta separation approach because the strategy typically obtains an alpha through a long-short strategy. These investors, however, could create a similar exposure as the alpha and beta separation approach if they can trade equity futures. For example, suppose the investor wanted a beta from large-cap U.S. stocks and an alpha from European equities. The investor could take a long position in the S&P 500 index futures contract and invest with a European equity manager to generate the alpha. To become market neutral in the European equity market, the investor would then short a futures contract based on European equities.

Sample Scoring Key:
1 point for identifying whether the statement is correct or incorrect.
1 point for the explanation of why each is correct or incorrect.
0 points possible if correct/incorrect decision is wrong.

B. i.   **For the Exam:**

Most bank liabilities are of shorter term than its loans.

The time horizon for securities portfolio assets must balance the difference and usually has a maturity of three to seven years.

Discussion:

The time horizon for the bank's securities portfolio is determined by the bank's need to manage interest rate risk (duration) and the need to earn a positive spread. A bank's liabilities are usually of shorter term than its loans. The securities portfolio must balance the difference and usually has a maturity of three to seven years.

ii.   **For the Exam:**

Liquidity is needed for liabilities and new loans.

Bank liabilities are uncertain, so the securities portfolio must be fairly liquid.

Discussion:

Banks must maintain liquidity in their securities portfolios to help meet demand for new loans. Furthermore, the bank cannot be certain when its liabilities will "mature." If interest rates rise, then bank depositors may withdraw cash from their accounts and move their money into higher yielding accounts.

iii. **For the Exam:**

Banks are highly regulated and face capital requirements, reserve requirements, and regulations on asset risk.

Discussion:

Banks in industrialized nations are highly regulated. For example, banks may not be able to hold sub-investment quality securities, and there may be specified minimum amounts of common equity. In addition, risk-based capital guidelines require banks to establish capital reserves of 100% against most loan categories. Because of reserve requirements, banks also have to pledge collateral (usually short-term treasuries) against certain uninsured public deposits.

> Sample Scoring Key:
> 3 points for the discussion of each issue.

QUESTION 6

Reference: Book 5, Study Session 18, LOS 48.d,e,k,l

Cross-reference to CFA Institute assigned reading: Reading 48

Answer for Question 6-A

Comment	Does statement comply with GIPS® requirements? (circle one)	Explanation
"Since most of our investments are made in fixed income securities, our performance reflects accrual accounting for bond interest, but not for the interest income of non-fixed income securities."	No	**For the Exam:** Accrual accounting must be used for all assets that accrue interest income. **Discussion:** When a fixed-income security or other asset that accrues interest is sold, the accrued interest is paid by the purchaser to the seller on settlement date. As a result, for accurate performance measurement, the accrued interest must be accounted for in all portfolio valuations.
"As you can see from all the various countries in which we invest, we have to pay much attention to exchange rate effects. Since some of our investments are in countries where exchange rate information is difficult to retrieve, we use a multitude of sources to calculate the exchange rate effects for our composites and benchmarks. These differential sources of information allow us to find the most accurate exchange rate data and are disclosed in performance presentations."	Yes	**For the Exam:** No explanation required. **Discussion:** Beginning January 1, 2011, firms must disclose and describe any known material differences in the exchange rates or valuation sources used among the portfolios within a composite, and between the composite and its benchmark.

"Return performance is presented gross of all fees, expenses, and loads."	No	**For the Exam:** Return performance may be presented gross of fees but must be net of all direct trading expenses. **Discussion:** When presenting gross-of-fees returns, firms must disclose if there are any other deductions beyond the direct trading expenses. When presenting net-of-fees returns, firms must disclose if there are any other deductions beyond the investment management fee and direct trading expenses.

Sample Scoring Key:
1 point each for consistent/inconsistent decision.
2 points each for correct explanation, where required.
0 points possible if consistent/inconsistent decision is wrong.

B.   There are a total of seven items not in compliance:

1. The compliance statement is not correct. For firms that have not been verified, the correct compliance statement is:

    [Insert name of firm] claims compliance with the Global Investment Performance Standards (GIPS®) and has prepared and presented this report in compliance with the GIPS standards. [Insert name of firm] has not been independently verified.

2. **For the Exam:**

    Cannot display noncompliant data after January 1, 2000.

    Discussion:

    To claim compliance with GIPS, performance presentations after January 1, 2000 must be GIPS compliant. Any non-compliant performance data presented for periods prior to 2000 must disclose not only the period but also how the presentation is not in compliance. This is true, even if the non-compliant data is consistent with existing local laws and regulations.

3. **For the Exam:**

    Performance of portfolios and composites for periods of less than one year cannot be presented on an annualized basis.

    Discussion:

    Annualizing returns that were realized over some fraction of a year is tantamount to the simulation of returns over the periods required to complete the full year. This violates the spirit of GIPS® and is not allowed.

4. **For the Exam:**

Footnote 8 regarding the return calculations is not in compliance.

Discussion:

The firm can claim compliance on the overall basis of its performance presentation. It cannot flatly state that a specific aspect of the presentation, such as the return calculation, is "performed as prescribed" by the GIPS®.

5. **For the Exam:**

Footnote 6 concerning non-fee-paying portfolios is not adequate.

Discussion:

Although the presence of non-fee paying portfolios is acknowledged, the firm must also disclose the percentage of the composite they represent.

6. **For the Exam:**

Footnote 9 concerning the percentage of firm assets represented by discretionary accounts is not in compliance.

Discussion:

Total firm assets must include the market values of all discretionary and non-discretionary accounts under management.

7. **For the Exam:**

The use of estimated trading expenses as mentioned in footnote 3 is not in compliance.

Discussion:

Actual direct trading expenses are known when an investment is bought/sold and must be included in return calculations. Using estimated trading expenses is prohibited.

Sample Scoring Key:
2 points for each of four correctly identified non-compliant component.

QUESTION 7

Reference: Book 2, Study Sessions 5, LOS 20.c,i
Book 2, Study Session 8, LOS 26.c,o
Book 5, Study Session 16, LOS 45.a,b,c

Cross-reference to CFA Institute assigned reading: Readings 20, 26, and 45

A.   **For the Exam:**

The characteristics that help to determine pension plan risk tolerance:
- Plan surplus.
- Sponsor financial status and profitability.
- Sponsor and pension fund common risk exposures.
- Plan features.
- Workforce characteristics.

Discussion:

There are at least five characteristics of any defined pension plan that determine the appropriate level of risk tolerance. These are:
- Plan surplus—the amount by which the present value of the plan assets exceeds the present value of plan liabilities. In general, the greater the surplus, the greater the risk tolerance.
- Sponsor financial status and profitability—if the sponsor is in strong financial health and is profitable, this implies a greater likelihood that the sponsor will be in position to cover any funding shortfall. Thus, there is a positive relationship between sponsor financial status and profitability and the plan's ability to tolerate risk.
- Sponsor and plan common exposures—this concern is that certain macroeconomic factors can have a simultaneous negative impact on plan funded status and the plan's sponsor. The greater the degree of common exposure, especially on the downside with regard to pension plan asset values, the lower the level of risk tolerance.
- Plan features—plans that allow participants to elect for early retirement and other features that can accelerate fund payouts generally reduce risk tolerance.
- Workforce characteristics—the principal issue here is average age of the participants. The greater the average age, the shorter the average time horizon to payout and the lower the plan's risk tolerance. There is also a positive relationship between the active to retired lives rates and risk tolerance.

Sample Scoring Key:
1 point for each characteristic listed, up to a maximum of 3 points total.

B.   **For the Exam:**

The constraints:
- Liquidity.
- Time horizon.
- Legal regulatory.
- Taxes.
- Unique needs.

The return objectives:
- The pension plan must focus on meeting or exceeding its actuarial required rate of return.
- The endowment focuses on a total return approach.

Discussion:

The factors that determine investment policy for institutional investors are the objectives and constraints. The objectives are concerned with risk tolerance and return. The constraints are limiting factors that often help to define the appropriate level of risk tolerance. These include the level of liquidity that must be maintained, the time horizon(s) until liabilities must be satisfied, any legal and regulatory issues such as the need to meet ERISA standards or diversification rules, the tax status of the fund, and any unique issues relating to the investment fund.

The pension fund's objective is to meet the promised pension payments. These are determined by various actuarial assumptions embedded in the present value calculations. Its return objective will be to meet or exceed the specified actuarial rate. An endowment's funding commitments are more flexible and can be adjusted to meet changes in the endowment's circumstances. Consequently, its focus will normally be on total return.

> Sample Scoring Key:
> 1 point for each constraint listed, up to 3 in total.
> 1 point for correctly describing each return objective, for 2 in total.

C. **For the Exam:**

Role of the strategic allocation:
- The strategic asset allocation provides an observable measure of the level of systematic risk that is believed to be appropriate given the investor's risk tolerance and the manager's capital market expectations.
- The empirical evidence indicates that, on average, more than 90% of a portfolio's returns are determined by the asset allocation.

Discussion:

The strategic allocation reflects the confluence of the investor's risk and return objectives and the expectations for the capital market expectations. The market expectations are formally expressed in the form of the efficient frontier, representing the set of optimal trade-offs for risk and return that are available to the investor. From this optimal set, the portfolio manager recommends a specific point that is best suited to satisfy the investor's risk and return objectives. As such, the point selected provides an observable measure of what has been deemed an appropriate level of risk tolerance for the investor.

Empirical evidence suggests that, on average, more than 90% of portfolio returns are determined by the strategic allocation and less than 10% by other factors, including active management. This suggests that determining the appropriate strategic allocation is the most important single decision to be made by the portfolio manager.

> Sample Scoring Key:
> 2 points for noting that the allocation provides an observable measure of appropriate risk tolerance.
> 1 point for relating the allocation to capital market expectations.
> 1 point for noting that more than 90% of portfolio returns are determined by asset allocation.

D.   **For the Exam:**
   - Institutions, such as defined pension funds, are primarily concerned with satisfying liabilities.
   - Individuals are usually interested in accumulating wealth that can be used to achieve their required and, if possible, their desired lifestyle objectives.

Discussion:

Institutional investment pools are normally created to fund some liability structure, such as pension payouts, life insurance claims, the ability to fund charitable causes, etc. Consequently, the primary concern is the fund's ability to meet these liabilities.

Individuals typically accumulate funds to meet a series of lifestyle objectives, which are often classified into required and desired objectives. A required objective might be to fund a minimally acceptable standard of living in retirement. A desired objective might be to take a vacation in Europe every year. Because individual liabilities are usually not fixed, as are many institutional liabilities, the focus is usually on wealth accumulation.

> Sample Scoring Key: 1 point for correctly stating each objective.

E.   **For the Exam:**
The portfolio manager has a duty to:
   - Construct a portfolio that meets the needs of the client.
   - Monitor the portfolio to be sure it continues to meet the client's needs.

Two basic factors indicate the potential need for monitoring, rebalancing, and review of the strategic allocation. These are:
   - Changes in market/economic conditions and expectations.
   - Changes in the investor's circumstances.

Discussion:

The institutional portfolio manager is in a position of managing the assets that belong to others. As such, they are in a position of fiduciary responsibility and have a duty of loyalty and prudence to the client.
   - The first of the manager's fundamental responsibilities is to construct a portfolio that meets the needs of the client. The first test of appropriateness is with respect to risk tolerance.
   - The second of the manager's fundamental responsibilities is to monitor the portfolio to be sure it continues to meet the client's needs. At minimum, this means the portfolio should be reviewed once per year—more often if circumstances dictate.

The main factors that will determine when monitoring should occur and action potentially be taken are changes in market conditions or investor circumstances.
   - Changes in market conditions can include large changes in market value or significant events that have an impact upon market expectations for the future.
   - Changes in client circumstances include a change in the terms of the pension plan agreement, the bankruptcy of the sponsor, or any other material matter affecting the plan's financial outlook.

> Sample Scoring Key:
> 1 point each for listing each of the portfolio manager's key responsibilities.
> 1 point each for listing each basic factor (market changes, changes in client circumstances).

QUESTION 8

Reference: Book 1, Study Session 4, LOS 19.b,c,d,g

Cross-reference to CFA Institute assigned reading: Reading 19

A. i. **For the Exam:**

Fisher: Human capital is low risk ⇒ Portfolio can be more aggressive and favor equity.

Pollard: Human capital is high risk ⇒ Portfolio must be conservative and favor bonds.

Discussion

Fisher: The asset allocation should be weighted towards equity. Her government job is secure; thus, her human capital has low earnings risk (i.e., it is bond-like). Because her human capital is secure, her financial capital (her portfolio) can be invested more aggressively and should be weighted towards equity.

Pollard: The asset allocation should be weighted towards bonds. His commissioned sales job has high risk; thus, his human capital has high earnings risk (i.e., it is equity-like). Because his human capital is risky, his financial capital (his portfolio) must be invested conservatively and should be weighted towards bonds.

Although the question does not ask for sector allocations, Easterling should recommend an asset allocation for Pollard that excludes the health care industry. Easterling would structure a completion portfolio (described in Reading 17) that has a low correlation with the health industry. In other words, he would minimize the correlation between Pollard's human and financial capital to mitigate Pollard's earnings risk.

 Professor's Note: You could also justify a bias towards equity for Fisher using her long time horizon and a bias towards bonds for Pollard using his potentially short time horizon (as discussed in Reading 14). Hers is long because of good health and his is potentially short due to a poor family health history.

Sample Scoring Key: 12 points maximum.
1 point for each investor's correct asset allocation.
1 point for the justification of each investor's asset allocation.
0 points possible if the investor's asset allocation is incorrect.

B. i. **For the Exam:**

Fisher: Probability of death is low ⇒ Low demand for insurance.

Pollard: Probability of death is relatively high ⇒ High demand for insurance.

Discussion

Fisher: She is in good health and expects a long life, so her mortality risk is low. Given a low probability of death, her demand for life insurance would be low.

Pollard: He has a poor family health history, so his mortality risk is potentially high. Given a relatively high probability of death, his demand for life insurance would be high.

ii. **For the Exam:**

Fisher: Human capital is low risk ⇒ High demand for insurance.

Pollard: Human capital is high risk ⇒ Low demand for insurance.

Discussion

Fisher: Her government job is secure and is bond-like. Insurance acts as a substitute for human capital. Because the human capital is of low risk, a low discount rate is applied to it. Its present value is thus high, and more insurance would be needed to replace it. So her demand for life insurance would be high.

Pollard: His commissioned sales job has high risk and is equity-like. Because the human capital is risky, a high discount rate is applied to it. Its present value is thus low and less insurance would be needed to replace it. So his demand for life insurance would be low.

iii. **For the Exam:**

Fisher: Bequest preference is rather low ⇒ Low demand for insurance.

Pollard: Bequest preference is high ⇒ High demand for insurance.

Discussion

Fisher: Her desire to leave an estate is fairly low. Although she states a desire to leave a modest amount to charity and enough for the care of her pets, she has no human heirs. So her desire for a bequest is rather low and, hence, her demand for life insurance would be low.

Pollard: His desire to leave an estate is high. He states that his wife has few job prospects and he fears leaving his family destitute. So his desire for a bequest is high and, hence, his demand for life insurance would be high.

> Sample Scoring Key: 12 points maximum.
> 1 point for the insurance decision for each factor for each investor.
> 1 point for the justification for each factor for each investor.
> 0 points possible if the investor's insurance demand is incorrect.

QUESTION 9

Reference: Book 3, Study Session 10, LOS 30.h,i,j,k

Cross-reference to CFA Institute assigned reading: Reading 30

A.   **For the Exam:**

    1.   Market selection.

    2.   Currency selection.

    3.   Duration management.

    4.   Sector selection.

    5.   Credit analysis.

    6.   Investing outside the relevant benchmark.

Discussion:

Market selection refers to the country in which the investment is to be made.

Currency selection (or management) involves the decision of which currency exposures to hedge.

Duration management concerns the selection of maturities that are likely to benefit from changes in the yield curve.

Sector selection concerns industry, ratings categories, and other classifications.

Credit analysis can generate excess returns if the manager is able to purchase securities with improving credit quality.

Investing outside the benchmark means that the manager selects bonds that are similar in risk to those in the benchmark but are anticipated to perform better than those contained in the benchmark.

> Sample Scoring Key: 1 point for each correct item listed.

B.   **For the Exam:**

Estimated yield change for Bond X = 1.30 × 80 = 104 bps = 1.04%.

Estimated change in value of Bond X = –7 × 0.0104 × 100 = –7.28%.

Discussion:

The relationship between domestic and foreign yields can be estimated with the following regression equation:

$$\Delta yield_{foreign} = \beta(\Delta yield_{domestic}) + e$$

In the regression, β is the country beta, and e is the error term $(\hat{e} = 0)$. The country beta estimates the relative change in the foreign interest rate for a given change in domestic rates.

The change in the value of the foreign bond can then be estimated using the forecast change in the domestic rate, the resulting change in the bond's yield (i.e., the foreign interest rate) and the bond's duration:

$$\Delta P = -D \times \Delta y \times 100$$

Since the change in yield was positive, the estimated change in value is negative.

> Sample Scoring Key:
> 3 points for the estimated change in yield.
> 2 points for the estimated change in value.

C.   **For the Exam:**

Forward discount for Currency Y = $C_d - C_y$ = 4.55 − 5.65 = −1.10%.

Expected depreciation for Currency Y = −0.95.

−0.95 > −1.10 → Do not hedge.

Discussion:

The foreign currency forward discount (−) or premium (+) is approximated by the differential in the cash rates for the two currencies (domestic cash rate minus foreign). In this case, the differential is −1.10, so the foreign currency is trading at a discount of 1.10% in the forward market. This is the forward currency differential that is locked in if the position is hedged by selling the foreign currency forward at current forward prices.

Since the portfolio manager expects Currency Y to depreciate by only 0.95%, they expect the currency to outperform the expectations that are embedded in the forward rates. If this turns out to be the case, the spot value of the currency one year from today will be greater than the current forward rate, and the manager will be better off by not hedging.

> Sample Scoring Key:
> 3 points for calculating the forward discount.
> 2 points for recommending not to hedge if the rationale is provided correctly (i.e., that −0.95 > −1.10).

D. **For the Exam:**

Bond X's yield disadvantage not considering the change in currency value = 4.55 – 7.05 = –2.50%.

The forward discount or premium: 5.65 – 3.05 = 2.60% forward premium for currency X.

Taking into consideration the appreciation of currency X:

2.60 – 2.50 = 0.10% overall yield advantage for bond X or 0.10 / 2 = 0.05% over the 6-month time horizon.

Breakeven yield change for Bond X = (–0.05 / –7) × 100 = 0.71 bps.

The two bonds will break even if the yield on Bond X increases 0.71 bps. Since Greystone expects X's yield to increase 15 bps, the expected capital loss on Bond X will make Bond Y the better investment.

Discussion:

Breakeven analysis is used by portfolio managers to measure the stability of the yield advantage/disadvantage between two bonds. Once the breakeven change in rates has been determined, the manager can compare it to his interest rate expectations.

Bond Y's yield advantage over Bond X is 250 basis points per year, not taking into consideration the change in value of the currencies. Once the appreciation of currency X is taken into consideration, Bond X is at a yield *advantage* of 0.1% or 0.05% over the 6-month investment horizon. Thus, if Bond X decreases in value by 0.05%, the yield advantage will be offset and the two bonds will break even over the period.

Note that we calculate the breakeven change in yield for Bond X because it is the bond with the greater duration. Performing the calculation using the bond with the greater duration is a conservative approach because that bond's value is relatively more sensitive to changes in interest rates.

Since Greystone expects the yield on X to increase (15 bps) more than the breakeven yield change of 0.71 bps, Bond X should experience a capital loss sufficient to make Bond Y the better investment.

Sample Scoring Key:
1 point for stating 0.5% yield advantage for Bond X or 0.5% disadvantage for Bond Y.
3 points for breakeven calculation of 0.71 bps increase in yield for Bond X.
0 points if stated in terms of Bond Y.

Practice Exam 3
Afternoon Session Answers

To get detailed answer explanations with references to specific LOS and SchweserNotes™ content, and to get valuable feedback on how your score compares to those of other Level III candidates, use your Username and Password to gain Online Access at schweser.com and choose the left-hand menu item "Practice Exams Vol. 1."

10.1. C	13.3. C	16.5. B
10.2. B	13.4. A	16.6. B
10.3. C	13.5. B	17.1. B
10.4. B	13.6. A	17.2. C
10.5. C	14.1. A	17.3. A
10.6. C	14.2. B	17.4. B
11.1. C	14.3. B	17.5. B
11.2. C	14.4. B	17.6. C
11.3. B	14.5. B	18.1. C
11.4. C	14.6. A	18.2. C
11.5. C	15.1. A	18.3. B
11.6. A	15.2. B	18.4. A
12.1. A	15.3. A	18.5. C
12.2. A	15.4. C	18.6. C
12.3. B	15.5. C	19.1. A
12.4. C	15.6. A	19.2. C
12.5. C	16.1. B	19.3. C
12.6. C	16.2. C	19.4. A
13.1. B	16.3. A	19.5. B
13.2. B	16.4. A	19.6. C

PRACTICE EXAM 3
AFTERNOON SESSION ANSWERS

QUESTION 10

Source: Study Session 1

10.1. **C** Standard VI(B) pertains to the priority of transactions. It states that all client accounts should be treated equitably so that no account is disadvantaged. If the family member accounts are client accounts and the account manager has no beneficial ownership of the account, then trades for the family member's account must be treated like all other trades for non-family member accounts. There is no indication that any disadvantage or special treatment is being given to family member accounts and therefore no action is required and no violation has occurred. (Study Session 1, LOS 2.a)

10.2. **B** Standard VI(A) requires that conflicts of interest be disclosed to clients and prospects. This disclosure applies to beneficial ownership of securities that could affect the impartiality of the professional's investment recommendations or actions. Smith's policy of optional disclosure to clients and prospects is not strict enough. Disclosure is mandatory. (Study Session 1, LOS 2.a)

10.3. **C** Standard III(E) requires members to preserve client confidentiality unless the client is engaged in illegal activities or an investigation by the CFA Institute requires disclosure of confidential client information. The managers are allowed to discuss strategies and other issues to better serve their clients as long as they maintain the confidentiality of each client. (Study Session 1, LOS 2.a)

10.4. **B** The portfolio managers at Smith Investments have violated Standard III(C) Suitability by failing to consider the suitability of the fixed-income investments for each individual portfolio. It is possible that some of the portfolios would meet the requirements to take on the risk of investing in below investment grade bonds but is unlikely that most of the firm's portfolios would have objectives and constraints that would allow below investment grade bonds into the portfolio. (Study Session 1, LOS 2.a)

10.5. **C** There is no indication from the case that Hatcher is in violation of the Code and Standards. Hatcher is allowed to accept a position where there are known violations as long as she will be granted sufficient latitude to eliminate such violations. Management at Smith Investments is hiring Hatcher to eliminate ethical violations at the company and giving her the proper power and authority. Hatcher is also taking reasonable measures (through the anonymous survey) to identify the violations of the Code and Standards. Hatcher is allowed to take a position with a direct competitor as long as she is not working for them secretly while still employed with Bernhardt. (Study Session 1, LOS 2.a)

10.6. **C** The GIPS standards require firms to maintain the historical performance of terminated portfolios up until the last full performance measurement period prior to termination. If the firm values composites quarterly (before 2010), the terminated portfolio must be included in the composite valuation through the last full quarter it was in the composite. If monthly (beginning 2010), they must maintain the portfolio through the last full month it was in the composite.

The GIPS require that composites represent portfolios managed to the same style and/or strategy. Since hedging can affect risk as well as return, hedging would typically represent a strategy and would require separation of portfolios into different composites, even if they are managed to the same style. The determination is whether (1) hedging is part of a permanent investment strategy applied to the portfolios in the composite, or (2) hedging is only a temporary, tactical strategy.

If considered part of a long-term investment strategy, the use of hedging would separate portfolios into different composites. Smith Investments must state and clearly document whether the hedging is a short-term tactic or long-term strategy. Unless clearly stated in the firm's documented policies for obtaining and maintaining GIPS compliance, an external verifier would definitely question the firm's use of hedging and its policies for constructing composites. (Study Session 1, LOS 2.a)

QUESTION 11

Source: Study Session 1

11.1. **C** Standard II(B) Market Manipulation. Transaction 1 is simply an attempt to exploit a market mispricing through a legitimate arbitrage strategy. Transaction 1 does not violate Standard II(B). (Study Session 1, LOS 2.a)

11.2. **C** Standard II(A) Material Nonpublic Information. Stirr violated Standard II(A) by using material nonpublic information in his decision to take a short forward position on the ONB Corporation bonds (Transaction 2). Stirr would have known about any publicly announced plans by ONB to offer more debt since the company's bonds were already a holding in the Fixed Income Fund at the time of the forward transaction. Stirr obviously knew that the unannounced bond offering by ONB would affect the price of the firm's existing bonds since he acted on the information shortly after overhearing the conversation between the investment bankers. Standard II(A) prohibits such trades. It does not matter that the trade utilized a derivative security rather than the actual underlying security or that the trade prevented losses for his investors. Stirr should have waited for the information to become public before making any trades on ONB securities. Transaction 3 is not in violation of the Standards. Transaction 3 reflects a trading advantage that Stirr has discovered. He is not using material nonpublic information to complete the trade. Rather, he is simply processing news and information faster than other market participants to make profitable trades. Transaction 3 also is not intended to manipulate market prices or information and is therefore a legitimate trade. (Study Session 1, LOS 2.a)

11.3. **B** Standard IV(B) Additional Compensation Arrangements. According to the Standard, Chang must obtain written consent from all parties involved before agreeing to accept additional compensation that could be reasonably expected to create a conflict of interest with his employer. Chang's arrangement with Cherry Creek involves providing investment advice in exchange for additional shares to be added to his account with Cherry Creek. Such compensation could affect Chang's loyalty to WMG or affect his independence and objectivity. Therefore, Chang must obtain written consent from WMG before accepting the arrangement with Cherry Creek. (Study Session 1, LOS 2.a)

11.4. **C** Standard VI(C) Referral Fees. According to the Standard, Stirr must disclose referral arrangements to his employer, clients, and prospective clients before entering into an agreement to provide services. Stirr's agreement with Cherry Creek constitutes a referral relationship whereby he has agreed to provide professional investment advice in exchange for referrals of Cherry Creek customers seeking traditional asset management services. Stirr's employer, clients, and prospects must be informed of this arrangement so that any partiality in the recommendation and the true cost of the services being provided by Stirr can be assessed. (Study Session 1, LOS 2.a)

11.5. **C** Standard V(B) Communication with Clients and Prospective Clients. Standard V(B) requires members to disclose the basic format of the investment processes used to analyze and select securities, the processes used to construct portfolios, and any changes to these processes. In addition, members are required to use reasonable judgment in selecting the factors relevant to their investment analysis or actions when communicating with their clients and prospects. Chang's first statement is correct; all of the items mentioned must be disclosed in the newsletter. His second statement is incorrect. Chang is not required to disclose every detail of every factor used to make decisions for the last quarter. It is possible that such disclosure may be appropriate, but there is no blanket requirement to include every piece of information in a report to clients and prospects. (Study Session 1, LOS 2.a)

11.6. **A** Standard V(B) Communication with Clients and Prospective Clients. In addition to the requirements of Standard V(B) listed in the previous answer, members are required to clearly distinguish between fact and opinion in the presentation of investment analysis and recommendations. Stirr is correct in his first statement that the newsletter must indicate that projections are not factual, but based on the opinion of the report's author. Stirr is also correct in stating that an abbreviated report may be used to communicate with clients as long as a full report providing more detailed information is maintained and made available to any clients or prospects requesting additional information. Best practice would be to note in the abbreviated report that more information is available upon request. (Study Session 1, LOS 2.a)

QUESTION 12

Source: Study Session 16

12.1. **A** Comment 1 is correct. The success of a calendar rebalancing strategy will depend in large part on whether the rebalancing frequency is appropriate to the volatility of the component asset classes. If volatility is high (or rebalancing infrequent), the asset mix can drift to the point where rebalancing could create a market impact, thus increasing the cost of rebalancing dramatically. If volatility is low (or rebalancing too frequent), the portfolio could incur numerous costly small trades to achieve minor adjustments in the asset mix.

Comment 2 is incorrect. Annual rebalancing is most likely too infrequent. The asset mix may well drift far enough over a year's time to necessitate large trades to rebalance. These trades would increase market impact. Market impact will be lower with more frequent rebalancing. (Study Session 16, LOS 45.e)

12.2. **A** A higher risk tolerance for tracking error provides more flexibility for the asset allocation relative to the target mix, and therefore a wider rebalancing corridor. If the volatility of other asset classes is high, then large differences from the target asset mix are more likely. Lower volatility reduces the likelihood of large differences, and allows for a wider corridor. (Study Session 16, LOS 45.f)

12.3. **B** Factors indicating a narrower corridor width are low transaction costs, low correlation with the rest of the portfolio, and high volatility. Emerging market stocks have the lowest correlation with the rest of the portfolio, as well as the highest standard deviation. Their transaction costs are only slightly higher than U.S. small cap stocks. The narrow corridor means that small changes in value may necessitate rebalancing. The low correlation and high volatility increase the likelihood of increasing divergence from the target asset mix. The low transaction costs reduce the cost of rebalancing back to the target mix. (Study Session 16, LOS 45.f)

12.4. **C** The constant mix strategy will be optimal for Client C, an investor whose absolute risk tolerance varies proportionally with wealth, and who expects a choppy stock market with frequent reversals. Client A has a floor value which limits his willingness to take risk if his portfolio declines below that value. Further, Client A appears to have a risk tolerance that varies by more than any change in his wealth (his multiplier is greater than 1). Client B has risk tolerance that varies proportionally with her wealth, as evidenced by the fact that she wants to hold stocks regardless of her wealth level. However, Client B expects a trending market with few reversals, in which a constant mix strategy would perform poorly. (Study Session 16, LOS 45.h,j)

12.5. **C** A buy and hold strategy has a linear payoff curve. The constant mix strategy is a concave strategy that supplies liquidity to the market, in effect "selling insurance" by taking the less popular side of trades when the market is trending up or down. A buy and hold strategy would not be an appropriate strategy for Client C, whose risk tolerance varies in proportion to her wealth, and who expects a volatile stock market. (Study Session 16, LOS 45.i)

12.6. **C** The constant mix strategy has a concave payoff curve and a multiplier between 0 and 1. The return on the portfolio using this strategy will increase at a declining rate when stocks go up, and decrease at an increasing rate when stocks go down. The constant proportion strategy has a convex payoff curve and a multiplier greater than 1. The return on a constant proportion portfolio will increase at an increasing rate when stocks go up, and decrease at a declining rate when stocks go down. (Study Session 16, LOS 45.i)

QUESTION 13

Source: Study Session 11

13.1. **B** Many institutional investors may not be able to mimic a value-weighted index, if they are subject to maximum holdings and the index holds concentrated positions. This is the case for the potential clients and the index in this question. Ten firms represent over 70% of the index's total market cap and the index is market cap weighted.

Since they constitute 70% of total market cap, the 10 stocks likely represent large-cap firms and are very liquid. They are also the best known stocks. There is no evidence that the institutional investors demand excess returns (as described in the first paragraph, the vast majority of clients attempt to minimize tracking error), so this response does not represent a valid concern either. (Study Session 11, LOS 32.d)

13.2. **B** Murray should use full replication. Full replication is appropriate when there are few stocks in the index, the index stocks are liquid, and the manager has significant funds to invest. The advantage of replication is that there is low tracking risk (tracking error) and the portfolio only needs to be rebalanced when the index stocks change or pay dividends. There are only 25 large-cap stocks in the index and Murray's institutional investors want low tracking error.

Most of the index returns are from capital gains, so the transactions costs from reinvesting dividends will be relatively low. Note that cash drag, experienced when a fund sets aside cash for shareholder redemptions, should be relatively low for the Canada fund due to the back-end load.

Stratified sampling and optimization are more appropriate when the number of stocks in the index is large and/or the stocks are illiquid. (Study Session 11, LOS 32.f)

13.3. **C** The fundamental law of active management states that an investor's information ratio is a function of her depth of knowledge (the investor's information coefficient) and the number of independent investment decisions (the investor's breadth).

 Professor's Note: Think of the information coefficient as the correlation between the manager's forecasted and actual returns.

The derivatives-based enhanced indexing strategy of Manager B will have less breadth than the (stock-based) enhanced strategies of Managers A and C. Note that Manager B has the same information coefficient as Manager A, so Manager A should have a higher information ratio than Manager B.

Manager C uses a long-short strategy, which attempts to exploit the short selling constraints faced by many managers. The long-only strategy of Manager A can only earn a long alpha, but both managers actively follow and analyze 500 stocks. This means their breadth is the same. Due to a higher information coefficient than Manager B, Manager C will have a higher information ratio, so C has the highest ratio among the three managers. (Study Session 11, LOS 32.m and p)

13.4. **A** The manager of Fund 1 is likely following a value strategy and is likely a contrarian investor. Contrarian investors look for stocks that they believe are temporarily depressed. They frequently invest in firms selling at less than book value, as is the case with Fund 1. Note that the EPS growth in Fund 1 is also negative, which likely indicates that the fund invests in firms that are temporarily depressed in price. (Study Session 11, LOS 32.g)

13.5. **B** The investor's active return is calculated as a weighted average return:

expected active portfolio return = $(0.20 \times 3.3\%) + (0.45 \times 1.2\%) + (0.35 \times 4.5\%) = 2.78\%$

To calculate the portfolio active risk, we use the active risks and allocations:

$$\text{portfolio active risk} = \sqrt{(0.20)^2(0.053)^2 + (0.45)^2(0.036)^2 + (0.35)^2(0.067)^2}$$

$$= \sqrt{0.0009247} = 0.0304 = 3.04\%$$

The investor's information ratio is then 2.78% / 3.04% = 0.91.

(Study Session 11, LOS 32.q)

13.6. **A** Statement 1 is correct. In the case of Provider B, there is no neutral category for firms that are not clearly value or growth. In the case of Provider A, the categories of value and growth are more distinct. Regressing a value manager's returns against Provider A's indices will show a strong relationship to one or both of the value categories. The regression will have a high R^2 and a high style fit.

Regressing a value manager's returns against Provider B's indices will not show as strong a relationship to the value category. The proportion of the manager's return not explained by the style indices, the difference between the portfolio return and the returns on the style indices, will be relatively high. This difference represents the selection or active return. The manager will appear to be earning returns from active management, but this will actually be due to the indistinct nature of the indices and the low R-square.

Statement 2 is also correct. When an index has buffering rules, a stock is not immediately moved to a different style category when its style characteristics have slightly changed. The presence of buffering means that there will be less turnover in the style indices and, hence, lower transactions costs from rebalancing for managers tracking the index. (Study Session 11, LOS 32.i and j)

QUESTION 14

Source: Study Sessions 9 and 10

14.1. **A** Weaver is correct. In enhanced indexing by matching primary risk factors and enhanced indexing by minor risk factor mismatching, the duration of the portfolio is matched with that of the index.

McNally is incorrect. In active management by larger risk factor mismatches, the portfolio manager can deviate from the duration of the index, but these deviations are typically not large. (Study Session 9, LOS 28.b)

14.2. **B** The economist believes that long-term interest rates will fall over the next year, but that short-term rates will gradually increase. The appropriate portfolio in this scenario is Portfolio 2, which is a barbell portfolio. The decrease in long-term rates will result in an increase in price for Bond C. This will be greater than the decline in Bond A's price from the increase in short-term rates, because Bond C has a longer duration. Portfolio 1 places too much emphasis on intermediate-term bonds which are not mentioned in the forecast. Portfolio 3 places too much emphasis on short-term bonds which will suffer a price reduction as short-term interest rates increase. (Study Session 9, LOS 29.d)

14.3. **B** To calculate the bond equivalent yield for the bond over the one year investment horizon, recognize first that the bond is originally bought at par, since the yield to maturity and coupon are equal. Next, the terminal value of the investment must be determined. The terminal value consists of the price of the bond in one year plus the sum of the coupons reinvested at the assumed reinvestment rate. The terminal values in one year are determined in a financial calculator as:

Price of bond in one year:
N = 19 × 2 = 38
PMT = 6.5 / 2 = 3.25
I/Y = 6 / 2 = 3
FV = 100
CPT PV = −105.62

Value of reinvested coupons in one year:
N = 1 × 2 = 2
PMT = 6.5 / 2 = 3.25
I/Y = 5 / 2 = 2.50
PV = 0
CPT FV = −6.58

The semiannual return is the rate of return between today and the accumulated value one year from now:
N = 2
PMT = 0
PV = −100
FV = (105.62 + 6.58) = 112.20
CPT I/Y = 5.93%

The bond equivalent yield is 5.93% × 2 = 11.86%.

(Study Session 9, LOS 28.e)

14.4. **B** The amount of leverage is $125,000,000 \times 15\% = \$18,750,000$. The total amount invested is Johnson's equity of $125 million plus the $18,750,000 borrowed, which equals $143,750,000.

The duration can be calculated with the following formula:

$$D_p = \frac{D_i I - D_B B}{E}$$

where :
D_p = duration of portfolio
D_i = duration of invested assets
I = amount of invested funds
B = amount of leverage
E = amount of equity invested

Using the above formula:

$$D_p = \frac{(5.2)143.75 - (0.8)18.75}{125} = 5.9$$

Note the use of leverage has resulted in the duration of the portfolio (5.9) being greater than the duration of invested assets (5.2).

This is higher than the required duration of 5.5, so the investment guidelines have been violated. (Study Session 10, LOS 30.a)

14.5. **B** McNally is incorrect regarding the discount on putable bonds relative to comparable bullets. Callable issues still dominate the high-yield segment, but in the rest of the corporate bond market, bullet and intermediate maturities dominate. Bullet maturities are not callable, putable, or sinkable. Bonds with embedded options command a *premium* price due to their scarcity. Bond managers with long horizons may also be willing to pay a premium for long-term bonds. Credit-based derivatives will be increasingly used to achieve a desired exposure to credit sectors, issuers, and structures.

McNally is correct regarding credit risk modeling in putable bond valuation. Putable bonds are attractive when interest rates rise, because the investor can put the bond back to the issuer and reinvest at a higher rate. But the valuation models for bonds with embedded put options often fail to incorporate the probability that the issuer will be unable to fulfill its obligation to repurchase its bonds. This is particularly relevant to the valuation of putable bonds issued by high-yield issuers. It may be that the creditworthiness of the high-yield issuer is a more relevant indicator of relative value than the value of the putable bond based on a valuation model. (Study Session 9, LOS 29.b,e)

14.6. **A** There are two primary steps to adjusting the portfolio's dollar duration:

1. Calculate the new dollar duration of the portfolio.

2. Calculate the rebalancing ratio and use it to determine the required percentage change in the value of the portfolio.

The dollar duration last year was $108,000. This year's dollar duration is $35,720 + $22,960 + $36,660 + $21,735 = $117,075.

$$\text{rebalancing ratio} = \frac{\text{old DD}}{\text{new DD}} = \frac{108,000}{117,075} = 0.92$$

To adjust back to the original dollar duration, we would rebalance each bond to 0.92 of its current value. The following calculations are not needed to answer the question, but illustrate the concept behind the calculation.

The value (in dollars) required for the individual bonds in the portfolio are:

Bond 1: $940,000 × 0.92 = $864,800

Bond 2: $820,000 × 0.92 = $754,400

Bond 3: $780,000 × 0.92 = $717,600

Bond 4: $621,000 × 0.92 = <u>$571,320</u>

$2,908,120

To check, the total value of the portfolio before rebalancing is $940,000 + $820,000 + $780,000 + $621,000 = $3,161,000.

After rebalancing, the portfolio value is: 0.92 × $3,161,000 = $2,908,120.

Alternatively, the manager could select one of the bonds to use as a controlling position and sell part of it to achieve the targeted dollar duration (as described in Book 3 of the SchweserNotes™). (Study Session 9, LOS 28.g)

QUESTION 15

Source: Study Session 9

15.1. **A** If interest rates decline, bonds with a shorter duration than the liability will cause the portfolio to fail to achieve the target accumulated value because of reinvestment risk. At the initiation of the classical immunization strategy, the portfolio of assets had a duration of $0.5(4) + 0.5(15) = 9.5$, while the duration of the liabilities was ten. Since the duration of assets is less than the duration of liabilities, the overall portfolio is exposed to reinvestment (also called immunization) risk.

 Professor's Note: Since the duration of the assets is less than that of the liabilities, the assets will increase in value less than the liabilities when interest rates fall.

Four years after the strategy was implemented, the duration of liabilities is six. If half of the portfolio remains in the once 15-year (now 11-year) bonds, the maturity of the remaining investment can be found as $0.5(11) + 0.5(X) = 6$; $X = 1$. Thus, half of the portfolio should be invested in 1-year zero coupon bonds to achieve proper immunization. This assumes, of course, that the present value of the assets is equal to the present value of the liabilities. (Study Session 9, LOS 28.f)

15.2. **B** Immunization risk is the same as reinvestment risk. To minimize the risk, zero-coupon securities maturing at the horizon date are the best alternative. The bullet portfolio would have the least amount of exposure to any changes in interest rates because the bonds' maturities are clustered near the investment horizon. The other answer choices would have relatively high reinvestment risk. Using zeros is sometimes considered an inefficient strategy, however, due to their low returns. (Study Session 9, LOS 28.f)

15.3. **A** Based on the minimum acceptable return (safety net return) the required terminal value $= \$55,000,000 \times (1 + 0.06 / 2)^{2\times6} = \$78.42$ million.

Assets required today at the immunized rate $= \$78.42 / (1 + 0.0725 / 2)^{2\times6} = \$51.15$ million; the currently available immunized rate of return (7.25%) is the appropriate interest rate for this calculation. (Study Session 9, LOS 28.f)

15.4. **C** The statement regarding conditions is correct. Yield curve shifts and the simple passage of time alter the duration of the portfolio and require the portfolio to be rebalanced in order to maintain the immunization strategy. The cost reduction statement is also correct. More liquid securities will have lower transaction costs, thus lowering the overall costs of any transactions needed to rebalance the portfolio. (Study Session 9, LOS 28.g)

15.5. **C** Edwards's statement regarding the duration of the asset portfolio in multiple liability immunization is correct. The two conditions that must be met in order to undertake multiple liability immunization are: (1) the composite duration of liabilities must equal the composite duration of assets; and (2) the distribution of individual assets' durations in the portfolio must have a range that exceeds the range of durations of the liabilities. If both of these conditions are met, the liabilities can be immunized against parallel shifts in the yield curve but will still be exposed to immunization risk if the yield curve shifts in a nonparallel manner. (Study Session 9, LOS 28.k)

15.6. **A** In a cash flow matching strategy, coupons are used to fund liabilities rather than being reinvested. Therefore, Edwards is correct that a cash flow matching strategy has no immunization risk. Edwards is incorrect about the capital requirements. Typically, immunization is cheaper to implement. Cash flow matching requires lower return assumptions for short term investments that typically are necessary under cash flow matching, when the timing of cash inflows does not exactly match outflows. The limitations of finding assets with cash flows that closely match both the size and timing of liabilities can also reduce asset returns. (Study Session 9, LOS 28.m)

QUESTION 16

Source: Study Sessions 14 and 15

16.1. **B** The currency overlay approach follows the IPS guidelines, but the portfolio manager is not responsible for currency exposure. Instead, a separate manager, who is considered an expert in foreign currency management, is hired to manage the currency exposure within the guidelines of the IPS. In a balanced mandate approach, the investment manager is given total responsibility for managing the portfolio, including managing the currency exposure. In a separate asset allocation approach, there are two separate managers much like the currency overlay approach, but the managers use separate guidelines. (Study Session 14, LOS 40.i)

16.2. **C** Since the question is concerned with eliminating basis risk and not with mitigating transactions costs, statement C is the best choice. The only way to avoid basis risk is to enter a contact with a maturity equal to the desired holding period. Continually adjusting the hedge would likely create significant trading costs, but is the best method for reducing basis risk. When the futures contract is longer than the desired holding period, the investor must reverse at the end of the holding period at the existing futures price. If the futures contract is shorter than the desired holding period, the investor must close the first contract and then enter another. Both the shorter-term and longer-term contracts will create basis risk for Wulf's portfolio. (Study Session 14, LOS 40.d)

16.3. **A** First calculate the appropriate number of yen put options to purchase for the initial delta hedge. The appropriate number of options to purchase is equal to $(-1/\delta)$ times the negative value of the portfolio in foreign currency units.

$$\text{yen put options} = \frac{-1}{0.85} \times \frac{-25,000,000}{1,000,000} = 29.41$$

Given the change in delta, the number of yen put options needed reduces to:

$$\text{yen put options} = \frac{-1}{0.92} \times \frac{-25,000,000}{1,000,000} = 27.17$$

The difference is $29.41 - 27.17 = 2.24$ yen options. So in order to remain delta-neutral, two put options need to be sold to accommodate the decrease in delta. (Study Session 14, LOS 40.g)

16.4. **A** Futures remove translation risk by protecting the investor against losses on the amount hedged, but they also eliminate any chance of a gain from favorable movements. They are, however, very liquid and are less expensive to use. Options require a premium in order to provide insurance against unfavorable exchange rate movements. (Study Session 14, LOS 40.g)

16.5. **B** Wulf invests a total of 6,410,256 euros (= £5,000,000 / 0.78£/€) in the British asset. After 180 days, the value of the asset has increased to €6,800,000 (= £5,100,000 / 0.75£/€). Therefore, the unhedged return on the asset in euros = [(€6,800,000 – €6,410,256) / €6,410,256] = 6.08%.

The next step is to calculate the return on the futures contract:

Wulf originally sold the £5,000,000 in futures for 0.79£/€, = (£5,000,000) × (€ / 0.79£) = €6,329,114.

Since the pound has strengthened relative to the Euro (the futures exchange rate has dropped to 0.785£/€), he has lost [(£5,000,000) × (€ / 0.785£) =] €6,369,427 – €6,329,114 = –€40,313, which translates to a loss on the futures transaction of –€40,313 / €6,410,256 = –0.63% return. The total return from hedging the principal is 6.08% – 0.63% = 5.45%. (Study Session 14, LOS 40.a)

16.6. **B** If Bauer shorts the appropriate amount of the index and the short position is perfectly correlated with the investment, the return must be the foreign risk-free rate. If Bauer then chooses to hedge the currency risk, he knows the exact value of the foreign currency to hedge and that the return to the (double) hedging strategy must be the domestic risk-free rate. (Study Session 15, LOS 41.g)

QUESTION 17

Source: Study Session 15

17.1. **B** Worth should assume the receive fixed/pay floating arm of the swap, since they are currently paying a fixed interest rate on its outstanding debt. If interest rates decline, Worth would like to take advantage of the lower rates. In order to do so, it must either reissue long-term debt (which can be an expensive process) or enter into a swap to convert its fixed payments into floating payments. Thus, Worth will receive fixed and pay floating in the swap. The net interest payment that Worth will pay is calculated as follows:

interest rate on existing debt − fixed rate received from swap + floating rate paid to swap

7.2% − 5.8% + EURIBOR = 1.4% + EURIBOR = 140 basis points + EURIBOR

(Study Session 15, LOS 43.a)

17.2. **C** The MIA analysts are correct, both with regard to the swap duration and to the balance sheet effects of entering into the swap. Worth will enter into the swap as the fixed rate receiver/floating rate payer. Since pay floating on the swap is equivalent to having a floating rate liability, the swap duration from this perspective is:

$$D_{\text{pay floating}} = D_{\text{fixed}} - D_{\text{floating}}$$

The duration of the floating rate side is a minimum of zero and maximum of 0.5 since the swap is semiannual settlement. Thus, the average duration of the floating side is 0.25. The duration of the fixed side is given as 1.2. Therefore, the duration of the swap from Worth's perspective is:

1.2 − 0.25 = 0.95

Since Worth issues fixed-rate debt, the firm has negative duration exposure. Because the bonds issued have a maturity of 15 years, the duration exposure is substantial. The exact magnitude of the duration is not necessary to answer the question. Adding the swap position, which has positive duration, reduces Worth's duration exposure, making the firm's liabilities less sensitive to interest rate changes. Since the swap will not affect the duration of the firm's assets, the duration of the firm's equity must offset the decrease in the duration of the liabilities. Thus, the duration of Worth's equity will increase and become more sensitive to interest rate changes. (Study Session 15, LOS 43.b,c)

17.3. **A** In a long interest rate collar, the firm purchases an interest rate cap and sells an interest rate floor, locking in a range of interest rates that the firm will pay. This position is frequently taken by borrowers with floating rate debt. The firm can manage its cash flow risk within the effective range of interest rates defined by the collar. If the underlying interest rate rises above the cap strike rate, the cap payoff to the borrower (purchaser of the cap) will mitigate the higher interest payments on the firm's debt. If the underlying interest rate falls below the floor strike, the borrower (seller of the floor) will make a payment which will offset the decrease in interest payments on the firm's debt. The payoff is made in arrears, so for Enertech's collar, the caplet and floorlet that expire in 18 months would payoff (if they were in the money at 18 months) in 24 months. Thus, to determine the payoff from the collar that occurs in 24 months, we must determine whether the cap or the floor is in the money at the 18th month. In the vignette, LIBOR is expected to be 4.1% in 18 months. This is below the floor strike of 4.5%. Therefore, Enertech will need to make a payment calculated as follows:

$$\text{floor payoff} = \text{notional principal} \times \left[\max\left(\text{strike rate} - \text{actual rate}, 0\right) \left(\frac{\text{days in period}}{360}\right) \right]$$

$$= \text{notional principal} \times \left[\max\left(0.045 - 0.041, 0\right) \left(\frac{180}{360}\right) \right]$$

$$= \text{notional principal} \times [0.002]$$

Enertech will need to make a payment equal to $0.002 per dollar of notional principal.

(Study Session 15, LOS 42.d)

17.4. **B** In 18 months, Enertech will be required to make an interest payment on its loan equal to:

(LIBOR at 12 months + 150bp) / 2 = (6.1% + 1.5%) = 7.6% / 2 = 3.8%

This interest payment will be partially offset by the payoff from the interest rate cap. Because LIBOR at 12 months is above the cap strike rate of 5.5%, the cap is in the money and will have a payoff equal to:

$$\text{cap payoff} = \text{notional principal} \times \left[\max\left(\text{actual rate} - \text{strike rate}, 0\right) \left(\frac{\text{days in period}}{360}\right) \right]$$

$$= \text{notional principal} \times \left[\max\left(0.061 - 0.055, 0\right) \left(\frac{180}{360}\right) \right]$$

$$= \text{notional principal} \times [0.003]$$

Thus, assuming the notional principal is set equal to the face value of the loan, the effective interest rate is equal to:

0.038 − 0.003 = 0.035 = 3.5%

(Study Session 15, LOS 42.d)

17.5. **B** SBK's swaption strategy is inappropriate for its interest rate exposure. The firm believes interest rates may increase and currently is paying a floating rate in an interest rate swap. Therefore, the firm will face higher interest expense on the swap if interest rates increase. SBK needs to purchase a swaption that will allow it to offset the swap exposure to rising interest rates. The correct option purchase would be a payer swaption, which would give SBK the right to enter into a swap in which it would pay the fixed rate and receive the floating rate. This swaption would effectively offset the firm's existing exposure to the swap. However, SBK has sold the payer swaption. If interest rates increase, the swaption will be in the money and exercised by the party that purchased the swaption. SBK would be required to enter the swap as the floating rate payer, increasing its exposure to floating interest rates. Exposure to floating interest rates is also known as cash flow risk since the interest payments are not known with certainty. (Study Session 15, LOS 43.c,h)

17.6. **C** MIA is considering an investment in a floating rate note issued by Rio Corp. The risk of such an investment is that interest rates will decrease, causing the cash flows received from the investment to decrease (i.e., an increase in cash flow risk). The best way to hedge against a decrease in interest rates is to purchase an interest rate put option. If interest rates decrease, the payoff from the put option will offset the lost interest income. Selling an interest rate call option would provide an immediate cash inflow from the option premium, which would also help mitigate lost interest income stemming from a decrease in interest rates. However, the option premium received is not linked to the changes in the interest rate. In other words, the payoff (income) from selling the call option is static whereas the payoff from the interest rate put is linked to the underlying interest rate. The put payoff grows larger as interest rates fall. Therefore, the long interest rate put is a better hedging strategy. (Study Session 15, LOS 42.c)

QUESTION 18

Source: Study Session 18

18.1. **C** The Moss account should not be added to the Aggressive composite. Moss's requirement to have a large weighting in technology is not consistent with CCM's typical aggressive investment approach. The Bateman account should be added to the conservative composite. CCM does not use options or futures to manage any of their portfolios, so Bateman's request that CCM not use options or futures is immaterial. (Study Session 18, LOS 48.h)

18.2. **C** Composites can be delineated using equity and bond exposures, as long as the ranges are tightly defined. GIPS do not mandate what type of composites or the number of composites to create. (Study Session 18, LOS 48.h)

18.3. **B** CCM should move North's account from the aggressive composite to the conservative composite. However, the historical performance of North's account must stay with the aggressive composite. (Study Session 18, LOS 48.i)

18.4. **A** Currently, GIPS verification is not required. This may change in the future. The verification process is central to the reliability of the GIPS. Normally, CCM must include the number of accounts in each composite. However, if the composite has five or fewer accounts, CCM is not required to disclose the number of accounts. The cash balance should be allocated across the other asset classes in reporting returns. (Study Session 18, LOS 48.w)

18.5. **C** The 70% allocation to bonds represents the percentage of the $277,875,000 ($95,875,000 stocks + $182,000,000 bonds) that is invested in bonds. It does not consider the $47,125,000 in cash or the total portfolio value of $325,000,000. To determine the strategic return on the bonds, we must allocate cash to the bond category by using the actual allocation to bonds in the portfolio, assuming cash is part of the portfolio:

allocation to bonds = total portfolio value × [strategic allocation − actual allocation]

$$= \$325{,}000{,}000 \times (0.70 - (182\,/\,325)) = \$45{,}500{,}000$$

$$\text{return}_{\text{bonds}} = \text{bond return} \times \left(\frac{\text{amount in bonds}}{\text{bonds} + \text{allocated cash}} \right) + \text{cash return} \times \left(\frac{\text{allocated cash}}{\text{bonds} + \text{allocated cash}} \right)$$

$$= 0.052 \left(\frac{182{,}000{,}000}{(182{,}000{,}000 + 45{,}500{,}000)} \right) + 0.034 \left(\frac{45{,}500{,}000}{(182{,}000{,}000 + 45{,}500{,}000)} \right) = 4.8\%$$

The bond return calculation must include the appropriate amount of cash. To determine the appropriate amount, the actual percentage amount is subtracted from the strategic percentage amount in bonds. This difference is multiplied by the total dollar amount of the portfolio. The cash dollar amount is used to calculate the weighted average return of cash and bonds. The performance calculation represents the actual return for the bond portion of the portfolio. (Study Session 18, LOS 48.j)

18.6. **C** GIPS now requires daily weighted cash flows in time-weighted total return calculations. The calculation for the modified Dietz method is as follows:

$$r_{ModDietz} = \frac{MV_1 - MV_0 - CF}{MV_0 + \sum (CF_i \times w_i)}$$

Moss portfolio: inflows for 61 days of the total 91 days

$$\left(\frac{3,100,000 - 2,500,000 - 300,000}{2,500,000 + \left[300,000 \times \left(\frac{61}{91} \right) \right]} \right) = 11.1\%$$

(Study Session 18, LOS 48.f)

QUESTION 19

Source: Study Session 4

19.1. **A** Under a flat and heavy tax regime, interest-paying assets have a favorable tax treatment. The other two categories do not. (Study Session 4, LOS 15.a)

19.2. **C** Since she lives under a flat tax regime, one does not have a benefit over the other. (Study Session 4, LOS 15.a, e)

19.3. **C** Increasing the investment horizon will increase tax drag because the number of compounding periods increases. Lowering returns will reduce tax drag because the aggregate amount taxed is reduced. Since the two effects are opposite, we would need to know the increase in the investment horizon as well as the decrease in return to be able to estimate their combined effect on tax drag. (Study Session 4, LOS 15.b)

19.4. **A** Typically, a heavy capital gain tax regime does not have a favorable treatment for capital gains, but it does have a favorable treatment for both dividend and interest income. (Study Session 4, LOS 15.a)

19.5. **B** The most recently acquired shares will have the highest basis and the lowest tax consequences. (Study Session 4, LOS 15.h)

19.6. **C** There must be a weight for the allocation of each asset to each type of account. (Study Session 4, LOS 15.d)

Notes

Notes

Notes

Notes

Notes

Notes

Notes

Notes

Notes